THE RISE OF THE
MODERNIST BOOKSHOP

The trade in books has always been and remains an ambiguous commercial activity, associated as it is with literature and the exchange of ideas. This collection is concerned with the cultural and economic roles of independent bookstores, and it considers how eight shops founded during the modernist era provided distinctive spaces of literary production that exceeded and yet never escaped their commercial functions. As the contributors show, these booksellers were essential institutional players in literary networks. When the eight shops examined first opened their doors, their relevance to literary and commercial life was taken for granted. In our current context of box stores, online shopping, and ebooks, we no longer encounter the book as we did as recently as twenty years ago. By contributing to our understanding of bookshops as unique social spaces on the thresholds of commerce and culture, this volume helps to lay the groundwork for comprehending how our relationship to books and literature has been and will be affected by the physical changes to the reading experience taking place in the twenty-first century.

Ashgate Studies in Publishing History: Manuscript, Print, Digital

Series editors: Ann R. Hawkins, Texas Tech University, USA, and
Maura Ives, Texas A&M University, USA

Exploring the intersection of publishing history, book history, and literary and cultural studies, this series supports innovative work on the cultural significance and creative impact of printing and publishing history, including reception, distribution, and translation or adaptation into other media.

Other Ashgate titles of interest

Charles Dickens's *Great Expectations*
A Cultural Life, 1860–2012
Mary Hammond

Charles Dickens's *Our Mutual Friend*
A Publishing History
Sean Grass

Lewis Carroll's *Alice's Adventures in Wonderland* and *Through the Looking-Glass*
A Publishing History
Zoe Jaques and Eugene Giddens

Baroness Orczy's *The Scarlet Pimpernel*
A Publishing History
Sally Dugan

Frances Burney's *Cecilia*
A Publishing History
Catherine M. Parisian

Elizabeth Gaskell's *Cranford*
A Publishing History
Thomas Recchio

The Rise of the Modernist Bookshop
Books and the Commerce of Culture in the Twentieth Century

HUW OSBORNE
Royal Military College of Canada

LONDON AND NEW YORK

First published 2015 by Ashgate Publishing

2 Park Square, Milton Park, Abingdon, Oxfordshire OX14 4RN
52 Vanderbilt Avenue, New York, NY 10017

Routledge is an imprint of the Taylor & Francis Group, an informa business

First issued in paperback 2019

British Library Cataloguing in Publication Data
A catalogue record for this book is available from the British Library

The Library of Congress has cataloged the printed edition as follows:

The rise of the modernist bookshop: books and the commerce of culture in the twentieth century / edited by Huw Osborne.
  pages cm. — (Ashgate studies in publishing history)
Includes bibliographical references and index.
ISBN 978-1-4724-4699-2 (hardcover: alk. paper) — ISBN 978-1-4724-4700-5 (ebook) — ISBN 978-1-4724-4701-2 (epub)
1. Booksellers and bookselling—History—20th century. 2. Independent bookstores—United States—History—20th century. 3. Independent bookstores—England—London—History—20th century. 4. Independent bookstores—France—Paris—History—20th century. 5. Literature publishing—History—20th century. 6. Authors and readers—History—20th century. 7. Books and reading—Social aspects. 8. Modernism (Literature) I. Osborne, Huw Edwin.
 Z473.R655 2015
 381'.450020904—dc23

                                                                          2014049926

ISBN: 978-1-4724-4699-2 (hbk)
ISBN: 978-0-367-88084-2 (pbk)

Contents

List of Figures

Notes on Contributors

Ted Bishop is a Professor in the Department of Literature and Film at the University of Alberta. He writes and teaches in the areas of Modernist literature, print-culture history, and creative non-fiction. He has authored and edited books on Virginia Woolf and published articles on James Joyce, archives, and motorcycle travel. *His Riding with Rilke: Reflections on Motorcycles and Books* (Penguin 2005) was a finalist for Governor-General's Award in Nonfiction and was named a "Best Book" by the Toronto Globe and Mail and CBC's "Talking Books." His latest book is *The Social Life of Ink: Culture, Wonder, and Our Relationship with the Written Word* (Penguin 2014).

Barbara Brannon, whose career has primarily involved editing, publishing, and book history, heads up a nonprofit organization for the Texas Historical Commission. Her work has appeared in such books and journals as *American University Presses* (Detroit, MI: Gale), *Agent of Change: Twenty-Five Years of Print Culture Studies* (University of Massachusetts Press), *Publishing Research Quarterly*, *Paradise Printed and Bound: Book Arts in Northampton and Beyond*, *Papers of the Bibliographic Society of America*, *Robert Frost Review*, and *John Jakes: A Critical Companion* (Greenwood Press).

Bartholomew Brinkman is Assistant Professor of English at Framingham State University, where he specializes in modern and contemporary poetry, print culture, and digital humanities. His essays have appeared in such venues as *Journal of Modern Literature*, *Modernism/modernity*, *African American Review*, and the *Cambridge Companion to Modern American Poetry*. He co-edits with Cary Nelson the Modern American Poetry Site (www.modernamericanpoetry.org).

David Eberly is co-editor of, and contributor to, *Virginia Woolf and Trauma: Embodied Texts* (Pace University Press, 2007). He has also published essays on homophobia, censorship and the arts, Walt Whitman and Frank O'Hara, and other diverse topics. His first collection of poetry, *What Has Been Lost, was published in 1*982. Since then, his poetry has appeared in numerous anthologies and periodicals. He worked briefly in The Grolier Poetry Bookshop and then, after gaining experience in non-profit organisations, served on its foundation board.

Celia Hilliard is the author of *The Woman's Athletic Club of Chicago: A History* (Women's Athletic Club, 1999); *Then and Now: Thirty Years of the Newberry Library Associates* (Newberry Library, 1995); and *Providing a Home: A History of the Old People's Home of the City of Chicago* (Old People's Home of the City of Chicago, 1983). Most recently, she completed a major project, *'The Prime Mover': Charles L. Hutchinson and the Making of the Art Institute of Chicago*, which was published as an entire issue (Spring 2010) of *Museum Studies*. In addition, she has contributed to *Other People's Books: Association Copies and the Stories They Tell* (Caxton Club, 2011), *The Encyclopedia of Chicago History* (2004), *Inland Printers: The Fine Press Movement in Chicago* (Oak Knoll, 2003), *Women Building Chicago: A Biographical Dictionary* (Indiana University Press, 2001), and *A Wild Kind of Boldness: A Chicago History Reader* (Eerdmans, 1998).

Katy Masuga teaches at Skidmore College in Paris and is the recipient of a 2015–2016 postdoctoral teaching and research fellowship in 'Science and Storytelling' at the Sorbonne. She holds a Ph.D. in Comparative Literature and a joint Ph.D. in Literary Theory and Criticism from the University of Washington, Seattle. Author of *The Secret Violence of Henry Miller* (Camden House, 2011) and *Henry Miller and How He Got That Way* (University of Edinburgh Press, 2011), Masuga's publications also include a dozen fiction/nonfiction-blurring short stories and two dozen essays and anthology chapters on topics including language games in Beckett, Wittgenstein and Blanchot; ekphrasis in Whitman, Hart Crane and Miller; D.H. Lawrence's poetry; altered books; and the vegetarian diet of Frankenstein's Creature. Her current primary research focus is on the intersections between literature, science and technology, and the visual arts.

Huw Osborne is Associate Professor in the Department of English at the Royal Military College of Canada. He is the author of *Rhys Davies* (University of Wales Press, 2009) and has contributed to such journals and books as *Almanac*, *The International Journal of Welsh Studies*, and *Military Culture and Education* (Ashgate, 2010). He is currently editing an interdisciplinary collection of essays on Queer Wales for the Gender Studies in Wales Series of the University of Wales Press.

Molly Schwartzburg is Curator at the Albert and Shirley Small Special Collections Library at the University of Virginia, where she acquires and cares for rare materials in all subject areas and formats. From 2006 to 2012 she was Cline Curator of Literature at the Harry Ransom Center at the University of Texas, where she curated large-scale exhibitions on topics such as Edgar Allan Poe, the Beat Generation, and the Rubaiyat of Omar Khayyam. Her most recent publication, on the acquisition, cataloguing, and use of the papers of David Foster Wallace, is 'Observations on the Archive at the Harry Ransom Center', in *The Legacy of David Foster Wallace*, ed. Samuel Cohen and Lee Konstantinou (University of Iowa Press, 2012).

Sylvia Whitman has been the proprietor of Shakespeare and Company since 2006. She took up the reins from her father, George Whitman, who founded the bookstore in 1951.

Acknowledgements

This book has been several years in the making. The idea originally derived from a seminar on 'Modernism and the Book Trade' at the 2006 Modernist Studies Association conference in Tulsa. In the years following, it gained a focus on bookshops in particular, eventually drawing together the contributors to this collection. I am very grateful to the participants of that original seminar (Rebecca Berne, Patrick Collier, Elizabeth Dickens, Sophia Estante, Maria Fackler, James Gifford, Patricia Rae, Molly Schwartzburg, Jennifer Sorensen, and Aaron Zacks). The ideas and discussions in this seminar established the groundwork for the current project. I am especially grateful for the kindness and mentorship of Patricia Rae, who supervised my post-doctoral research at Queen's University, Kingston. Patricia saw the value of the project and encouraged me to pursue it; this book would not be possible without her support. I also gratefully acknowledge the Queen's University Principal's Development Fund Fellowship that originally funded this work. In subsequent years, this research was funded by the Royal Military College of Canada's Academic Research Program, which made possible many productive trips to archives and conferences. Thanks also to the helpful and knowledgeable staff at the Harry Ransom Center, University of Texas, Austin, who provided so much patient assistance. I am also indebted to David Goodway, who provided materials, a critical eye, and encouraging email conversations over the past few years. I am grateful to several colleagues, especially Irwin Streight and Ted Bishop, who provided welcome advice on edited collections. Thanks also to colleagues, family, and friends, including Helen Luu, Chantel Lavoie, Geraint Osborne, Brian Osborne, and Ann Osborne, who generously read parts of this book in draft and who patiently listened to me throughout the process. A very special thanks is reserved for Ann Donahue at Ashgate for her enthusiasm and patience. From the earliest days when this book was nothing but a brief synopsis, Ann was there with encouraging support. Lastly, I would like to thank the contributors of this book who shared the vision and worked so hard to make it happen; I am humbled to be in the company of such an impressive group of scholars who have begun such an exciting dialogue. It has been a joy to work with this community.

Introduction:
Openings

Huw Osborne

When we enter bookshops, we engage in a social and spatial act on the threshold of commerce and culture, one that activates material, aesthetic, political, personal, and communal affiliations and commitments. Through this act, we stake claims on the place of art and reading in a capitalist economy, we shape the towns and cities in which we would like to live, and we connect our private literate reflection to public consumption and exchange. The interests of commerce and culture, however, are not easily reconciled, and bookshops have long operated within the fraught space formed in these twinned and competing forces. They are charged social spaces that open up the field of cultural production in ways that are both intimate and expansive. As Jean-Luc Nancy writes, the bookshop 'opens to the reader the general space of all kinds of opening'.[1] The opening of a door leads to the opening of books and the opening of ideas. The opening of the physical space of ideas leads to the opening of communities and to the opening of the communication that sustains a literary culture.

The bookshops in this collection opened their doors for the first time between 1913 and 1927, and their histories are also the history of the relationship between modernism and the market. Lawrence Rainey, who has done the most to establish the importance of bookshops in the production and reception of modern literature, argues that modernism's supposed resistance to commodity culture often exposes its actual embeddedness within that culture, and when the book emerges within the bookshop as a recognisable commodity, it is a product of 'decisions and actions within the context of a body of institutions, a corpus of collecting, marketing, and discursive practices that constitutes a composite social space'.[2]

This is an important reminder of the wide field of a book's production, dissemination, and reception, but the book does not always emerge from the shop *after* these more important processes have taken place; rather, as Rainey illustrates in his discussion of Shakespeare and Company, it is integral to them.[3] Mark Morrisson has similarly argued that literature that emerged within the context of mass printing could not escape the effects of advertising and the mass market periodical that

---

[1]   Jean-Luc Nancy, *On the Commerce of Thinking: Of Books and Bookstores*, trans. David Wells (New York: Fordham University Press, 2009), 39.

[2]   Lawrence S. Rainey, *Institutions of Modernism: Literary Elites and Public Culture* (New Haven: Yale University Press, 1998), 44.

[3]   See also Alissa Karl, *Modernism and the Marketplace: Literary Culture and Consumer Capitalism in Rhys, Woolf, and Nella Larsen* (New York: Routledge, 2009), 80–112.

contributed so much to the emergence of modern commercial culture.[4] Modernist writers and their communities were inseparable from literary institutions and their material practices, and many of these writers were savvy self-promoters applying shrewd marketing knowledge in the branding of modernism. Whether in relation to journalism, advertising, popular culture, or celebrity, modern literary culture is shaped within and in relation to the commercial forces that characterise twentieth-century culture as a whole,[5] and much of the work of this shaping took place in bookshops. While some of these booksellers resisted their implication in the market, they were all essential material supports to a wide range of authors. They assumed several institutional roles as publishers, printers, patrons, promoters, and agents; in doing so, they drew authors, publishers, reviewers, editors, publisher's readers, and many others from across the field of cultural production, and their shops, therefore, were nodal spaces within these networks. Each of the shops in this collection is, as Alissa Karl writes of Shakespeare and Company, an 'enterprise, logistical network, and literal and figurative space that consolidates and institutionalizes'[6] literary communities, movements, and reputations.

This book addresses a gap in our understanding of twentieth-century bookshops as sites of cultural production, dissemination, and reception. Although works of oral history, memoir, and biography[7] have done much to illustrate the significance of bookshops, there is a need for more extensive scholarly work on the social, commercial, and cultural impact of bookstores within their literary,

---

[4]   Mark S. Morrisson, *The Public Face of Modernism: Little Magazines, Audiences, and Reception, 1905–1920* (Madison: University of Wisconsin Press, 2001), 4.

[5]   Patrick Collier, *Modernism on Fleet Street* (Aldershot: Ashgate, 2006); Catherine Turner, *Marketing Modernism Between the Two World Wars* (Amherst and Boston: University of Massachusetts Press, 2003); David E. Chinitz, *T.S. Eliot and the Cultural Divide* (Chicago: University of Chicago Press, 2003); Aaron Jaffe, *Modernism and the Culture of Celebrity* (Cambridge: Cambridge University Press, 2005).

[6]   Karl, 99.

[7]   A great deal of excellent work in the form of memoir, oral history, and biography has been done. Works of memoir include Sylvia Beach, *Shakespeare and Company* (Omaha: University of Nebraska Press, 1991); Madge Jenison, *Sunwise Turn, A Human Comedy of Bookselling* (New York: E.P. Dutton & Co., 1923); Joy Grant, *Harold Monro and the Poetry Bookshop* (Berkeley: University of California Press, 1967); the 1975 special issue of the *Journal of Modern Literature* 4.4 (1975), which collected recollections of the famous customers of The Gotham Book Mart; W.G. Roger, *Wise Men Fish Here: The Story of Francis Steloff and the Gotham Book Mart* (New York: Harcourt Brace & World, 1965); Anthony Rota, *Books in the Blood: Memoirs of a Fourth Generation Bookseller* (Middlesex: Private Libraries Association; New Castle: Oak Knoll Press, 2002); and Alistair McCleery, David Finkelstein, and Jennie Renton, eds, *An Honest Trade: Booksellers and Bookselling in Scotland* (Edinburgh: Birlinn, 2009). For oral history, see Sue Bradley, *The British Book Trade: An Oral History* (London: The British Library, 2008); and Sheila Markham, *A Book of Booksellers: Conversations with the Antiquarian Book Trade* (New Castle: Oak Knoll, 2007).

historical, political, and economic contexts.[8] Rainey's work on Sylvia Beach has demonstrated the value of thinking of bookstores within the networks of Modernist institutions. Within this body of institutions, bookshop owners are what Robert Darnton refers to as the 'forgotten middlemen of literature' who demonstrate 'the character of publishing as an activity'.[9] In their various roles, booksellers occupy essential sites of literary production and negotiation; they are instrumental in facilitating what Darnton further describes as 'the transactions that brought into being a small amount of literature from the nebulous vastness of the literature that might have been',[10] always operating in the shop, that 'crucial area where supply [meets] demand'.[11] But, for our purposes, perhaps even Darnton's 'middlemen' does not go far enough. Not only were many of these twentieth-century booksellers *middlewomen*,[12] but none of them could be regarded as mere conduits

---

[8]   Important historical work on bookstores is provided by John Tebbel, *A History of Book Publishing in America*. 3 vols (New York: R.R. Bowker, 1972–1978); John Tebbel, 'A Brief History of American Bookselling', *Bookselling in America and the World: Some Observations and Recollections in Celebration of the 75th Anniversary of the American Booksellers Association*, ed. Charles B. Anderson (New York: Quadrangle, 1975); F.A. Mumby and Ian Norrie, *Publishing and Bookselling* (London: Jonathan Cape, 1974); Giles Mandelbrote, ed., *Out of Profit and into Print: A History of the Rare and Secondhand Book Trade in Britain in the Twentieth Century* (London: British Library; New Castle: Oak Knoll Press, 2006); and James Raven, *The Business of Books: Booksellers and the English Book Trade* (New Haven and London: Yale University Press, 2007). Useful historical surveys and analyses of bookselling are also found in Laura Miller, *Reluctant Capitalists: Bookselling and the Culture of Consumption* (Chicago: University of Chicago Press, 2006); and John B. Thompson, *Merchants of Culture: The Publishing Business in the Twenty-First Century* (Cambridge UK: Polity Press, 2010). Other scholarly work on bookshops include Christopher Hilliard, 'The Literary Underground of 1920s London', *Social History* 33.2 (May 2008), 154–82; and Jeremy Tranmer, 'Taking Books to the People: Radical Bookshops and the British Left', *The Lives of the Book, Past, Present, and Future*, ed. Nathalie Collé-Bak, Monica Latham, and David Ten Eyck (Nancy: Presses Universitaires de Nancy, 2010). See also David Embledge's many articles on bookstores, including 'Isaiah Thomas Invents the Bookstore Chain', *Publishing and Research Quarterly* 28.1 (2012), 53–64; 'The Gotham Book Mart: Location, Location, Location', *International Journal of the Book* 9.4 (2013), 147–60; 'The Old Corner Bookstore: "Rialto of Current Good Things, Hub of the Hub,"' *Concord Saunterer: A Journal of Thoreau Studies* 16 (2008), 103–18; and 'City Lights Bookstore: 'A Finger in the Dike', *International Journal of the Book* 3.4 (2006), 27–34.

[9]   Robert Darnton, *The Kiss of L'Amourette: Reflections in Cultural History* (New York: Norton, 1990), 128.

[10]   Ibid., 138.

[11]   Ibid., 148.

[12]   As businesswomen working at the site where reading and shopping overlap, many of the booksellers featured in this collection explicitly or implicitly address the gendering of modern consumer culture, identifying selling, consuming, and reading women as part of what Rita Felski refers to as 'an alternative model of the rational female consumer', one that challenges the association of mass culture with femininity and that resituates women

connecting other, more important, elements of the 'communications circuit'.[13] Whereas we know a great deal about the work of publishers, agents, reviewers, and advertisers, we know comparatively little about the bookstore owners who created the spaces in which many of these more readily recognisable institutional figures worked creatively with one another. In bringing to light the work of key bookshop proprietors, this collection extends the existing discussion on bookshops to include less familiar sites, such as Fanny Butcher's Chicago bookshop, Frank Shay's Greenwich Village bookshop, and Marion Dodd and Mary Byers Smith's Hampshire Bookshop. At the same time, it revisits well-known shops, such as Shakespeare and Company and Harold Monro's Poetry Bookshop. Taken together, these chapters detail how bookshops were active producers within the field of literary production, making creative interventions into the literary marketplace.

These interventions took many forms. Fanny Butcher, for instance, merged her work within her bookshop's literary community with her day job as a literary columnist at *The Chicago Tribune*. She demonstrates the mutual dependence of mass periodical publication and Modernist literary institutions, and she was a respected source of marketing for authors in search of a good plug in the press to advance their public image. All of these bookshop spaces were networking hubs whose importance is defined by their ability to bring people together, and the artists that they promoted and published (often in anti-commercial terms and forms of publication) were simultaneously marketed and exploited in the business of personality and celebrity. Molly Schwartzburg's chapter on Frank Shay's shop makes this point in the most explicit detail. Shay's office door with its many signatures highlighted the importance of a wider cult of personality that defined the shop and the culture of Greenwich Village in the 1920s, a culture poised between bohemianism and the tourism to which Shay's shop contributed and from which it benefitted. Many of these shops, furthermore, were important stops in the lecture tour circuit of celebrity authors, which was part of the co-emergence of modern writing and celebrity.[14] Defined by the famous names associated with them, these shops bore what Aaron Jaffe calls the 'imprimatur' of these authors: 'At once the

---

as important cultural producers. As with important Modernist periodicals, many of whose editors were women, these shops stand opposed to the dystopian modern vision of the all-consuming woman as the embodiment of capitalist expansion. See, for example, Rita Felski, *The Gender of Modernity* (Cambridge, MA: Harvard University Press, 1995), 89–90; and Jane E. Marek, *Women Editing Modernism: Little Magazines and Literary History* (Lexington: University of Kentucky Press, 1995).

[13]   According to Darnton, the communications circuit 'runs from the author to the publisher (if the bookseller does not assume that role), the printer, the shipper, the bookseller, and the reader', 111.

[14]   Timothy W. Galow, 'Literary Modernism in the Age of Celebrity', *Modernism/ Modernity* 17.2 (2010), 313–14. See also Karen Leick, *Gertrude Stein and the Making of American Celebrity* (London: Routledge, 2009); Deborah M. Mix, 'Gertrude Stein's Currency', *Modernist Star Maps*, ed. Aaron Jaffe and Jonathon Goldman (Farnham, UK: Ashgate, 2010), 93–106; and Catherine Turner, *Marketing Modernism Between the Two Wars* (Amherst and Boston: University of Massachusetts Press, 2003).

distinctive mark and a sanctioning impression, the imprimatur ... turns the author into a formal artefact, fusing it to the text as a reified signature of value. The imprimatur, then, represents a moment of clarity to all takers against the apparent obscurity of the modernist meaning'.[15] These names fused not only with the texts but also with the shops that sold the books and hosted their authors, sanctioning 'elite, high cultural consumption at times when economies of mass cultural value predominate'.[16] This process was carried out in the physical spaces of the shops in which authors left their marks in the forms of photographs on the wall or even literal signatures, as in the cases of Frank Shay's door and Fanny Butcher's guestbook. Some these shops were, from the outside, literary celebrity spectacles for the young aspiring writer and, from the inside, celebrity identity workshops in which meeting the proper reviewers, editors, publishers, or collectors was useful, and even essential, for managing one's career. In a number of ways, therefore, whether in terms of marketing, journalism, or celebrity, this book contributes to the ongoing discussion of modern literature's relationship to commercial culture.

While clearly engaged in consumer culture, the wide range of these booksellers' roles in the literary marketplace makes it difficult to place them simplistically within a 'communications circuit'. If anything, these shops demonstrate just how nebulous and idiosyncratic the literary market can be as it manifests itself in these unpredictable social-commercial spaces. All bookshop owners work in the space where the marketing strategies of publishers meet the messy and unpredictable vagaries of consumption, but shops like the ones in this collection also foster communities in which all stages and processes of literary production overlap in relation to intersecting literary markets. Most of the interactions in these communities could be described in terms of Jennifer Wicke's 'coterie consumption', where the communities forming in the commercial spaces of bookshops compose 'loosely knit and loosely netted group[s] of people whose consumption and production caroms off each other, recirculates and then scatters out into the wider marketplace'.[17] In this dynamic space where the literary and the commercial meet, the market is as 'at least as much an aesthetic phenomenon as it is anything else, and ... neither art nor economics can be separated out of it or given an artificial primacy as instigator or reflector'.[18] These bookshops, 'situated in the spaces between author and reader – but which authors also take part in', reveal the market, in Claire Squire's terms, 'as a form of representation and interpretation ... surrounding the production, dissemination and reception of texts'.[19] Squire's spatial terms are especially appropriate to the bookstore. Again

---

[15]   Jaffe, 20.

[16]   Ibid.

[17]   Jennifer Wicke, 'Coterie Consumption: Bloomsbury, Keynes, and Modernism as Marketing', *Marketing Modernisms: Self-Promotion, Canonization, Rereading*, ed. Kevin J. Dettmar and Stephen Watt (Ann Arbor: The University of Michigan Press, 1996), 118–19.

[18]   Ibid., 118.

[19]   Claire Squires, *Marketing Literature: The Making of Contemporary Writing in Britain* (New York: Palgrave Macmillan, 2009), 3. Original italics.

and again in this collection, the bookshop is the space where authors, readers, representations, interpretations, production, and dissemination cohere in diversely unpredictable acts of intellectual and material exchange. Indeed, they are not unlike the anthologies and periodicals published from within these shops, which may even be seen as the spatial and social equivalent to an anthology or miscellany; not surprisingly, one continually finds the names of shop visitors reappearing together in tables of contents in everything from little magazines, to special editions, to Penguin paperbacks. In these shops that host physical encounters between readers, books and authors, the cultural work of the bookstore is both inseparable from and yet irreducible to the economic imperatives of the market.

These charged sites of commercial and cultural interplay, one must stress, do not simply expose commercial complicity, but embrace 'material and intellectual – finally ideological – practices'.[20] They reveal how the entrepreneurial work of bookshop proprietorship was contiguous with the cultural work of literary creation, and the material, intellectual, aesthetic, and political goals of each were never far from each other. Fanny Butcher's dual role typifies the interdependence of Modernist writing and mass market newspapers through which, as Patrick Collier writes, 'questions and anxieties about the public, democracy, and the arts, and the individual writer's or artist's potential influence over them' could be worked out.[21] The Hampshire Bookshop and The Grolier Book Shop both have strong university affiliations, linking their commercial and cultural work to an explicitly educational one. Frank Shay's shop is linked to the Provincetown Players, and Harold Monro's shop was the organ for Georgians and Imagists. The shops position themselves within the competing aesthetic, social, political, and economic claims of the literary market, and the various habitués of these shops position themselves within these spaces and in relation to one another. As Bartholomew Brinkman elaborates in his chapter on Monro, for example, this position was instrumental in bringing different and competing modernisms into dialogue with one another, not simply in the diverse displays of books and periodicals, but in the informal and formal face-to-face interactions of the patrons. The same holds for all of these shops, as will be seen, for instance, in the lecture series of The Hampshire Bookshop, The Grolier Poetry Book Shop, The Sunwise Turn, and Shakespeare and Company; or in the door of Frank Shay's shop; or Charles Lahr's anarchist eclecticism.

Engaged as they are in these networks, the influences and experiences of the shops featured in this collection consistently overlap. Both Frank Shay and Mary Mowbray-Clarke were featured lecturers in the 'Intimate Bookshop' lectures at the New York Library Club in January 1922. Christopher Morley frequented both the Hampshire Bookshop and Frank Shay's shop, though, as Ted Bishop tells us in his chapter, Mowbray-Clarke dismissed him as the type of those who write

    [20]   Kevin J. Dettmar and Stephen Watt, 'Introduction: Marketing Modernisms', *Marketing Modernisms: Self-Promotion, Canonization, Rereading* (Ann Arbor: The University of Michigan Press, 1996), 2.

    [21]   Patrick Collier, *Modernism on Fleet Street* (Aldershot: Ashgate, 2006), 6.

'delectable moonshine about dream shops into which the shadow of the credit man never enters'. Anna Wickham crossed the thresholds of The Poetry Bookshop and The Progressive Bookshop. Lola Ridge spoke at The Sunwise Turn and signed Frank Shay's door. Robert Frost visited The Poetry Bookshop while making his name, spoke at The Sunwise Turn in 1919, and later supported the Hampshire Bookshop with his well-established fame. D.H. Lawrence was published by both Monro and Lahr. Yeats visited the Hampshire Bookshop, was a lecture topic in The Sunwise Turn, signed Fanny Butcher's guestbook, and was published by Monro. These shops stocked each other's books and periodicals, celebrated or supported many of the same authors, and they all traded in, and are part of the story of, the transatlantic networks of the twentieth century.

Such connections demonstrate that the bookshops in this collection are important locations of modernism that highlight the increasing hybridity of place. They invite us into considerations of one form of what Peter Brooker and Andrew Thacker describe as the 'social and physical architecture of modernity and the newly and differentiated and gendered locales of its streets, offices, cafes and artists' quarters'.[22] They are both locally fixed in cities and towns and yet tied into transatlantic and global networks, open to the changing conceptions of work, home, leisure, travel, and identity.[23] The shops in this book build connections across ideological, aesthetic, and geographical lines, and they disrupt the psychically charged boundary between 'private' and 'public': they fuse the private act of reading with the public act of consumption and sociability; they offer commercial spaces open to the public thoroughfare but nevertheless become the clubhouses for an elite in-crowd of privileged habitués; they straddle the spaces of business and parlour or salon. In these bridging roles, they may be regarded as what urban sociologists refer to as 'interstitial spaces', and, within them, art emerges as part of the talking, walking, browsing, shopping, playing, eating, and socialising spaces of the city. These interstitial spaces tend to be inclusive ones that level social distinctions and bring together wide varieties of people in interesting and unexpected ways.[24] They are, therefore, potentially catalytic, and the bookstore, which operates on the basis of the circulation of ideas in the physical form of books, is arguably even more likely than most interstitial spaces to produce such meaningful interaction.

This vision of the bookstore as a social space where leisure and consumption overlap is an increasingly familiar one today when so many bookstore proprietors struggle to discover the formula that will sustain their businesses in the digitised

---

[22] Peter Brooker and Andrew Thacker, eds., *Geographies of Modernism: Literatures, Cultures, Spaces* (London: Routledge, 2005), 3.

[23] Ibid., 2.

[24] Ray Oldenburg, *The Great Good Place* (New York: Paragon House: 1991), 14; the connection between third spaces and bookshops is discussed in Audrey Lang and Jo Royle, 'Bookselling Culture and Consumer Behaviour', *The Future of the Book in the Digital Age*, ed. Bill Cope and Angus Phillips (Oxford: Chandos Publishing, 2006), 14–16.

world of ebooks and Amazon. While most of the shops in this collection failed after too few years, and while two of them were bought out by Doubleday in the rise of book-market rationalisation and chain stores, this book does not tell the story of the heroic failure of independents within the soulless forces of the twentieth-century book industry. On the contrary, it suggests that, despite the real difference of scale, all bookshops share a common set of challenges and anxieties, all share the same field of literary production, and independents ignore this fact at their peril. Two of the shops in this collection have survived into the twenty-first-century book market, and both have adapted to continue the cultural and community work that keeps them vital as lived social spaces and sites of literary exchange.[25] The book in your hands (or on your screen) is called the *Rise of the Modernist Bookshop* because we have not yet witnessed the fall of the distinctive work of many booksellers, and the forces of commerce and culture that cohered in the early twentieth-century personal bookshop are still the name of the game today.

Laura Miller's study of bookselling in the twentieth and twenty-first centuries includes both independents and chains, demonstrating a shared history and co-development through which each survived by learning from the failures and successes of the other[26] in their shared literary-commercial paradox; Miller found that people working across the book trade see their commercial activities as unique in capitalist markets. The commercial work they do is aesthetic and political in nature because it 'engages their creativity and ... contributes to the greater good'.[27] These 'reluctant capitalists', as Miller calls them, consistently characterise books

---

[25] One might also look to the recent re-opening of Foyles' flagship store in London (originally opened in 1903), which has gone through an extensive community and industry work-shopping process to build 'the bookshop of the future'. Foyles today is more than ever a hybrid or interstitial space where reading and browsing mingles with socialising, eating, and drinking, where artists exhibit and authors offer public readings. In the new Foyles, mobile apps allow one to browse electronically within the brick and mortar of the shop, and, beyond the walls, the store organises travel and literary tourism. Foyles may not offer the more intimate literary communities associated with the shops in this collection, but it is an example of a business surviving by maintaining some of what makes these iconic bookshops special, which is then packaged in a commercial model that sustains a culture of reading. The recreation of Foyles has been reported in several articles in *The Bookseller*: See Sion Hamilton, 'Foyles Workshop', *The Bookseller*, 22 February, 2013, http://www.thebookseller.com/feature/depth-foyles-workshop.html; Lisa Campbell, 'Titchner to be First Exhibitor at Foyles Flagship', *The Bookseller*, 22 May, 2014, http://www.thebookseller.com/news/titchner-be-first-exhibitor-new-foyles-flagship.html; and Lisa Campbell, 'Foyles Launches Literary Tours', *The Bookseller*, 23 May 2014, http://www.thebookseller.com/news/foyles-launches-literary-tours.html.

[26] Laura Miller, *Reluctant Capitalists: Bookselling and the Culture of Consumption* (Chicago: University of Chicago Press, 2006), 115.

[27] Ibid., 219.

as 'sacred products'[28] and are often reluctant to treat them as commercial products at all. Just 'as books were believed to have a particular moral worth, bookselling is viewed as an especially moral endeavour'.[29] As one independent bookseller put it,

> How is it different? Well, the basic difference is that a book really is a little piece of culture … [I]t has to do with our entire intellectual life, and with our progress, and with our quality of life. Although a grocery store has to do with our quality of life as well, there's simply a bigger difference between any two books and any two different brands of orange juice. It's just a *much* larger difference. And it's a much more important difference.[30]

On the basis of this common perspective, Miller argues that these stores implicitly 'present a critique of prevailing economic and consumer practices'.[31] When consumers choose to shop at an independent bookstore when they might instead simply click on Amazon, they 'incorporate some understanding of a social benefit to their consumption habits'[32] and practice a form of 'consumption that incorporates a political dimension'.[33] As merchants of culture, as economic agents who transform an economic exchange into an intellectual or leisure activity in excess of the immediate act of purchasing a book, booksellers fashion spaces that implicitly revise (but never escape) their dominant commercial activity. Within the historical scope of this book, the bookstore has operated in this fraught relationship between commerce and culture, and as we look today to the bookstores surviving or closing down but also expanding and opening their doors for the first time, we do well to recall the legacy of these forerunners, whether they defined themselves in personal, Modernist, counter-cultural, communal, or capitalist terms.

While there is much that connects these shops in terms of their work within the commerce of culture, each essay has its own story to tell, focused as they are upon the strong personalities of individual proprietors who bind together different (though overlapping) communities in particular times and spaces. This book is organised in a roughly chronological and geographical structure, beginning with two important forerunners, The Hampshire Bookshop and The Sunwise Turn. Barbara A. Brannon's analysis of Marion Dodd and Mary Byers Smith's Hampshire Bookshop of Northampton, Massachusetts identifies the shop as a pioneer in the creation of the 'personal bookshop'. Opened in 1916 and surviving until 1971, the Hampshire Bookshop became a key literary, social, and economic institution. Brannon's analysis identifies this shop not only as a successful general bookstore, but an innovative and profitable university bookstore for Smith's College. Like other shops in the collection, the Hampshire shop proprietors served

---

[28] Ibid.
[29] Ibid.
[30] Ibid., 220.
[31] Ibid., 214.
[32] Ibid., 200.
[33] Ibid., 214.

as reviewers, editors, publishers, and promoters, and the shop became a hub for an influential international network of writers. Brannon is especially concerned with bookselling as a profession for women and with the institutional ties between the shop and Smith's College. Dodd and Smith's education, their connection with the college, their commitment to communities and professions for women, and their vision of the college bookstore are at the heart of their venture, and their shop was an extension of both the liberal arts education they had obtained at Smith and their involvement in social work during and after college, both of which had prepared them, they felt, to broaden and improve minds. They were poised to extend the college's public contact, expanding ideas and dialogue beyond its ivy walls, and, in doing so, they contributed to literary professionalism for women.

Ted Bishop examines another prominent early twentieth-century bookshop owned and operated by women, Madge Jennison and Mary Mowbray-Clarke's The Sunwise Turn in New York. Drawing on detailed archival research and theories of space, Bishop describes the history of the shop in terms of its owners' original Modernist vision and ultimate capitulation to the dominant forces of metropolitan capitalism. Opening in 1916 and closing in 1927 when it was sold to the Doubleday chain of bookstores, this self-consciously Modernist bookshop sought to foster cultured audiences with modern sensibilities. The shop's owners created a space for *reading* rather than *buying* and saw their business as an extension of the art they sold. Bishop argues, however, that The Sunwise Turn operated on the symbolic capital garnered from the disavowal of its primarily commercial activity and that, at the end of the day, the business of bohemia cannot deny its dependence on economic necessities for survival. Ultimately, this liminal space operating on the threshold of the private and public, domestic and commercial, was forced to sell out, gathered up in the rising wave of chain store merchandising.

Molly Schwartzburg's chapter on Frank Shay's book shop in Greenwich Village takes as its point of departure an interior door of the shop, an artefact which vividly materialises the purpose of this book. This door bears the signatures of 217 literary, artistic, and bohemian celebrities who frequented the shop between 1921 and 1925. It includes the signatures of novelists Theodore Dreiser and John Dos Passos, poets Sara Teasdale and Lola Ridge, publishers Albert Boni and John Farrar, a dozen individuals involved with the Provincetown Players, and self-professed bohemian celebrities Sadakichi Hartmann and Harry Kemp. In Schwartzburg's analysis, Frank Shay's shop documents a neglected transitional period of the cultural life of Greenwich Village in the 1920s when the major bohemian moment was over. As Greenwich Village became a trendy post-bohemian attraction, the intimate space of the bookshop operated in an ambiguous relationship to the cults of personality, celebrity, marketing, and tourism that began to grow around it.

In Celia Hilliard's chapter, we stay in the 1920s but move to Chicago, where Fanny Butcher, as mentioned above, negotiated two complementary roles as bookshop owner and literary critic for the *Chicago Tribune*. Hilliard stresses that because Chicago was then the railway hub of the nation and *The Tribune* was for many years the most powerful newspaper in the Midwest, Butcher was geographically and professionally well positioned to connect networks of writers. Drawing on the archive and Butcher's journalism, Hilliard maps the forging of a wide literary influence centred on Butcher's shop. Hilliard argues that Butcher's literary critical role engaged writers as collaborators in a broad literary enterprise. This enterprise spilled into the space of the shop where the regular appearance of international literary and artistic celebrities, together with a cosmopolitan atmosphere, made the shop an important gathering place. The guestbook of Butcher's shop includes the signatures of Sherwood Anderson, Stephen Vincent Benet, Willa Cather, Floyd Dell, Edna Ferber, Henry Blake Fuller, Sinclair Lewis, Somerset Maugham, Maurice Maeterlinck, Harriet Monroe, Carl Van Vechten, Hugh Walpole, William Allen White, and W.B. Yeats. As Hilliard's analysis demonstrates, Fanny Butcher served as bookshop owner, editor, reviewer, and critic across fifty years, and, in these roles, she occupied a complex and shifting position within literary networks and institutions.

Bartholomew Brinkman's chapter examines the ways in which Harold Monro's Poetry Bookshop indexes the production, dissemination, and consumption of literary modernism within its wider economic conditions. Opening in 1913 and closing in 1935, the bookshop drew poetic modernism's major figures, including W.B. Yeats, T.S. Eliot, Ezra Pound, and Robert Frost. Instrumental in the production of the literary journal *Poetry and Drama*, Edward Marsh's Georgian anthologies, and Pound's *Des Imagistes* anthology, the Bookshop was a cultural space that privileged the reading of poetry over its sale; however, as Brinkman demonstrates, this same space was equally instrumental in its own demise by popularising modern poetry and demonstrating its commercial viability. This privileged space of coterie consumption that had contributed to disseminating transatlantic modern poetry and forging an international community of poets could not survive within the wider field of literary production that it had influenced.

My own chapter on The Progressive Bookshop describes the loose community of writers that circulated through Charles Lahr's anti-capitalist and counter-cultural commercial space, and it illustrates Lahr's wide influence across a diverse field of literary production. His relationship with such writers as D.H. Lawrence, Rhys Davies, Hugh MacDiarmid, Liam O'Flaherty, H.E. Bates, James Hanley, T.F. Powys, and many others reveals his conflicted work against and within the mechanisms of literary publication. Spatially, the shop functioned as a counter-space that intervened in the dominant urban commercial culture that determined literary success. The chapter also examines Lahr's subversive publishing activities, especially his publication of James Hanley's *The German Prisoner*, a limited edition book whose publication history, physical form, and literary content manifest a wide range of the aesthetic, commercial, and political commitments within the field of literary production to which Lahr and his shop contributed.

Despite their impact, all of the shops discussed so far are gone. In one way or another, they succumbed to the familiar pressures of the bookselling economy. The Hampshire Bookshop with its strong university affiliation remained open until 1971 when it could no longer compete with the mall bookstores. Both The

Sunwise Turn and Fanny Butcher's shop sold out to the Doubleday chain in 1927, for $5,000 and $10,000, respectively. The Poetry Bookshop and Frank Shay's shop both closed shortly after the deaths of their founding owners. The Progressive Bookshop was bombed in the Blitz, and while Lahr never stopped selling books, the magic of the Red Lion Street shop, with its fortunate convergence of space and time, was lost.

The final two essays offer an alternative to these narratives of loss and failure. They provide a transition from the important modern and Modernist bookshops examined in the collection to the changing contexts of bookselling in the twenty-first century. Both Katy Masuga and David Eberly discuss bookshops that had profound institutional impacts in the early twentieth century and that have survived in some form or fashion into contemporary literary markets. Eberly's essay examines the persisting institutional role of The Grolier Poetry Book Shop in Cambridge, Massachusetts, which has provided commercial and cultural support for poetry since 1927. He maps the stages of the Grolier Poetry Book Shop through its three different owners, explaining how these distinctly different proprietors transformed the shop and its culture to reflect their personal, aesthetic, and political commitments while adapting to an ever-changing literary market. Similarly, Masuga revisits Sylvia Beach's famous Shakespeare and Company to explore how the original shop evolved from one of the most important promoters of modern literature, to a relocated and reimagined Beat salon, and finally to a contemporary literary institution and tourist attraction. These final essays, therefore, feature booksellers who adapted to a market that is ostensibly hostile to the kind of independent bookshops that did so much to foster modern literature.

The questions raised by the chapters in this book are very timely ones. Remembering his own experience working in a bookshop, George Orwell wrote that, despite its more crass elements, bookselling 'is a humane trade which is not capable of being vulgarised beyond a certain point. The combines can never squeeze the small independent bookseller out of existence as they have squeezed the grocer and the milkman'.[34] It is hard to read Orwell's hopeful words and ignore the current state of the independent bookstore. Although one could argue that there were already in place the forms of commercial competition that would eventually culminate in the rise of chain store outlets, box stores, online shopping, and ebooks,[35] Orwell's hopeful prediction derives from a context in which the roles of independent bookshops in literary commercial life were taken for granted. This book examines this earlier period from our contemporary moment when independent bookstores have been receding from our main streets and dispersing

---

[34]   George Orwell, 'Bookshop Memories' [1936], *Facing Unpleasant Facts* (New York: Mariner Books, 2009), 40. I am indebted to Pat Rae (Queen's University, Kingston) for drawing my attention to Orwell in this context.

[35]   The book clubs, the paperback revolution, train station sales, and rising bookselling giants like W.H. Smith were all in place by this time. Orwell's *Keep the Aspidistra Flying* (1936) presents a much less optimistic vision of the bookshop.

into the dynamic digital spaces shaping themselves on the screens of Kindles, Kobos, Nooks, and iPads. These changes are not all bad, but when one considers the significance of books and reading in the development and maintenance of a civil society, the decline of the bookstore is a major change in the intellectual spaces of our towns and cities. As readers turn to ebooks and as students carry out most of their research online, we lose the unique spaces of sociability that independent bookshops have created around, for, and through books and reading. How will the next generation of consumers conceive of the book as it is delivered to them within the matrices of Internet advertising and market segmented cross-merchandising? The rise (and demise in some cases) of book chains, box stores, and online bookselling has contributed to the rationalisation of the book within commodity culture, and the consumption of books is an increasingly uniform experience that removes the 'idiosyncratic, personal judgments of numerous individual booksellers'.[36] As we conceive the urban realities of the future, as we foster the life and industries of creative cities, these same cities accommodate fewer and fewer of these catalytic spaces of literate exchange. It is impossible to predict where bookshops will be in ten years' time. The general decline may continue, and if we grow accustomed to the rationalisation of the book industry in the twenty-first century, we will wonder at the ways in which our relationships to books and reading were once governed by the spaces that physical books required. Then again, we may instead learn to appreciate the distinct pleasures of the bookshops that remain as they forge new roles in the changing book market. In reopening the bookshop spaces in this collection and by mapping the far-reaching influences within and beyond their doors, perhaps this book reminds us, as Sylvia Whitman's coda reminds us, that it is still too early to close the door on bookshops.

---

[36] Miller, 14.

Chapter 1
'We Have Come to Stay': The Hampshire Bookshop and the Twentieth-Century 'Personal Bookshop'

Barbara A. Brannon

Early in the fifty-five-year history of the Hampshire Bookshop of Northampton, Massachusetts, Robert Frost described the enterprise as 'one of the few bookshops in the world where books are sold in something like the spirit they were written in'.[1] To mark the Bookshop's twenty-fifth anniversary in 1936, manager Marion Dodd cannily reprinted his words in a limited-edition keepsake, a booklet of Frost's poems that patrons snapped up and collectors today still seek. Turn the pages of the handsomely printed 'From Snow to Snow' and you will readily grasp what set this institution apart, for it encapsulates the founders' aim to draw author, book, and reader into intimate proximity. This was not only a humanistic goal; it was good business sense, establishing a model for bookselling that persists – though severely challenged by chain-store incursions – nearly a century later.

On that same anniversary, Frederic Melcher of *The Publishers' Weekly* toasted the store as 'the most influential bookshop that this country has had during my time of watching the book business'[2] – and if his appreciation was coloured by celebratory hyperbole, he nonetheless recognised that something *was* distinctive about this one small business and its principals, something that changed the way Americans bought, read, and thought about books.

Among the numerous women-run 'personal bookshops' that sprang up during the World War I era and wielded such influence, Hampshire Bookshop cofounders

---

[1]   Robert Frost, 'From Snow to Snow: The Hampshire Bookshop, 1916–1936, Twentieth Anniversary Week' (Northampton, MA: privately printed, 1936). The author's original 16 May 1921, letter to Dodd, a facsimile of which is laid into the booklet, is held in the collections of Amherst College. Dodd drew from Frost's testimonial often in bookshop publicity: it was showcased in the store's house organ, the *Book Scorpion*, in May 1921; used several weeks later in a book-trade overview, 'After Five Years', *The Publishers' Weekly*, 25 June 1921, 1852–53; and recalled in Frances Reed Robinson's retrospective, 'The Hampshire Bookshop', *Smith Alumnae Quarterly* (February 1976), 14–17.

[2]   Marion E. Dodd Papers, box 1609.1, Class of 1906 Papers, and *Smith Alumnae Quarterly* clippings, c. 1951, Smith College Archives, Northampton, Mass. (hereafter cited as MED Papers).

Marion Dodd and Mary Byers Smith claimed theirs was the first.[3] This new boutique approach to bookselling – 'personal' not only because it emphasised one-on-one service bolstered by an ingrained knowledge of books but because it reflected the taste and character of the bookseller – opened up new ways of connecting books with the reading public. The personal bookshop contributed to the rise of literary modernism, in the way the urban coffeehouse would fuel the Beat movement in the 1950s and the chain megastore would drive book-buying habits in the 1990s. Through a hand-picked and hand-sold inventory, regular involvement in the emerging profession, a slate of popular book-and-author events, and a cosy and inviting retail space, 'the Hamp' and other personal bookshops set the standard. Such bookselling enterprises also provided attractive employment and entrepreneurial opportunities for women. And soon they fostered new patterns of consumer and materialist attitudes, changing the way the American public – in particular, women – purchased and perceived books.

Not all the personal bookshops lasted for long. The trend, largely sparked in 1915 by an *Atlantic Monthly* article suggesting bookselling as the ideal occupation for throngs of recent female college graduates, yielded at least forty-four new enterprises throughout the United States by 1920.[4] Within a decade, some of the most promising of these, including the pioneering Sunwise Turn of New York City, were gone. Others fell victim to the Great Depression or simply to changing priorities. But the Hampshire Bookshop, launched in a small central Massachusetts town with only the pooled resources of two Smith College graduates and their handful of investors, remained a going concern through 1971 and a fond memory long after.

Soon after the Bookshop's opening, Northampton's daily newspaper reported that the store seemed 'already to have climbed at least the first rung of its ladder ... And if you question Miss Dodd as to the stability of the organisation,

---

[3]   The Bookshop's founders may not have been aware that Madge Jenison and Mary Mowbray-Clarke had opened the Sunwise Turn Bookshop that same season in New York City, nor did they consider the handful of local bookstores off the beaten path whose female owners had not publicised their founding. In my analysis and in the database of women booksellers I maintain, trade news briefs of openings, sales, or closings from 1905 to 1915 reveal only thirty-eight female proprietors, co-owners, or managers, most of whom were wives or daughters inheriting their husband's or father's enterprises; female clerks managing bookselling operations owned by men; or women setting up shop for themselves in frontier towns as the population expanded westward. These statistics are based on my tallies of notices in *The Publishers' Weekly* and the triennial *American Book Trade Manual*, both published by R.R. Bowker. More in-depth background on the history of the personal bookshop and the origins of the Hampshire Bookshop is documented in my unpublished dissertation, 'No Frigate Like a Book: The Hampshire Bookshop of Northampton, 1916–1971' (Columbia: University of South Carolina, 1998).

[4]   Earl Barnes, 'Bookselling: A New Profession for Women', *Atlantic Monthly* 116 (August 1915), 225–34.

she will reply quickly, "It is very permanent indeed; we have come to stay"'.[5] The Hampshire Bookshop's staying power, more than its sales volume or other measures of success, accounts for the disproportionate breadth of its influence. It served a culturally important region of the United States not only as general and college bookstore, but also as gathering place, purveyor of rare and collectible books, promoter, reviewer, and even editor and publisher. Among the Bookshop's staunchest partisans were publisher Alfred Knopf, author and book-trade wit Christopher Morley, British authors Vita Sackville-West and Harold Nicolson, Dr Doolittle creator Hugh Lofting, and Imagist poet Amy Lowell; dozens of writers of national and international repute, such as William Butler Yeats, Carl Sandburg, Dorothy Canfield Fisher, Thornton Wilder, Archibald MacLeish, Padraic Colum, James Stephens, Edna St Vincent Millay, G.K. Chesterton, Vachel Lindsay, and Bennett Cerf, came to Northampton audiences through the Bookshop's agency. Robert Frost was not alone in recognising the ways the Hampshire Bookshop could aid his publishing career, and he, like many others, remained a friend of the institution throughout his life.

Primed for a Bookselling Partnership

Marion Elza Dodd, Smith College class of 1906, and Mary Byers Smith (no relation to college founder Sophia Smith), class of 1908, had been close friends throughout college though separated by a few years in age. New Jersey native Marion, whose grandfather Moses Dodd had established an esteemed New York publishing house and whose uncles and cousins were also renowned in the book business, met Andover, Massachusetts-born Mary through college clubs. After graduation from Smith, the women maintained their friendship while working at various jobs back home – Marion as a librarian, Mary as a hospital volunteer. But by 1915, as the US was anxiously occupied with events on the European front, each had become restless with life in the parental household. Now in their thirties and both unmarried, they sought a new and worthy challenge.[6]

An inheritance from a wealthy aunt provided Mary a windfall that year, and the pair lighted on the idea of establishing a bookstore in the college town to which they felt such strong ties. Within a few short months, they formed a corporation and enlisted officers and directors (primarily from the ranks of Smith faculty), obtained letters of introduction to jobbers, secured credit, and located a place of business. The $25,000 in capital they had raised through sale of stock to

[5] 'An Hour in the Hampshire Bookshop', (Northampton, Mass.) *Daily Hampshire Gazette*, 6 December 1916.

[6] The Bookshop's history is extraordinarily well documented through the scrapbooks, correspondence, publications, and other records kept by staff and preserved in special collections, Neilson Library, Smith College, Northampton, Mass., and the Smith College Archives.

initial shareholders no doubt helped ensure a sound footing from the outset.[7] The Hampshire Bookshop was launched in April 1916 with the slogan 'There Is No Frigate Like a Book', borrowed from an Emily Dickinson poem. By October the shelves were stocked, and the doors were opened to the public and flocks of Smith students.

Marion Dodd, outgoing and assertive, was a natural organiser and manager. Her authoritative manner commanded respect from associates and employees. At the time she became involved in the Bookshop venture, she had already served as managing editor of a social-work journal and librarian to John D. Rockefeller's General Education Board; as she matured in her professional role, she became quite comfortable dealing with authors, influential publishers, and the media. Her standards of performance were exacting, her expectations of staff high.

While both women were avid readers and informed critics, it was Mary Byers Smith, the poet and volunteer social worker, who reviewed books in the house promotional newsletter and provided guidance on the shop layout and decor. In the store, they used some pieces of furniture that Marion had built, and they chose motifs of ships and the sea that held special meaning for them both.

Since neither Dodd nor Smith left behind correspondence of a personal nature, and since neither took a public stand on issues of women's political or sexual rights, questions about their romantic lives remain matters of speculation. As social critic Betsy Israel points out in her perceptive study of unmarried women of the era, 'the term "lesbian" – the very idea – did not in its current sense yet exist' at the time, and it is unlikely that Dodd or Smith (or their literary, business, or college peers) would have thought of themselves in that sense even if their relationship went deeper than platonic friendship.[8] Certainly they saw themselves as part of a homosocial, female-centric community built on friendship and mutual empowerment, and even in the mid-1920s when rumours circulated that Dodd's new attachment and cohabitation with college professor Esther Cloudman Dunn led Mary Byers Smith to bow out of her ten-year partnership in the Hampshire Bookshop, Dodd and Smith remained lifelong friends.

This sense of community was central to the Bookshop's identity and mission from the outset. Its founders laid out five specific goals:

1. To give all people the variety of pleasures that association with good books always provides: to make itself an indispensable aid to scholarship and research, thereby filling in the gaps of a college curriculum; to increase the reading habit by providing students with a selection of books which will develop a catholic taste in literature; to encourage the collecting of fine books as a means of developing sound criticism and discriminating judgment.

---

[7]   'Smith College Book Store, Northampton, Mass., Incorporated' (Business Notes), *The Publishers' Weekly*, 6 May 1916, 1456; 27 May 1916, 1772.

[8]   On smashes and Boston marriages common at women's colleges, see Betsy Israel, *Bachelor Girl: The Secret History of Single Women in the Twentieth Century* (New York: William Morrow, 2002), 29–30.

2. To offer students the opportunity to save money by establishing a co-operative department somewhat similar to the plan in operation at Yale or Harvard which paid a certain percentage on student purchases at the end of the year in proportion to the profits of the business ...

3. To prove the aptitude of women for the book business.

4. To demonstrate the fact that a college book store can sell all kinds of good books, instead of merely text books and stationery and possibly doughnuts.

5. To make contacts between the author and his public.[9]

Dodd and Smith wisely envisioned the Bookshop as a bookstore to serve both community and college, modelling it on features of the groundbreaking Harvard 'Coop'. Following the rapid growth of American post-secondary education in the late nineteenth century, several colleges and universities had established campus bookstores: the Harvard Co-operative Society (founded 1882) was, and is, among the earliest and best known. Some were owned by the institution, others were completely independent, and some set up a cooperative plan and were even owned and managed by students themselves.[10]

Beyond simply making available the goods students sought, the Hampshire Bookshop's principals actively promoted a cooperative arrangement that would reward buyers for their loyalty and help ensure a steady market. As Dodd put it in a later document, the Bookshop was 'an economic experiment in the selling of books to students, which would give them an opportunity to buy books and supplies more cheaply'.[11] Although the firm was not extended the option of an exclusive contract with Smith College or an official endorsement, it enjoyed the

---

[9]   'Hampshire Bookshop Has Had Interesting History', *Daily Hampshire Gazette*, 17 April 1936.

[10]   The most successful of the cooperative enterprises was the Harvard store, founded in 1882; similar organisations soon followed its precedent, at Michigan and Amherst as well as Yale. The Harvard Coop had been launched by a group of students (and, later, professors) who were unhappy with the high prices of books in Cambridge. Its plan involved nominal yearly dues from, and proportionate dividends to, all members. The Coop was housed on the college premises at first, but as its business expanded, it became an independent operation located off campus – where it still thrives today, though under a quite different business model. N.S.B. Gras, *Harvard Co-operative Society Past and Present, 1882–1942* (Cambridge, MA: Harvard University Press, 1942), 3–19. At Yale, the Brick Row Book Shop was founded in 1916; Cambridge's Dunster House was established in 1919.

[11]   '$19,000 Returned to Cooperative Members by the Hampshire Bookshop', press release, c. 1940 (MED Papers, box 1609). Dodd goes on to explain that the founders had been intrigued by the cooperative movement in Denmark and at the men's colleges, but not wanting to confine themselves to student trade alone, they 'skipped some of the undesirable elements at that time of forming a Cooperative society under the state laws, and established a COOPERATIVE DEPARTMENT for students, faculty and heads of houses'.

blessing of college president Marion LeRoy Burton and his successor Laurenus Clark Seelye and the encouragement generally of alumnae, faculty, and students.[12]

The first such cooperative bookstore at a women's college, the experiment quickly proved successful: halfway through the shop's first year, the cooperative department reported that it had enlisted more than 1,250 Smithies who had each paid a membership fee of one dollar. At the end of the year, members would receive dividends on the store's profits in proportion to the purchases they had made. Though the plan was initially open only to Smith students, the directors promised to extend membership to alumnae if it met their expectations.[13]

Mary Byers Smith was careful to distinguish between the Hampshire Bookshop and the garden-variety campus store. However, as she explained to readers of *The Publishers' Weekly*:

> [T]he fact that we have had from the first a broad, modern conception of bookselling has kept us from even appearing to be a 'college bookstore'. To those of you who do [sic – not?] know us and to whom the term means one of those barren distribution centers for pads and pens and Livys and zoo instruments, we state emphatically that we are not a college bookstore ... Our aims are less finite, less easily attained – and more alluring.[14]

Dodd and Smith would be instrumental, a few years later, in changing the role and image of the college bookstore on a much broader scale. Dodd made professionalisation of college bookselling a special project, and under her leadership the Hampshire Bookshop became one of the founding members of the College Bookstore Association (later the National Association of College Stores). The organisation's aim was to counter the situation, as described in the Boston *Transcript* in 1922, that

> American communities have been, on the whole, slow to recognize the bookstore as an integral part in the educational system. Of course every one knows that a university town must necessarily be a distribution point for pads, pencils and recommended textbooks. That the university bookstore should not merely supply an existing demand but create a need for books – inspire a thirst for learning, is to some people an entirely new idea ... Curiously enough the faculties of schools and colleges are by no means whole souled abettors of these new ideas ... [T]here still lingers a conservatism that hesitates to recommend book ownership to students with the necessary definiteness of price and edition.

---

[12]   'Smith College Book Store, Northampton, Mass., Incorporated' (Business Notes), *The Publishers' Weekly*, 6 May 1916, 1456. The Bookshop's incorporation was also covered a few weeks later, in the magazine's 27 May 1916 issue (p. 1772).

[13]   'An Hour in the Hampshire Bookshop', *Daily Hampshire Gazette*, 6 December 1916.

[14]   Mary Byers Smith, 'A Successful College Bookshop', *The Publishers' Weekly*, 4 December 1920, 1753.

The editor went on to comment (perhaps persuaded by the Hampshire Bookshop's active publicity efforts), 'I have often heard it said that the Smith College student who is working her way through college buys more books outright than the careless wealthy student who is apt to borrow or buy in groups'.[15] In the years to come, Dodd would find it necessary on occasion to remind the Smith community that the Bookshop's cooperative plan was available to benefit them, especially at times when the college students complained about textbook prices or floated the idea of a college-sanctioned store.[16] But a brisk trade in textbooks, supplies, and supplemental readings would sustain the Bookshop for decades and also forge a mutually beneficial partnership between town and gown.

With the enthusiastic backing of President Seelye and a solid welcome from local patrons, the Hampshire Bookshop flourished from the start. The Bookshop did some $29,000 worth of business during its first year of operation, an encouraging sign to its principals and stockholders.

As Dodd described their original Elm Street location,

> A few beautiful pieces of old-fashioned furniture gave our Shop an atmosphere in which a cheap novel or an ignorant clerk would have suffocated. It was evident from the first few days when the line of 'customers' went far down the street, that there was a desire for the thing we were trying to do, *e.g.*, to provide a book-shop in which books are *selected*. A 'best seller' is not a magic phrase with us, and tho we welcomed 'Mr. Britling' (as we didn't 'God the Invisible King'!), De la Mare's 'Peacock Pie' and McFee's 'Casuals of the Sea' and 'Aliens' are equally welcome … The members of our staff spend much time in learning their stock, but we have made a special effort not to let a trashy war book leak thru.[17]

What Dodd and Smith would have considered a 'trashy war book' isn't clear – the World War I novels best remembered now had yet to be written when they made this comment in 1918; not even Rebecca West's 1918 *The Return of the Soldier* had appeared at the time. Dodd and Smith considered their role a vocation – a mission to guide the reading choices of an impressionable clientele. The partners felt the liberal arts education they had obtained at Smith, and their involvement in social work during and after college, had prepared them to broaden and improve minds. They were poised to extend the college's public contact, expanding ideas and dialogue beyond its ivy walls. Thus their book selections were also liberal and eclectic, if hardly radical. As Dodd described the shop's offerings,

---

[15]　'Transcript Writes of Hampshire Bookshop', *Daily Hampshire Gazette*, 15 June 1922.

[16]　A press release by Dodd from about 1940, titled '$19,000 Returned to Cooperative Members by the Hampshire Bookshop', is especially enlightening (MED Papers, box 1609).

[17]　Marion Dodd, 'The Hampshire Bookshop', *The Publishers' Weekly*, 16 March 1918, 871–72. In 1916–1917, H.G. Wells's war novel Mr *Britling Sees It Through* rose to the top of the fiction bestseller lists; Wells's *God the Invisible King* was one of the nonfiction bestsellers of 1917.

> One room was given over to general books, good editions of standard fiction, the best literature of all languages, a few fine bindings and three or four shelves of selected children's books. The stock was small but carefully chosen and the comfortable, homelike appearance of this browsing room invited all our visitors to a leisurely survey of our books.[18]

The Bookshop represented a cross-section of middlebrow reading deemed appropriate for the cadre of aspiring young women recruited by Smith College as well as the hardworking Yankee townfolk. Among Dodd and Smith's college-educated generation of the Gilded Age, 'good books' had become a key to refinement and higher purpose, no longer limited to a privileged few. 'As society increasingly seemed to be characterized by greed, materialism, and the breakdown of collective responsibility for individual welfare', explains book historian Laura J. Miller, 'books beckoned as an enduring means to the perfection of humankind'.[19]

Marion Dodd's own evaluation of quality excluded many popular novels. Her cultural conservatism is evidenced in her priggish put-down of 'What College Girls Read' in the early 1920s: '[T]he temptation to read the current fiction of to-day with the lure of sex-discussion to the fore, is irresistible, and the Fitzgerald stuff and "The Sheik" and their like are wasting valuable time and money of students whose minds should be on more serious business', she claimed.[20] The distinction seems to be not a matter of morality, for Dodd was an outspoken opponent of censorship, but rather a subjective evaluation of literary merit measured by personal taste.

The standards espoused by the Bookshop's staff spread far beyond the bounds of Northampton, through widely read articles in trade journals and the Bookshop's own occasional newsletter, the *Book Scorpion*. The combined effect of a number of similar operations by the 1920s, such as the Vassar and Mount Holyoke bookstores, further multiplied the Bookshop's influence on reading choices and helped introduce a much wider audience to literature on a regular basis.

As an adjunct to Smith, the women's college, the Hampshire Bookshop both reflected and contributed to a particular brand of feminine ethos, another aspect of its founders' personal inclinations. Dodd and Smith were uniquely positioned to appreciate the merits of a single-sex education for women – self-sufficiency,

---

[18]   Dodd, 'Hampshire Bookshop', 870.

[19]   Laura Miller, *Reluctant Capitalists: Bookselling and the Culture of Consumption* (Chicago: University of Chicago Press, 2006), 27. While Miller's study focuses on the rise of the chain bookstore in the later twentieth century, her overview of the 'genteel industry' that preceded it accurately depicts the important intersections of education, society, and the book trade at the turn of the century. Richard Malin Ohmann's *Selling Culture: Magazines, Markets, and Class at the Turn of the Century* (Hanover, NH: University Press of New England, 1996), while specifically dealing with periodical literature, is also relevant.

[20]   Marion Dodd, 'What College Girls Read', *The Publishers' Weekly*, 17 June 1922, 1741–43. F. Scott Fitzgerald's 1920 *This Side of Paradise* and 1922 *The Beautiful and Damned* were both commercial successes, though neither sold as wildly as Edith M. Hull's 1921 exotic romance *The Sheik*. All three were denounced by contemporary critics as salacious and lacking in serious literary merit.

confidence, camaraderie, achievement – and to perpetuate and propagate them. Intensely loyal to their alma mater, the two alumnae considered Northampton a congenial society where, if largely removed from the artistic currents of the big cities, they could nonetheless find happy and useful work among like-minded people. As single women, they could also enjoy a considerable degree of freedom, safety, and acceptance there. In such a climate, female entrepreneurs could thrive, and their customers of both sexes and all ages in turn benefited from the welcoming bookstore atmosphere Dodd and Smith created.

Mary Byers Smith, an aspiring poet, saw their bookstore as more literary and more serious than some of its counterparts. She took care to distance it from the fads of the day:

> [W]hile we have a part and an important one in the development of bookselling in America, there is nothing unique in what we did and something very dangerous in novelty. The Hampshire Bookshop is not a specialty shop like certain of the women's shops nor is it essentially radical and artistic like certain others. In fact it is not particularly feminine, and its problem is essentially that of the small city store the country over.[21]

In describing the Hampshire Bookshop as 'not particularly feminine', Smith was being quite literal. The overall impression of the store was like a club or library, with a hearth, shelves open to browsers, and ample comfortable seating. Absent were Victorian frills. While Dodd and Smith certainly courted the female student and the female book-buyer, they did not specifically target this niche – and by opting not to limit their reach, they sent a message that within the walls of the Hampshire Bookshop, women consumers were as welcome as men, their ideas and interests equally respected.

In this regard, the founders of the Hampshire Bookshop were creating a space that reflected consumer culture of their times. Since the late 1890s, a strong economy and efficiencies in market distribution had helped transform American retailing into a highly organised system of large department stores, chain stores, mail-order houses, and door-to-door sellers, bolstered by increasingly sophisticated approaches to marketing, merchandising, and advertising. Shopping had become not only a pragmatic necessity but a way of life, especially for women. As cultural historian Kathy L. Peiss points out, the establishment of national women's magazines –such as *Ladies' Home Journal, McCall's*, and *Good Housekeeping* – during this period testified to the key participation of women in this evolving marketplace. 'Like attending a matinee, eating at a restaurant, or going to the beauty parlor – all new activities for women – shopping took place in a semi-public, commercial, and safe realm, an important consideration for women concerned about their respectability', explains Peiss. 'Promoting the pleasures of looking and touching, merchants encouraged women to desire goods

---

[21]   'A Successful College Bookshop', 1753.

and be seduced by them'.[22] By displaying books on readily accessible tables and shelves, in ways that beckoned buyers to handle, open, and explore, a bookstore could spark as strong a desire as a fine department-store glove counter. What Dodd and Smith sought to provide within the embrace of the Hampshire Bookshop was an encounter with commodities and community that invited women customers, workers, and authors to feel as empowered as men – without alienating the latter.

The founders of the Hampshire Bookshop were neither radical nor activist; they hewed to a white, middle-class, Protestant, progressive program of good works aimed at social betterment. They were generally supportive of American domestic and foreign policy. They had not been involved in struggles for woman suffrage or other rights – but they also understood that women had a long way to go to prove themselves in the old-boy networks of bookselling and business, and in this they were determined to change the status quo. Dodd, the primary decision-maker, preferred to train Smith's own students and graduates for store positions; she also hired talented women from New York firms. She was hardly an equal opportunity employer: over the Bookshop's fifty-five-year run, only seven of sixty-six identified staff members were men (and of these two were proprietors during the store's final decade, after Dodd's death).

The Hampshire Bookshop strove to provide a personal level of service that made it more than a mere purveyor of retail goods. Within its first three years of business, its founders were well on their way to achieving their stated objectives. In analyzing sales for 1919, Marion Dodd estimated total revenues of about $50,000, with 61 percent of volume in books, 33 percent in stationery, and 6 percent miscellaneous – a successful financial start.[23] If the Hampshire Bookshop's well-meaning leaders gave literature a place to flourish, they also shaped the choices readers would encounter there. The founders, and the female staff members they employed, had proved that they were both well prepared and well suited for their chosen endeavour.

Women in the Book Trade

Women, however judged to be suited by temperament and education to serve as booksellers, still faced an uphill battle for full inclusion in the bookselling field overall. At the time the Hampshire Bookshop launched their enterprise, though women had commonly found employment in the industry, it was usually behind to the sales counter. The woman-owned bookstore was yet a novelty, and even after a few women had gained membership in the American Booksellers Association

---

[22]   Kathy L. Peiss, 'American Women and the Making of Modern Consumer Culture', *Journal for Multimedia History* 1.1 (Fall 1998), http://www.albany.edu/jmmh/v011n01/peiss-text.html, accessed 24 June 2012.

[23]   Marion Dodd, 'The Long Way Around', *The Publishers' Weekly*, 24 May 1919, 1449.

(ABA), none held a leadership position. Women were not, on the whole, leading the profession, making decisions, or setting policy.

Dodd and Smith had made their first foray to an ABA meeting in 1917. Two years later, Dodd was invited to speak on the program, and she used the opportunity to take a friendly jab at the establishment: 'Some one asked me yesterday whether we were not proud of ourselves', she said, 'and I almost shouted "No, we are filled with humility and overjoyed at the amount there is to learn and are glad that we plunged into the venture and escaped ruin at a time when the wet blankets in the book-trade were as wet as they ever will be."'[24] On a more serious note, she described the Bookshop's environment with obvious confidence in her all-female bookselling staff:

> Our object was to supplement the educational facilities of the college, to provide a place where the student might in a leisurely way survey good literature with a view to ownership and to have a sales force, whose personal acquaintance with the majority of the books was evident. I know now that one way to increase sales is to require your staff to read books, and that when your stock is larger than it is within human possibility to absorb, your sales force should be increased in ratio to that increase of stock … Every member of our selling force has in her (not him!) that persuasive quality which is a direct outcome of her own belief that it is necessary for every human being to own good books. Sales are made on the basis of the intrinsic worth of the book. There is more excitement in the air, when one copy of *Far Away and Long Ago* is sold than ten copies of ordinary fiction, or one copy of that remarkable little book *Chinese Lyrics* than five of some modern anthology. This kind of excitement is possible, I suppose, only where your stock is comparatively small, carefully selected and your sales force regards certain books as the staff of life.[25]

What Dodd and Smith seem to have been striving for was not a separate, 'feminine' enterprise, but one that capitalised on women's particular aptitudes to create a new approach to bookselling for all. It would take some time.

In October 1917, a group of bookwomen gathered in New York City to form their own professional alliance, the Women's National Book Association, still an active force in the industry today. The advent of the WNBA helped raise visibility of women's issues in the conventions and trade journals; *The Publishers' Weekly* began to devote regular coverage to the organisation, and in 1918 Richard R. Bowker himself, presiding over the ABA, formally welcomed 'the ladies of this association' to that gathering.[26] Marion Dodd, elected second vice president of the ABA in 1921, remained active in the association until her retirement in 1951 and

---

[24]   Ibid., 1450.

[25]   Ibid., 1448. Dodd was referring to W.H. Hudson's travel book on Argentina, *Far Away and Long Ago* (New York: Dutton, 1918), and Helen Waddell's translation of poems, *Lyrics from the Chinese* (London: Constable, 1914).

[26]   Richard R. Bowker, 'Bookselling as a Profession—An Address', *The Publishers' Weekly*, 25 May 1918, 1633.

over the years held several key positions; her successor, Smith alumna Cynthia Walsh, carried on the tradition of leadership. By the time *The Publishers' Weekly* published its fifty-year retrospective in 1921, six members of its own editorial and office staff working under managing editor Frederic Melcher were women – half of them graduates of women's colleges.[27]

Women would never again be excluded. Dodd, Smith, and the proprietors and staffers of the other personal bookshops had pushed through their agenda within a few short years. The full participation of women in the industry decidedly transformed the book business, and the space of the bookstore, irreversibly toward the intimate and inclusive, fixing the bookstore in the American mind as a nexus of conversation, culture, and connection for decades to come.

A Literary Space for all Readers

The Hampshire Bookshop's managers used every means at their disposal to attract customers and convert them into readers. They adopted or introduced new methods of outreach that hardly seem innovative today: special programming and promotion for children's books, a bookmobile to make the rounds of summer camps and smaller communities, a loyalty rebate program, a lending library, and a plethora of advertising swag and cleverly designed promotions. They became adept at branding, cultivating a consistent image of genteel sociability through their custom-lettered logotype, hand-drawn illustrations, and unmistakable tone of communications – much as the Barnes & Noble chain would later use to spectacular advantage, infusing its large, cookie-cutter stores with an image of warmth and personality.

Drawing upon the traditional skills considered natural to their sex – and cultivated within the socialised environment of the private college – Dodd and Smith hosted an ambitious schedule of book-and-author events that became their hallmark and most successful promotional strategy. As Smith's de facto campus bookstore, the Hampshire Bookshop tapped into a built-in audience for the authors it would soon begin booking for lectures and signings.

The advantages of bringing a renowned author to speak at the bookstore were multivalent: not only did an event ensure that books would sell in quantity; it also provided a ready hook for free publicity (often far outside the firm's local community), it established the basis for an ongoing relationship with long-lasting benefits, and it lent intellectual lustre to a modest, home-grown enterprise. Most important, it enabled fans and followers to rub shoulders with their favourite authors, or meet new ones. The Bookshop became a highly desirable venue that rewarded patrons with an elite level of cultural affinity rare outside New York or Boston. Customers could chat with authors – often famous ones or rising stars – and feel edified and inspired. They in turn spread the word; faculty adopted

---

[27]   'Publishers' Weekly Thru 50 Years: Part III, 1872–1921', *The Publishers' Weekly*, 15 January 1921, 108–09.

the author's books into conversation or teaching, and news coverage boosted awareness. Such interaction, even in the hinterlands, contributed strongly to the construction and reinforcement of a literary canon.

When the Bookshop staff discovered how easy it was to line up British writers eager for paying engagements after World War I, they brought a stream of prominent authors and leaders to the U.S for readings and book signings.[28] Perhaps Dodd and Smith also saw longer-term benefit in cultivating relationships with English authors; in due time, when Dodd and her partners travelled abroad to buy collectible editions, they parlayed existing connections into invitations to bookshops and authors' homes across the pond and were able to secure some choice offerings to bring back for resale. As one link in a broader US lecture circuit, the Hampshire Bookshop was critical to establishing the American reputation of writers such as Lord Dunsany, Hugh Lofting, Hugh Walpole, Virginia Woolf, and William Butler Yeats. They also helped boost awareness of American authors and tastemakers such as Amy Lowell and Christopher Morley. Through a vigorous program of publicity, a clever newsletter, and informative catalogues, the Bookshop steadily advanced the image of authors as it built its own.

A Woman-Led Enterprise Comes of Age

The bookstore that had begun inconspicuously on a quiet residential side street near campus moved downtown only a year later, in 1917, to the commercial heart of Northampton, and, in 1923, to even larger quarters a couple of blocks away.

With its lecture series, publications program, and sales promotions, the Hampshire Bookshop had reached full stride by the mid-1920s. The achievement of ten years in business was cause for great celebration in April 1926, with a week-long series of speakers and events. Bennett Cerf of Random House and the Modern Library was slated to speak on 'Modern Library Adventures'; Frances Phillips of Morrow on 'The Editor as a Constructive Critic'; author Leland Hall, illustrator Maitland de Gogorza, editor Ben Huebsch of Viking, and artist and printmaker Marion F. Wakeman were also scheduled. On Thursday evening, April 16, Robert Frost was to give a talk titled 'Twenty Years A-Growing'; on Friday a mysterious 'surprise for the public' was planned; on Saturday, guests were invited for tea in Marion Dodd's office and a reading from Emily Dickinson by Martha Dickinson Bianchi. Throughout the week, the Bookshop held an exhibition of

---

[28]   Dodd and Smith often spoke with pride of their lecture series and author events. See, for example, Mary Byers Smith Memoirs, Smith College Centennial Project, Smith College Archives, Northampton, Mass., 15; Mary Byers Smith, 'A Successful College Bookshop', 1754; 'After Five Years', *The Publishers' Weekly*, 25 June 1921, 1853; and 'Hugh Walpole in Fall Lectures', *The Publishers' Weekly*, 6 May 1922, 1276.

American bookmaking, showcasing the American Institute of Graphic Arts Fifty Books of the Year.[29]

Smith history professor John C. Hildt, one of the Bookshop's original directors, offered a tribute:

> There is another aspect of [the Hampshire Bookshop's] success that I do not think is so readily perceived as that of its being the most successful of all college bookshops. This aspect is that it is a concrete proof that here is a business started by women, financed by women, directed by women, and employing women which has achieved a success greater than any similar business man-run and man-controlled. Miss Smith and Miss Dodd have proved to perhaps a skeptical world not only that women can compete successfully in business, but that ... there is a field particularly adapted to the abilities and energies of women.[30]

All paeans aside, it *had* been a financially successful decade for the Bookshop. Just how successful is not easy to measure, lacking full financial records. But a portion of the picture can be patched together from tidbits in the *Book Scorpion* and reported sources. In June 1921, the directors voted a 6 percent dividend on common stock, after gains on preferred stock had been paid.[31] By the time it had been in business for seven years (1923), the Bookshop had returned to its cooperative members some $8,000 in rebates; by the following year, Marion Dodd reported the Hampshire Bookshop's gross sales to be more than $100,000 annually. The staff numbered seventeen that year and the stockholders 137.[32] A promotional brochure for 1925 cited sales of 'over four and a half times that of the first year' – in the neighbourhood of $130,500 – with 136 stockholders. The staff had grown from three and four in 1916 to fourteen permanent staff a decade later, with every member of the sales force a college graduate.[33]

By the time Mary Byers Smith withdrew from involvement in the everyday operation of the Bookshop in 1927, the enterprise was solidly established within the Northampton community and the book trade at large. It continued under Marion Dodd's energetic leadership through the Great Depression and a second World War, until Dodd turned over the reins in 1951 to Cynthia S. Walsh, another Smith graduate and publishing professional whom she had personally groomed for the management role. It survived another two decades of radical change within

---

[29]   Broadside, 'The Hampshire Bookshop: Twenty Years A-Growing, 1916 to 1936: Program of Events for 20th Anniversary, April 13–18, 1936' (MED Papers, box 1609.2, folder 1, HBS Publicity/Booklists).

[30]   Quoted in Robinson, 'The Hampshire Bookshop', *Smith Alumnae Quarterly* (February 1976), 17.

[31]   *Book Scorpion* 1.4 (March 1922).

[32]   'The Hampshire Bookshop' (part 2 of 'Six New England Bookshops'), *The Publishers' Weekly*, 3 May 1924, 1440.

[33]   'Some Historical Facts about the Bookshop', from 1925 promotional brochure (MED Papers, box 1609). 'The original stockholders number eighty-six'.

the bookselling industry, at last giving way to the growing popularity of mall bookstores in 1971.

The Hampshire Bookshop thrived for so long thanks to its solid financial footing, the dedication of its personnel, and its ability to fill a niche demand. But what it brought to bookselling at large was part of a sea change in the industry. The bookstore became a space at once solitary and social. Like the public library, it welcomed all comers to private browsing, reading, and contemplation – but it required no credentials for entrance or use and it encouraged, rather than restricted, conversation and activity. While inviting patrons regardless of age, sex, or status to step through its doors, it imparted to them a cachet of upward mobility and leisurely, even luxurious, indulgence. A shared reverence for the merchandise prevailed, as well as a trust in the customer's motivations to look, read, or buy at will. The personal bookstore, of all retail enterprises, managed to become both egalitarian and elite, combining affordable paperbacks with pricey editions in a venue where any customer could linger freely. While you might *shop* for household goods or hardware or clothing or a car, you *browsed* a bookstore.

In such a protected and nurturing space, more living room than emporium, a knowledgeable clerk could readily engage a visitor in stimulating conversation leading to a satisfactory purchase. The founders could fulfil their altruistic goals and feed their literary aspirations, and yet achieve requisite success in sales. And the reader could discover, among the orderly shelves, an invitation to thought, creativity, and adventure. On a given evening a customer could gather with friends, shake hands with a notable writer, think more deeply and enjoyably, and become inspired to read – and write – themselves. If this scenario bears more than a passing resemblance to the best-known independent bookstores of this century, it's no coincidence. The direct descendants of the personal bookshops, they have inherited the formula the Hampshire Bookshop branded long ago.

Nothing in today's bookstore-cum-coffee shop can quite deliver the personal touch of that groundbreaking establishment, however. Today's consumers covet the 'high touch' experience – and that is why a considerable number still choose the bricks-and-mortar bookstore over online buying – but much has necessarily faded into obsolescence. The Hampshire Bookshop taught how to open a book's uncut pages with a paper knife, how to spot a first edition, how to wrap a purchase tautly in kraft paper. It hosted holiday parties with guests choosing a keepsake from a book-festooned tree and celebrated the publication of a new book by ringing a ship's bell. Nothing substitutes for such particularities now, not Facebook's 'like' or Amazon's bloodless rankings and consumer ratings. And with them has gone the shared appreciation for an unfolding canon, fractured now into genres and subgenres, and varieties of disintermediated self-publishing.

When a secondhand book turns up these days on eBay with the description 'small Hampshire Bookshop label on rear pastedown', a bidder might well wax curious about the provenance of a volume such as Marianne Moore's *O to Be a Dragon*. What Bookshop staffer, in 1959, once lifted the slim book of verse off the shelf and recommended it to a Smith senior or a Northampton resident in search of a gift? Whose hands received the bundle in brown paper and took it home to savour on a winter's night? In our generation and those to come, we will not likely gaze at a book's sterile ISBN or barcode and wonder where or when or why it was purchased. That era of 'personal' – face-to-face personal, I-know-you'll-enjoy-this personal – has largely passed, and with it much of the reason people still remember 'the Hamp' with such reverence.

I picture a student clerk, glad to earn her modest wages working part-time among books, moistening that label on the wheel of a white ceramic reservoir. She carefully opens the book so as not to break the spine or dent a corner and affixes the tiny rectangle precisely in its unobtrusive location. When she has processed the stack – among that week's arrival of ten or twenty new titles – she cradles the copies in the crook of her arm, delivers them to the poetry section, and slides them into their alphabetical slot.

It is a vanished art, that labelling. It once cemented the bond between bookseller, publisher, author, and buyer. It is a microcosm of the Hampshire Bookshop – itself the prototype of the independent, literary bookstore of the twentieth century.

Chapter 2
The Sunwise Turn and the Social Space of the Bookshop

Ted Bishop

In 1916, two women, Madge Jenison and Mary Mowbray-Clarke, opened 'The Sunwise Turn, The Modern Bookshop' on East 31st Street in New York City. The owners saw themselves as cultural missionaries in the capitalist jungle of Manhattan, clearing a space for culture, creating a place of inspiration and enlightenment. Within seven years they were at each other's throats, suing over the assets of the shop, finally selling out to Doubleday. John Tebbel in his authoritative *History of Book Publishing in the United States* notes that the Sunwise Turn was 'probably the prototype of the small "personal" bookshop' and states that Madge Jenison's memoir, *The Sunwise Turn*, was 'an influential guide to "personal" bookstore operation'.[1] This sounds straightforward, but the archives tell a darker story. The boxes of material at the Harry Ransom Center in Austin, Texas, include manuscripts of talks by the partners, ledgers, correspondence, and the formal minutes of the Board of Directors' meetings. It is a tale of fascinating characters: Mary Mowbray-Clarke, who argued for a return to medieval systems of finance and then hired a clever lawyer to try to swindle her partners out of their back wages; Madge Jenison, who leapt from the sinking Sunwise Turn and then wrote a chatty book advising all young women to start bookstores; Harold Loeb, the model for Robert Cohn in Hemingway's *The Sun Also Rises*, who adventured in western Canada, founded a little magazine in Italy, and wound up as a bureaucrat for the Food and Drug Administration; and his cousin Peggy Guggenheim, who was too incompetent to work the till but who claimed her interest in art collecting came from her experience at the Sunwise Turn. The narrative arc of the Sunwise Turn is one of idealism and missionary zeal turning to bitterness and capitulation to the market, with the accompanying trajectory of a proudly liminal space – private and public, domestic and commercial – devolving into a space that was completely commodified, that of a chain store.

---

[1]   John Tebbel, *A History of Book Publishing in the United States, Volume II: The Expansion of an Industry 1865–1919* (New York and & London: R.R. Bowker, A Xerox Education Company, 1975), 277.

Felicitous Space

One of the first bookstores in America to be owned and operated by women, the Sunwise Turn sponsored lectures and readings by Robert Frost, Theodore Dreiser, Amy Lowell, and others; they sold paintings and sculpture; they published a few of their own books, and even briefly considered publishing *Ulysses*.[2] And in 1917, they hosted a meeting of women in the publishing trade who subsequently organised the Women's National Association of Booksellers and Publishers. The name of the store, deliberately chosen, was not 'sunrise' (though correspondents often made that mistake) but 'sunwise', which meant to follow the course of the sun, to be in harmony, in other words, with the rhythms of nature, and, implicitly, to provide relief from the mechanical rhythms of the city. The most striking document in the archive is a bill for draperies and furniture coverings when they decorated the new store:

$211.75 for 25 yds linen, 19 yds Tudor, 2 yds Damask, 2 yds Agra, 6 yds Gauze

and then:

$302.40 for 38 sq ft of tapestry, purple, for sofa;

39 sq ft plain tapestry, orange-red for two arm chairs;

36 ft of plain tapestry, blue, for 3 side chairs;

47 sq ft of plain tapestry for outside covering.[3]

A purple sofa, orange-red armchairs, blue side chairs – the shop must have looked like a Matisse painting. To spend over $500 for fabric in 1919, when a fireman might have been paid $100 a month, might seem outrageous, but the purchases were deliberate, part of the owners' ideal of creating a space that was designed to do more than simply maximise sales. In 'The Small Bookshop', a speech to a class for booksellers at the New York Public Library on 27 January 1922, Mowbray-Clarke insisted on the importance of physical space:

> Our physical setting has meant a great deal to us. Both at the old 31st street shop where we restored a delightful old Jacobean installation that had been an early collector's picture-gallery, and in the shop built to our own design for us by the Yale club we have kept the aspect of a modern art expression. Our color scheme

---

[2]   Mowbray-Clarke wrote to Beach: 'I think we know you and you know us. I hear you have a nice little book-shop in Paris and I am giving the address to friends living there. Meanwhile I enclose an order for copies of *Ulysses*. I hope you will allow us a discount on the books. We thought of publishing it here but didn't have the money. Should you be undersubscribed let us know. Hoping for your best success'. Box 133, Beach Papers, Princeton.

[3]   Sunwise Turn Papers, Box 2, Harry Ransom Research Center, University of Texas at Austin, Austin TX, hereafter HRC.

was worked out for us with the Taylor system of harmonized [color] having on its realistic basis books in their colored wrappers.[4]

A glance at the pamphlet (Figure 2.1) makes it clear that they were creating a space for *reading*, not just *buying* books. It is a blending of public and private space, and there is a consciousness of the body: the image looks simultaneously like a gingerbread cottage and like a featherbed, with the chimneys doubling as bedposts and clouds – unlikely in midtown Manhattan – for pillows. At the centre of the roofline is a device suggestive of two hands holding a book. It is all meant to evoke refuge, repose, and reading.[5]

Gaston Bachelard in the *Poetics of Space* speaks of "felicitous space" and the recurrent dream of a cottage, a hut, that is a place of refuge. Bachelard contends that 'The house, even more that the landscape, is a "psychic state", and when reproduced as it appears from the outside, it bespeaks intimacy', and he notes psychologists' work with children: when the house is happy, soft smoke rises in gay rings above the roof.[6] We do not have smoke rings in this drawing of the Sunwise Turn, but we have those puffy clouds, and the drawing itself is meant to look as if it were drawn for a child. Bachelard argues for the universality of the 'hut dream': 'the dreamer of refuges dreams of a hut, of a nest, or of nooks and corners in which he would like to hide away, like an animal in its hole'.[7] The 'hermit's hut' becomes a centralised solitude; in the land of legend there exists no adjoining hut.[8] Within the dwelling, 'every corner in a house, every angle in a room, every inch of secluded space in which we like to hide, or withdraw into ourselves, is a symbol of solitude for the imagination'.[9] And Judith Fryer (taking the title of her book *Felicitous Space* from Bachelard) discusses how in the early decades of the century the American skyscraper became identified with male aggressive enterprise, the house with the realm of the imagination. She quotes George Santayana: 'The American Will inhabits the sky-scraper; the American Intellect inhabits the colonial mansion', the one 'all aggressive enterprise' is 'the sphere of the American man; the other, at least predominantly, of the American woman'.[10] The Sunwise Turn was not a colonial mansion, but it was designed to be a place where the intellect could abide.

---

[4] Mary Mowbray-Clarke, manuscript of 'The Small Bookshop, The substance of a speech made at the class for Booksellers in the Public Library, Jan. 27, 1922' Sunwise Turn Papers, Box 1, HRC.

[5] It was also freezing cold in winter. Jenison, probably inspired by Harold Loeb's Alberta adventure, says, 'We called it "Medicine Hat,' Medicine Hat being a station somewhere on the Canadian Pacific which is the real site of the North Pole'. Madge Jenison, *Sunwise Turn, A Human Comedy of Bookselling* (New York: E.P. Dutton & Co., 1923), 16.

[6] Gaston Bachelard, *The Poetics of Space*, trans. Maria Jolas, intro. John R. Stilgoe (Boston: Beacon Press, 1994), 72.

[7] Ibid., 30.

[8] Ibid., 32.

[9] Ibid., 132.

[10] Judith Fryer, *Felicitous Space: The Imaginative Structures of Edith Wharton and Willa Cather* (Chapel Hill and London: University of North Carolina Press, 1986), 10.

Fig. 2.1   The Sunwise Turn Bookshop, promotional pamphlet. *Source*:
              Sunwise Turn Papers, Box 20.8, The Harry Ransom Center, The
              University of Texas at Austin.

Louis Sullivan 'had begun in the late 1880s to build the skyscrapers which,
rooted in the ground and ornamented along their shafts with an elegance that
emphasized their verticality and grew more elaborate at their skyward tips, were
raw celebrations of phallic energy'. For Sullivan, *masculine* meant "that which
is virile, forceful, direct, clear and straightforward, that which grasps and retains

in thought'. *Feminine* meant 'intuitive sympathy, tact, suavity and grace – the qualities that soothe, elevate, ennoble and refine'.[11] What Jenison and Mowbray-Clarke hoped to do was ennoble and refine, and they defined themselves against the buildings that surrounded them, and all they represented:

> Even our mullioned windows and our great tiled wall sign are a protest against the mediocrity of the eternal plate-glass. Every hide-bound advertiser would tell us that we cannot sell books as well from small windows as from large ones, but we think we do a few things to people besides sell them books, and architecture with personality is not often enough a consideration in America in spite of our sky scrapers.[12]

In 'Building Dwelling Thinking', Heidegger explores the distinction between *building* and *dwelling*, arguing that the root word of 'building' means to 'cultivate' as well as to 'raise up edifices.' Further, he suggests that the nature of dwelling is to create a space, to make room for something to appear. The real plight of dwelling, he says, lies not in the lack of houses but that mortals must ever learn to dwell. The distinction is useful in talking about bookstores, in distinguishing between bookstores that *dwell*, that cultivate and allow a culture to appear, and bookstores that are merely *built* – like airport bookstores, that fire out best sellers like Big Macs, or university bookstores that have become warehouses rather than sites of culture. These new bookstore owners with their cottage amongst the skyscrapers were less concerned with reaping profits than with creating a space where culture could flourish.

The place struck a chord with professionals. In April of 1916, *The Publishers' Weekly* ecstatically announced a vision on Fifth Avenue, a bookstore with 'bravely original' architecture, with a 'touch of absurdity' but the feel of a 'cloister':

> The publisher who has reached the dark hour when he believes that paper will never come down, and binding and printing will rise beyond his reach, and no more books will ever be sold again, should go forth to Fifth Avenue and 31st Street, New York City, and there, next to the corner, see the thing he has dreamed about when his dreams were most visionary. 'The Sunwise Turn, the Modern Bookshop' is the sort of place you might find in a booklover's essay; yet there it stands, quaint and bewitching, yet apparently made of real substance. It is built of red brick, cunningly contrived to suggest something old-worldly, yet startlingly new. Its architecture is bravely original, with the 'new art' touch of absurdity; yet the long, low-leaded windows and round archway entrance have the 'booky' look of a cloister.[13]

---

[11] Ibid., 14.

[12] Mary Mowbray-Clarke, 'The Small Bookshop'.

[13] 'The Sunwise Turn: A Modern Bookshop', *The Publishers' Weekly*, 22 April 1916, 1361.

The reference to the medieval element, the cloister, was both prescient and prophetic because Mowbray-Clarke's fondness for the medieval would prove to be part of her downfall. The writer goes on to describe the space and to give credit to the designers of the fireplace, the batiks, and even the signs:

> It has one large room, about 20 x 30, with a window seat half-way along one side, furnished with library tables, sufficiently strewn with books, easy-chairs, bookshelves, and art objects (some of which are for sale). In the decoration of the room itself the co-operation of several artists has been secured, and an interesting chord of colors has been carried out. The signs were painted by Henry Fitch Taylor and John Wolcott Adams. The mosaic fireplace and the seal were designed by John Mowbray-Clarke, the batiks in the shop by Miss Martha Ryder.[14]

It all sounds wonderful, especially since the article following the Sunwise Turn piece – 'Will Book Prices Have to be Increased?' – details problems in the book trade and laments that excessive advance payments to authors, the reduction of the working day from nine to eight hours, and the fact that 'Other forms of amusement, such as automobiles and motion pictures, are taking the place of books to a great extent', has caused the standard price of a novel to rise from $1.35 to $1.50.[15] The story on the Sunwise Turn announced that, 'not fiction but non-fiction – especially in art lines – will be the specialty of the shop', but in fact work of all sorts, as long as it was non-commercial, found favour with the shop.

The Sunwise Turn was conceived as much as a cultural centre as a bookstore. One of their first author-events was a reading by Theodore Dreiser, in April 1916, from his new book, 'Plays, Natural and Supernatural'.[16] And early in 1917, 'some two-score invited guests' convened to hear Amy Lowell read and then to take part in 'an informal discussion of the place of *vers libre* in the world of art'.[17] Jenison and Mowbray-Clarke were soon offering two series of lectures, one on modern poetry every Tuesday night, to be conducted by Padraic Colum (the Irish poet and founder of the Abbey Theatre, who had come to New York in 1914), and the other on libertarian education on Friday nights. The cost for the six lectures was $5 or $1 per single lecture. *The Publishers' Weekly* provides a sample:

> Tuesday, January 22nd: 'The Successors of Tennyson', including Arthur Symons, Ernest Dowson, Oscar Wilde, and the poetry of Robert Bridges and Thomas Hardy
>
> January 29th: 'Two Contrasting Poets', discussing the poetry of the Catholic, Francis Thompson, and the materialist John Davidson

---

[14]   Ibid.

[15]   'Will Book Prices Have to be Increased?' *The Publishers' Weekly*, 22 April 1916, 1362–63.

[16]   'The Sunwise Turn: A Modern Bookshop', 1632.

[17]   *The Publishers' Weekly*, 27 January, 1917, 283.

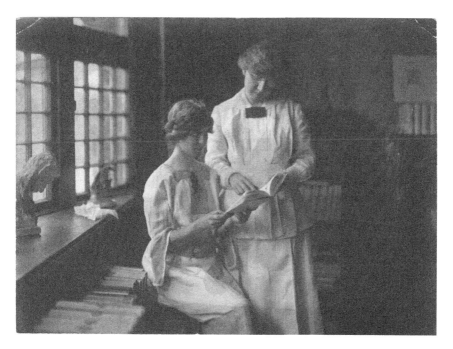

Fig. 2.2   The Sunwise Turn Bookshop, interior of original shop, Mary
             Mowbray-Clarke (seated), and Madge Jenison. *Source*: Sunwise
             Turn Papers, Box 20.8, The Harry Ransom Center, The University
             of Texas at Austin.

February 5th: Yeats, George Russel (A.E.) and Synge

February 12th: 'The Rise of Nationalism Amongst the Younger English Poets'

February 19th: 'Some American Poets', including Vachel Lindsay, Robert Frost,
Edwin A. Robinson and the imagists

February 26th: 'An Interpretation of the Spirit of Irish Poetry'[18]

These are established authors to us now, but in 1919 they were still emerging
figures. Yeats, for instance, was well known, and *The Wild Swans at Coole* had
come out in 1917, but *Michael Robartes and the Dancer* would not appear until
1921; and Frost had published *North of Boston* (1914) and *Mountain Interval*
(1916), but *New Hampshire*, which would win him the Pulitzer Prize, was four
years away.

---

[18]   'Lectures at the Sunwise Turn', *The Publishers' Weekly*, 20 March 1920, 945.

After the bookstore moved uptown to 51 E 44th Street in 1919, *The Publishers'
Weekly* noted happily that the Sunwise Turn planned to continue its 'series of
delightful poetry evenings'.[19] The week before Christmas 1919, Alfred Kreymborg
– who had published Ezra Pound's *Des Imagistes* in *The Glebe* 1914 and who
had produced *Others* with Skipwith Cannell, Wallace Stevens, and William
Carlos Williams from 1915 until June of 1919 – presented 'his poem-mimes with
mandolute accompaniments as a sort of housewarming and introduction to the
course, to be followed later by weekly recitals by such artists as Robert Frost, Carl
Sandburg, Vachel Lindsay, Witter Bynner and others'.[20] The course was to include
fifteen lectures, for which season tickets could be purchased for $12.00. Single
tickets were $1.00 – so not cheap: two-thirds the cost of a hardcover book.[21] In the
event, Robert Frost's lecture of March 16 1920, 'had to be postponed until April
20 because Mr Frost is suffering from influenza', but we are promised more, and
the lectures are wide-ranging:

> March 23: Helena de Day will lecture on 'Romain Rolland and the War'
>
> March 30: Ridgeley Torrance will read some of his Negro Plays
>
> April 6: Amy Murray, Gaelic harpist (author of 'Father Allan's Island' soon to
> be published by Harcourt, Brace & Howe) will give her Hebrides songs and
> folk tales
>
> April 7: Dr. Ananda Coomaraswamy will lecture on Indian Poetry
>
> April 13: Lola Ridge will lecture on 'Woman and the Creative Will'

The shop was a place where connections could be formed, ideas germinate.
Anarchist-feminist Lola Ridge had published her first book of poetry, *The Ghetto*,
in 1918, and fostering 'Woman and the Creative Will' was very much part of the
Sunwise Turn mandate from the start: the initial shareholders were all women.[22]
Allan Antliff in *Anarchist Modernism* notes that for the newly arrived philosopher
Ananda Coomaraswamy, the Sunwise Turn was the centre of his life. It was also
one of the favourite haunts of Carl Zigrosser, editor of the radical Ferrer Center's
journal, *The Modern School*, from 1917 to 1920 (Zigrosser was involved in the
discussions for the naming of the shop – his suggestion was 'Here Are Ladies'),

---

[19]   'Poetry Evenings at the Sunwise Turn', *The Publishers' Weekly*, 20 December1919,
1620.

[20]   Ibid.

[21]   Ibid.

[22]   The Sunwise Turn Stock Certificate Books list thirty shares for $100 each, signed
by Madge Jenison, Treasurer, and Mary Mowbray-Clarke, President. The shareholders
were Sophia A. Walker, Georgianna B. Ballard, Alice Einstein, Beatrice Wood, Lewis,
Alice Bennett, Mrs Emanuel Einstein, Alice Lewisham, Irene Lewisham, August Rucker,
Lillie Bliss, Amy Sprinarm, Alice Lewisham, Irene Lewisham. Sunwise Turn Papers, Box
1, HRC.

and Eugene O'Neill, unpublished but working with the Provincetown Players, would come by. There was much going on besides the selling of books.[23]

Yet in selling, too, the Sunwise Turn was innovative. In addition to floor sales, they developed a three-pronged technique for getting books into the hands of readers: they provided an expert consultation service, installed special libraries tailored to particular businesses and groups, and created a subscription service. In an address to the 1917 Annual Convention of the American Booksellers' Association, Mowbray-Clarke explains that 'Efficiency' was a current issue and so they 'gathered all the efficiency engineers that we knew or could possibly meet', got their advice on the best books and put their comments in a card catalogue. 'Now when a young man studying Efficiency at Columbia comes to us we can tell him the ten most important books for him to read'.[24] Unfortunately, the technique proved not very efficient. They would spend hours talking to experts for very few books sold.

After one year, they had on their list a subscriber in New Zealand, a club in Tientsin, China, a missionary in India, workers in lumber camps, and a man in the Klondike who wanted 'the very best English poetry'. This is so exciting that 'we have almost gotten to scorn our regular customers who come in every week for books; they are so docile, and 'we abominate docile people' (the writer records '[Laughter]' from the audience).[25] In these early years, *The Publishers' Weekly* is as enthusiastic as Madge Jenison, who in her memoir *Sunwise Turn: A Human Comedy of Bookselling* contends that 'thought … is the world's soul' and that bookstores are the way of 'passing the current, more important than universities, than schools, than public libraries, because they … are in the thick of affairs and work.[26] They did their best 'to make the shop a cult, something unlike other things, and offering one a breath of experience even to buy a book there'.[27] If we stick to the contemporary accounts by Madge Jenison and *The Publishers' Weekly*, we would certainly conclude that the bookstore was a success, a model of its kind, groundbreaking in politics, culture, and marketing.

---

[23]   Zigrosser heard Coomaraswamy deliver a lecture at the Sunwise Turn in December of 1917 and asked if he could publish it in *The Modern School*. Coomaraswamy agreed, but told Zigrosser that he needed to get permission from Mary Mowbray-Clarke because the essay was coming out in a collection published by the Sunwise Turn (*The Dance of Siva*, still in print). The essay, 'Young India', appeared in the February and March 1918 issues of The Modern School. See Alan Antliff, *Anarchist Modernism: Art, Politics, and the First American Avant-Garde* (Chicago and London: University of Chicago Press, 2001), 127. This was precisely the kind of cultural cross-fertilisation Mowbray-Clarke hoped to foster.

[24]   Mary Mowbray-Clarke, 'The Sunwise Turn Bookshop – New York', *The Publishers' Weekly*, 26 May 1917, 1704–07.

[25]   Ibid., 1705.

[26]   Jenison, 39.

[27]   Ibid., 43. See also Margaret Stetz's excellent article on, among other things, the bookstore as a site of fashion, a place to be seen: 'Sex, Lies, and Printed Cloth: Bookselling at the Bodley Head in the Eighteen-Nineties', *Victorian Studies* 35.1 (1991), 71–86.

Dissent

Harold Loeb provides another perspective: carried away by Mary Mowbray-Clarke's enthusiasm, he poured money and time into the shop, but before long he began to view the enterprise as self-indulgent and commercially suspect. Loeb is the character pilloried by Hemingway as Robert Cohn in his 1926 novel *The Sun Also Rises*. In *The Way It Was*, Loeb's attempt to correct that characterisation, he proves much more interesting than Hemingway allows him to be: in 1913, having just finished his degree at Princeton and entranced by an actress singing 'On the Banks of the Saskatchewan' in a musical, he had travelled out to Calgary (because it was on the banks of the Saskatchewan) and spent half his patrimony setting up a cement factory in Empress, Alberta, something he would write about later in *Tumbling Mustard* (which he published unfortunately in 1929: the combination of the stock market crash and the uninspired title caused the book to sink without a trace). He served during the First World War, and after his discharge he and his wife wanted to develop their 'potentialities'. A friend advised them to talk to Mowbray-Clarke. 'Small, spare, and schoolmarmish, Mary was possessed by a driving force', Loeb writes. 'She could listen, but once she started to talk she went on and on, twisting and turning through art, politics, economics, literature, town-planning, guild socialism, Freud. I was fascinated, though a little breathless'.[28] Nonetheless, in 1919, he sunk half of his remaining patrimony, $5,000, into the Sunwise Turn.

Like everyone else, Loeb loved the intimacy of the little shop on 38th Street, but, in the summer of 1919, the block that housed the Sunwise Turn was to be sold, and Loeb found an empty store in the Yale Club building opposite Grand Central Station at 51 East 44 Street. Again, the décor was crucial: 'Mary fretted: the high ceilings and straight lines would make it difficult to recapture the intimate warmth of the old shop. But after the ceilings and walls were painted a rich orange and the light bulbs swathed in fluff, everyone was satisfied'.[29] And as a cultural centre, the bookstore flourished, with Mowbray-Clarke still the driving force:

> Literary sessions, feasible in the larger quarters, paid for themselves and helped publicize the shop and the authors. Usually autographed copies were sold to everyone present. Robert Frost, Amy Lowell, Mekerji, Lola Ridge, Alfred Kreymborg, and others read their work or discussed the American literary renaissance and whatever else came into their heads. Mary's energy seemed boundless. Among a score of other projects she managed to find space for what was probably Charles Burchfield's first exhibition.[30]

From this new location, the Sunwise Turn moved into publishing, 'issuing a book of parodies by Witter Bynner, an essay on Rodin by Rainer Maria Rilke, *The*

---

[28]   Harold Loeb, *The Way It Was* (New York: Criterion Books, 1959), 27.

[29]   Ibid., 34.

[30]   Ibid.

Dance of Siva by Ananda Coomaraswamy, a book of caricatures by Ivan Opfer, *The Gods of the Mountains* by Lord Dunsany, and a perfectly dreadful miracle play called *Guibour* that was presented at the Grand Street Theatre'. Loeb stood well back: 'Publishing was Mary's department, and I did not interfere with it'.[31]

In fact, relations with his partners had begun to fray: 'Despite the pleasure of associating with people who wrote books, painted pictures, and upheld causes, and the satisfaction of working at a task I believed in, I began to have doubts about the bookshop'.[32] He was charmed that F. Scott Fitzgerald dropped in, and one evening Wallace Stevens, Scofield Thayer, and William Carlos Williams came to the shop and talked. He enjoyed jousting with the publishers' representatives, including Blanche Knopf, who would come in with her little suitcase, promoting their latest title, which in some way or other was always 'superlative' and deserving of a large order. Despite her charm, Loeb says, he learned to say 'no' to her,[33] but this was not enough to keep him in the business. He was organised and his partners were not:

> I was especially troubled by Madge Jenison, who sold books like a tornado, swooping around, picking up a volume here, dropping one there, scribbling the wrong title, name, or address on her sales slip or forgetting it altogether, leaving a trail of debris and confusion behind her. It was particularly hard on Marjorie [Loeb's wife], who kept the books. And it hindered my efforts to make ends meet.[34]

And of the other partner, the more philosophical Mowbray-Clarke:

> It wasn't long before my initial enthusiasm for Mary Clarke and her theories began to wear thin in spots. The postwar period was marked by a swing of the younger generation toward social experimentation and ideological revision and Mary Clarke and her kind played an essential role in this movement by providing it with an intellectual or pseudo-intellectual basis. Although she herself was as inhibited as a puritan, she liberated her disciples in certain areas and tied them up in others.[35]

It was a dinner with photographer Alfred Stieglitz that crystallised his doubts:

> One evening Alfred and Georgia O'Keefe, an intense young painter from Sun Prairie, Wisconsin, came to dinner … The conversation veered to The Sunwise Turn. Alfred tried to hold back his opinion – a hard feat for an unrestrained talker whose mind refueled itself in flight.

---

[31]   Loeb, 35.
[32]   Ibid.
[33]   Ibid., 51.
[34]   Ibid., 35.
[35]   Loeb, 35–36.

Tactlessly I praised Mary Clarke for her success in promoting the careers of young and unknown artists, a task into which Stieglitz also put much effort and in which he took great pride. Alfred exploded: 'Stuff and fiddlesticks! Bloodless females who suffocate the slightest suspicion of beauty beneath torrents of gush'.

I was impelled to defend my partners: 'Before dismissing them, you might come to one of our poetry evenings, or look at Burchfield's water-colors, or at the books that go out ... '

He retorted by ridiculing the shop's Christmas packages. Each volume sold during the previous holiday season had been swathed in multicolored Japanese paper. Then he made fun of our orange decorations and Mary's aesthetic pronouncements.[36]

Torrents of gush, light bulbs, and books alike swathed in bright paper – these were enough for Stieglitz to dismiss the real cultural work that the Sunwise Turn was doing. Madge Jenison did gush. In her memoir, we hear the voice that made Stieglitz grump: 'How we worked! ... We worked as a Beethoven sonata should be played, with the same abandon, the same joy, the same sense of connection with the beat of one's own heart and the rhythm of the world'.[37] And later, 'I believe everyone likes to keep a shop. Keeping a shop is one of the thirteen rivers of fairy land'.[38]

One of those who succumbed to Mowbray-Clarke's charisma was Loeb's cousin, Peggy Guggenheim. She had turned twenty-one in 1919 and inherited $450,000; she started to get a nose job, but called it off, and she approached Harold Loeb 'desperate for something to do'.[39] Loeb remembers how 'Peggy came to work in the bookshop as a volunteer. Awkward as a young magpie in her furs and jewelry, she captivated us all by her willingness to go through with the dullest clerical work, and by her joy in being around'.[40] Guggenheim herself acknowledges, 'Though I was only a clerk, I swept into the bookshop daily, highly perfumed, and wearing little pearls and a magnificent taupe coat'.[41] There, as Loeb says, she came 'under Mary Clarke's spell'. Guggenheim says, 'I loved Mary Mowbray-Clarke. She became a sort of goddess to me ... She was so serious and so good and so wonderful about her work, idealistic, absolutely devoted to what she thought she was doing';[42] but even Guggenheim's adoration admits an ambiguous note: 'She was a very superior person. I suppose she thought she was educating the world'.[43] In any case, the six months at the Sunwise Turn changed Guggenheim's

---

[36]   Ibid., 36–37.

[37]   Jenison, 32.

[38]   Ibid., 49.

[39]   Jacqueline Bograd Weld, The Wayward Guggenheim (New York: E.P. Dutton, 1988), 39.

[40]   Ibid., 36.

[41]   Ibid., 39.

[42]   Peggy Guggenheim, *Out of This Century: Confessions of an Art Addict*, foreword by Gore Vidal, introduction by Alfred H. Barr Jr. (New York: Universe Books, 1979), 23.

[43]   Weld, 40.

life, initiating the devotion to art that would define her philanthropic career; as her sister Hazel said, 'If it hadn't been for the bookshop and Laurence [Vail], she'd be playing golf at the Westchester Country Club'.[44]

Loeb mocks Guggenheim's motives and her guilt over her inherited wealth: 'In compensation she collected the latest in experimental painting and gave money and meals to poor artists and writers',[45] but in the passage in which he speaks of himself and his wife developing their potentialities, he sketches a portrait of a rich young couple flailing about in an effort to justify their position:

> We studied painting with Billy and Marguerite Zorach, read *The Bookman* for its literary criticism, Parsons on interior decorating, bought Swedish peasant chairs, listened to Yvette Guilbert, and applauded Little Theatre productions even when it hurt. Thinking of ourselves as *not* innately superior to the general populace, we felt we had to justify our privileges by training our eyes to see, our ears to hear, our minds to understand.[46]

We can see in Loeb and Guggenheim (as in Sylvia Beach) a kind of cultural money laundering at work, and though the older Loeb scoffs (he was sixty-seven when writing this), the younger Loeb, who on his twenty-first birthday had inherited $50,000 from his father – roughly the equivalent of $1,250,000 today, was no doubt just as seduced as Peggy Guggenheim by Mowbray-Clarke's fervent anti-capitalism.

But while Guggenheim was so inept as a shop assistant that she was only allowed to sell at noon ('a slight which she never forgot', says Loeb), Loeb was a man who had already worked as a supply purchaser with the American Smelting and Lead company and who, after the Crash and the failure of his novel, would spend the years 1929 to 1954 as an economist and administrator in the Office of Price Administration and War Production Board, Washington, D.C. What really rankled was not the quality of Mowbray-Clarke's ideas but the way they interfered with business: 'Mary and Madge were more intent on getting their ideas across than on selling books. Many a time I had walked into the shop to discover Mary or Madge, and sometimes the two of them, declaiming for the benefit of a confirmed browser while a would-be customer stood by impatiently'.[47]

Women of Breeding

The 1916 *The Publishers' Weekly* article has Madge Jenison stating that the inspiration for the bookstore came from Earl Barnes's article 'A New Profession for Women' in the August 1915 *Atlantic Monthly*. It makes for squeamish reading

---

[44]　Ibid., 69.
[45]　Loeb, 36.
[46]　Ibid., 26.
[47]　Ibid., 30.

today, as Barnes addresses the 'problem' of the 'large number of young women who have been to college or university'. He notes that 'the callings of teacher, librarian, and social worker are already over-supplied. What are educated young women going to do?' These women have a 'bookish habit of mind' and 'beyond this ... a desire for social service. Brought up on abstract ideals, separated, in most cases, from the grind of daily work, at the marriageable age they instinctively desire to lose themselves in service'.[48] So, given that 'the old-time bookstore, managed by a man who knew books and loved them, is now little more than a tradition', replaced by piles of books in department stores (this is 1915; we remember the injunction that there never was a Golden Age), why not have these women open bookshops? Barnes admits that the 'universal criticism raised is that young college women have no financial skill and no interest in commercial life. Their whole tendency is to spend ... ' But, he points out, women manage restaurants, candy and pastry shops, flower stores or toy shops. And, he concedes, 'the same criticism holds, though possibly in a less degree, with regard to many men who leave college'.[49] Thus opening a bookstore would 'help in every way to settle the vexed question of such women's relation to the economic life of the community'.[50]

In her memoir, Jenison credits not Barnes but Clive Bell for her inspiration, even dedicating the book 'TO / Mr Clive Bell / WHO, THOUGH I HAVE NEVER SEEN HIM / AND HE HAS NEVER HEARD MY NAME, / FOUNDED THIS BOOKSHOP /BECAUSE HE WROTE A BOOK'. It was reading Bell's essay 'Art' that compelled her to call Mary Mowbray-Clarke, and though 'she cried a little, being of Irish parents, and said that she did not see how she could possibly take anything else on',[51] Jenison convinced her. This is very touching (we do not have Mowbray-Clarke's version of the generation story), but, later in the book, Jenison

---

[48]   Earl Barnes, 'Bookselling: A New Profession for Women', *Atlantic Monthly*, August 1915, 229.

[49]   Ibid., 233.

[50]   Ibid., 234; The questions was indeed vexing. The Woman's Book-Shop, the first bookstore planned exclusively for women, had opened at Lexington Avenue and Fifty-Second Street in late 1916. In the Woman Suffrage Parade on 27 October 1917, there was a special section in the parade 'for women from the bookstores and publishing houses, who carried banners and copies of feminist books, which they waved at the spectators'; it was in part this demonstration, John Tebbel argues, that led to a meeting two weeks later at the Sunwise Turn, in which twenty-one women in the book trade organised the Women's National Association of the Booksellers and Publishers. Tebbel, II, 176. *The Publishers' Weekly* was of two minds about this new organisation: 'We give the new Association cordial welcome. The question will naturally arise whether women should not rather put their energies behind trade organizations already existing'. Nevertheless, the writer conceded that the Association was necessary: 'As yet, however, they are excluded from the regular trade gatherings in New York and Philadelphia – tho [*sic*] not in Boston – and it is no doubt largely due to this fact that the new Association, with headquarters in New York, has been formed', *The Publishers' Weekly*, 24 November 1917, 1822.

[51]   Jenison, 4.

gives us a sense of the particular class position of the bookstore in terms that seem to corroborate Barnes: 'The leisure-class woman wants to sell books. She will do it when she would not teach or work in any other business or profession. Women of breeding, with a background of reading, perception, distinction, and brains ... We had from one to ten a week coming in to ask how they could open bookshops or volunteering as our assistants'.[52] So Peggy Guggenheim was not an anomaly.

One of the delights of the bookstore, however, is all the interesting people one comes in contact with, says Jenison, in a passage that delineates current fashion and her demographic:

> Most of the people we know are just like ourselves. They wear the same woollen embroidered blouses with no shoulder seams, or midnight *pea de soie* silk with muslin ruches. They keep the same number of maids or have a charwoman polish off the studio twice a week. They have gone to college if we have, and to Europe the same number of times. If they have done Greece, we have done it. But in a bookshop you drink democracy. People not selected by your own personality come into a shop – all sorts, the great, and cold, young ex-convicts, shoplifters.[53]

She tells an amusing story of trying to sell *The Theory of the Leisure Class* to a man with long hair who looked Scandinavian and who, she has decided, must be a Swedenborgian minister. He resists her urging and only later does she find out he is Thorstein Veblen. Though she admits that 'We never really reached working people',[54] she seems unaware of just how leisured her class was.

In *Reluctant Capitalists*, Laura J. Miller draws on Gregory Stone's 1954 study, 'City Shoppers and Urban Identification', in which he identifies four types of consumers: the *economic consumer*, concerned with price, quality and assortment, who regarded clerks as 'merely the instruments of ... purchase'; the *personalising consumer*, who valued the formation of relationships with sales staff; the *ethical consumer*, who perceived 'a moral obligation to patronize specific types of stores'; and the *apathetic consumer*, who made little differentiation between stores and staff. To this typology, Miller adds a fifth category, the *citizen consumer*, 'who acts on behalf of a perceived common good and who consciously turns consumption into a political act'.[55] Unlike Stone, she sees see these types not as separate individuals but as 'cultural orientations' that the same person may draw on at different times, and she argues that independent booksellers have 'contributed to pushing this last vision of consumption somewhat more into public consciousness'.[56] Certainly that was the aim of Jenison and Mowbray-Clarke.

---

52   Ibid., 152.

53   Ibid., 114.

54   Ibid., 121.

55   Laura J. Miller, *Reluctant Capitalists: Bookselling and the Culture of Consumption* (Chicago and London: University of Chicago Press, 2006), 17.

56   Ibid.

Fig. 2.3   The Sunwise Turn Bookshop, interior of second shop. *Source*:
              Sunwise Turn Papers, Box 20.8, The Harry Ransom Center, The
              University of Texas at Austin.

They were not unique. Books have always occupied a special place in retailing,
regarded as 'sacred products'. Indeed, booksellers are often reluctant to call them
products at all; books have moral worth, and selling books is regarded as a moral
endeavour; a small bookstore is different from a small grocery store, says one of the
independent booksellers Miller interviewed, because it is a place for the exchange
of ideas.[57] Department stores carried them to enhance their image; in 1938, the
manager of the book section of a department store told his staff they should think
of book salesmen as 'Mind Doctors' for the community.[58] As Miller says, people
who choose to run independent bookstores are generally very committed to their
enterprise; they could certainly make more money doing something else, they
'see themselves as bettering society by making books available', and they see
customers as 'neighbours', not merely as sources of profit. But then Miller makes
a crucial point: 'whether or not many customers experience the independent
retailer this way is a different question'.[59]

---

[57]   Ibid., 19, 219–20.
[58]   Ibid., 58.
[59]   Ibid., 14.

Miller cites George Ritzier on 'The Macdonaldization of Society' with its attendant 'homogenization of experience, dehumanization of employees and customers alike, as interactions between them are minimized and those that remain are governed by uniform scripts'.[60] The interactions between Mary Mowbray-Clarke and her customers were not governed by a script – at least not one that had sales as its object – but the comments by Harold Loeb suggest that her enthusiastic advocacy crossed the line into hectoring, as she tried to impose her own script upon the shopping experience. We can see the seeds of this as early as 1917 in Mowbray-Clarke's enthusiastic speech to the Booksellers' Association: 'it is almost impossible for any one to come into the Bookshop and not buy a book because if he didn't know anything about a subject before he came in, he is talked into it while there'. And while she claims they will order any book, 'good, bad or indifferent, moral or immoral', when a women's club decided to install a library, and put together a committee who came up with a long purchase list, Mowbray-Clarke told them, 'No, that isn't the kind of books anyone will read. What you want to put in their hands are perfectly up to date books, the best books on the war and on the present situation in America'. She says triumphantly, 'We finally brought them around to our way of thinking'.[61] Maybe so, but she seems to have no sense that she might have been alienating more customers than she engaged.

A Modernist Performance

Mowbray-Clarke's 1922 speech 'The Small Bookshop' captures not only Mowbray-Clarke's voice but also the excitement in that first month of the *annus mirabilis* of Modernism (six days before *Ulysses* was published). These are the ideas that inspired, and then tired, Harold Loeb. Mowbray-Clarke's sense of mission is paramount:

> I like that term – book-shop-keeper. It sounds like light-house-keeper in my mind and that brings in connotations of courage and steadfastness and other virtues common and necessary to both.

> The movement is still too young for any of us to know exactly what we are contributing to the service of the Book. Something, each of us, I am sure – something of a new form of Humanism, vaguer as yet than that of the small traditional old-book shop with its classics and monumental books, and just possibly something more concentrated than is possible in the large merchandising

---

[60] Ibid. 13.

[61] Mary Mowbray-Clarke, 17th Annual Convention of the American Booksellers' Association, *The Publishers' Weekly*, May 26 1917, 1706. Clarke states her belief that books are 'a kind of spiritual food', and demands that 'they be not treated as luxuries but as necessities of life. We don't allow any one to think that because times are bad, salaries low, or because there may be a little flurry because of the war, that this is the time not to buy and read books'.

> Book-shops where books are … perhaps sold as ordinary commodities rather
> than as what they seem to us to be – food for the soul of man – tools for the
> pursuits of life.[62]

As the pamphlet indicates, the Sunwise Turn described itself as a 'Modern' book
shop.[63] Mary Mowbray-Clarke saw the Sunwise Turn as part of the Modernist
movement and a movement of 'Little' bookshops, like Little theatre or Little
magazines. In 1917 she established a connection with the Arts and Crafts Theatre
in Detroit, who set up a bookstore in their box office.[64] She talks about rhythm, not
about retail strategies:

> To imitate is to kill at once the soul of your own idea, yet you can – and do, when
> you've done any real work – refresh and admire the traditional and learn from
> it every day until you genuinely find out for yourself and reaffirm in your own
> work the truth that there are no laws in art or life, only law – the inner rhythm
> taking form whenever the right elements are brought together.
>
> Does this seem too far from the every-day business of running a book-shop and
> making it pay? My talk to you will be a waste of your time unless I can succeed
> in making known to you the very definite kind of a performance the Sunwise
> Turn experiment is.[65]

The Sunwise Turn is at once a performance, a work of decorative art, and a political
act: in her earlier talk, just one year after the shop had opened, she said 'I am a
cubist, a futurist, an impressionist, all rolled into one.[66] Critics regard the little
magazines of the Modernist period as an extension of the manifesto, and certainly
the banner of Margaret Anderson's *Little Review* – MAKING NO COMPROMISE
WITH THE PUBLIC TASTE – could be taken as the motto of the Sunwise Turn.

---

[62]   Mowbray-Clarke, 'The Small Bookshop'.

[63]   One of the best essays/cautionary tales on the subject is Susan Stanford Friedman's
'Definitional Excursions: The Meanings of Modern/Modernity/Modernism', Modernism/
Modernity 8.3 (2001), 493–513, in which she insists that 'definitional excursions are
fictionalising processes, however much they sound like rational categorization' and draws
our attention to the unresolved complexities with modernism itself, as well as to the
continuing evolution of the term.

[64]   See ALS (Autographed Letter, Signed) 13 October 1917, from Sam Hume, dictated,
on Arts and Crafts Theatre stationary, 4 pp.; Sunwise Turn papers, Box 2, HRC, Detroit
Theatre file; in September 1918 they closed the bookshop because Sam Hume took up a
professorship at the University of California, although in December Maud Hume wrote to
'Mrs Clarke and Miss Jettison' [sic] that she was thinking of opening a bookshop near the
university. She succeeds, and they have etchings and exhibitions and it's 'tremendous fun'
– but Madge was about to jettison the Sunwise Turn.

[65]   Mowbray-Clarke, 'The Small Bookshop'.

[66]   Mowbray-Clarke, 'The Sunwise Turn Bookshop – New York', 1704.

> Now, specifically, what do we do at the Sunwise Turn that is not done everywhere? We glean and sort and distribute, when invited to do so, what we can of the materials for an intelligent modern thought life. We try constantly to descry the structure of civilization in the new lights that illumine it yearly and to keep on watching for the important tendencies in philosophy, psychology, education, science ... [67]

And when you are 'ready' she will tell you what to read:

> When we have found you ready to read 'Tertium Organnum' we can tell you where to find related ideas in our mathematical philosophers. When you read 'Dangerous Ages' we can point to the master from whom the author learned the trick. We may even help to get a serious person still afflicted with war hysteria to a point where he can read Bertrand Russell's 'Analysis of Mind' or Gilbert Cannan's 'Release of the Soul' without worrying about the author's war views ...

She is determined to bring in 'English books of value' even if their authors are not great writers – figures such as Dorothy Richardson and Virginia Woolf, who had published *The Voyage Out* and *Night and Day* and whose radical experiment in *Jacob's Room* would not appear until October of this year:

> 'I think I can claim the honor of introducing Mr Clive Bell to a wider public in America a year or two earlier than he would inevitably have reached us, and over 2/3 of the Am. ed. of Roger Fry's Vision and Design was sold ... and A.E. has been a true best seller at the Sunwise Turn. The many who have read through us his 'National Being' were not so worried about a free Ireland as they might have been without it. Many a man or woman in America has read John Dewey or Thorstein Veblen ... Lao Tsu who might not without our suggestion have done so. If English books of value are not brought out here or come out here and fail to take well and so are dropped, we try to keep them for their chance. We did this notably for 'South Wind' and Virginia Wolff [*sic*] ... not great authors these, but contributors.[68]

But it is not just a matter of importing culture. Mowbray-Clarke takes it as part of her mission to promulgate American values abroad:

> Then we take a special pride in finding the values in our own new poetry and fiction and painting and making them known in Europe. During the war we were especially well able to do this through the interesting visits of the various High Commissions from European countries and the intellectual caliber of the men in them who could come to us again and again to discuss our America and get us to make up for them little libraries of the work we would select as showing our truest records of American experience.

And this is to take place not just in Europe:

---

[67]   Ibid.
[68]   Ibid.

Here & there, In India, In China, In Japan, In Australia and In New Zealand, we have introduced American poets, educators and psychologists. Naturally our very broad contacts have showed us the [*sic* – weaknesses?] of propaganda for any issue, but no freedom can be achieved without experience of all issues, so we collect data on all controverted [*sic* – controversial?] subjects, and so hope to contribute to clarification. National Guilds ideas, Sinn Fein, Bolshevism, Bhai, Ghandi's non-cooperation – all are represented as fast as we can get the material and if we sell Mrs Sanger we also can show you the scholarly little [anti? - in margin] 'Birth Control' pamphlet so beautifully printed at St Dominic's Press.[69]

Today Mary Mowbray-Clarke would be urging Martha Nussbaum's *Not For Profit: Why Democracy Needs the Humanities* on customers, for, she declares, an intelligent bookshop must be a 'University Militant'. These things, from Sinn Fein to birth control 'are factors in world growth to-day. The intelligent person must take notice of them. Snap-shot judgments on them are the curse of our public life'.[70]

Robert Darnton draws attention to the bookseller as 'a cultural agent, the middleman who mediated between supply and demand at the key point of contact'.[71] The bookseller is the interface between the production side and the reception side of the communications circuit, and there are two basic kinds of booksellers: those who are just order-fillers, responding to public demand, and those who strive to shape public demand. What they offered at the Sunwise Turn was not just commodities but also counsel, and though a note of resentment creeps in, Mowbray-Clarke is proud of their abilities:

Our professional service in selecting for the special work of individuals books to help with facts or inspiration often leads to comical results. A man or woman will ask us for such a list. Hours will be spent in thought about the needs, a whole Saturday Post Review will be written especially for him or her.[72]

Self-selection applies to the staff, which Mowbray-Clarke generously compares to the process of art:

We seem nowadays to have almost achieved an alumni of those who have been with us and gone on to more lucrative jobs, from which they come back to give us often excellent 'business ideas'. People that prove unrelated seem naturally to fall away while those who belong become more truly integrated. This is the inevitable art process again.[73]

Little magazines and the little theatre movement existed to promote new ideas or new forms of art, rather than sales; small presses and little bookstores by definition

---

[69]   Ibid.
[70]   Ibid.
[71]   Robert Darnton, *The Kiss of L'Amourette: Reflections in Cultural History* (New York: Norton, 1990), 130.
[72]   Mowbray-Clarke, 'The Small Bookshop'.
[73]   Ibid.

did not make money. 'Business ideas' seem to be the opposite of 'modernism'; Mowbray-Clarke is unrepentant, even defiant, on this issue:

> We are a 'Modern' Book-Shop because we conceive the term 'modern' to apply to the 20th century consciousness of all the factors in the life itself – even those sub-conscious ones the psychanalyst [*sic*] is unearthing for us – and we believe that our way of selling books is our way of searching for those factors. We find them every where. We take them 'off of' the Tammany politician who often surprisingly enough reads widely and intelligently, the jejune young anarchist just out of jail, the morose Scandinavian editor, the most sensitive of Italian diplomats, the burly English novelist, or the American writer of Middle Western movies. We follow every lead that connects with our work. We promote discussion of all the arts and sciences. We are less interested in hearing What is the matter with America than in discovering what American has that is fine and noble and beautiful, and we often feel proud of our little piles of great ones.[74]

Then she comes to the point:

> 'But do you make any money?' ask all the business friends, who think everything we do a little foolish, yet continue to come to us nevertheless.

> 'No, we do not', we have to answer. We do everything but make money. We've sold some hundreds of thousands of dollars worth of books, we've almost doubled each year the number of our steady customers, we've made good friends we hope, but we do not make money. With our [?methods] our selling costs are necessarily high, we've done many things that were foolish and unnecessarily expensive perhaps and which we will never do again, but we have not compromised our original idea. That entity that very soon became bigger than any one of us who worked for it – the Sunwise Turn – seems destined to go on trying to prove its right to exist ... [75]

What she did not tell the booksellers was that the Sunrise Turn was at that moment not trying to prove its 'right' to exist but to exist at all. The issue of money had been the fundamental one for Harold Loeb: 'For me, the "profit system" existed whether I liked it or not; and since it did I accepted the first rule of business: to operate without loss', but 'Mary, however, was against capitalism itself. To her the word "profit" had an evil connotation'.[76]

Alan Antliff argues that Arthur Penty's 'guild socialism' and Coomaraswamy's 'traditions' were 'variants of an anarchism which Mary Mowbray-Clarke also endorsed'.[77] Coomaraswamy (who was born in Ceylon, grew up in England, received his BA from the University of London) was deeply influenced by the ideas of William Morris and argued that industrial capitalism was 'destroying

---

[74] Ibid.
[75] Ibid.
[76] Loeb, 52.
[77] Antliff, 127.

both the religious ideal in Indian art and the modes of production that tied this art to the spiritual life of the people'. He called for a renewed 'medievalism' that integrated spiritualism with day-to-day activities, an integration that could only be achieved through art.[78] Whether or not we label her views 'anarchist', we can see why Mowbray-Clarke published Coomaraswamy's essays. In her speech to the booksellers in 1922, Mowbray-Clarke had said, 'the Sunwise Turn experiment ... tries to show what the whole trend of socialism works toward – the lessening of the separation between a business and a philosophy of life of the creators of it'.[79]

Two years later we find her, all idealism lost, almost spitting in her scorn. 'Booksellers' she says, 'a group of rather timid, ineffectual, inarticulate people Babbitting about the splendid conditions in the trade, & the growth in numbers ... wary of being caught on the wrong side of the censored book, vague about most other problems confronting them'.[80] Not only are they 'rarely able to describe their methods scientifically', they are 'nearly always badly dressed in the imitative way'.[81] The so-called romance of the bookshop is bogus: 'Those who write for the magazines on bookshops are generally people like Mr Morley and Mr Newton who write delectable moonshine about dream shops into which the shadow of the credit man never enters'.[82] Either that or 'they are the naïve and self-deluded people who "bring books to Bohouk" in a "true missionary spirit"'.[83] Wasn't Mowbray-Clarke herself one who lauded bookselling as a vocation? What happened in the interim?

Infelicitous Space

Mary Louise Pratt in her book *Imperial Eyes: Travel Writing and Transculturation* gives us the concept of the 'contact zone', a space of colonial encounters, the space in which peoples geographically and historically separated come into contact. The relations established usually involve 'coercion, radical inequality, and intractable conflict' – but she wants to emphasise 'copresence, interaction, interlocking understandings and practices, often within radically asymmetrical relations of power'.[84] In a sense, a bookstore is a contact zone; this is what Jenison was getting at when she talked about the range of people who came into the store, and Mowbray-Clarke when she says, 'We get all kinds of people. We have colored people. We have all sorts of people who are not ordinarily readers

---

[78]   Antliff, 129–30.

[79]   Mowbray-Clarke, 'The Small Bookshop'.

[80]   Mowbray-Clarke, manuscript, undated, filed with 'Corporation Reports 1923–4', Sunwise Turn Papers, Box 1, HRC.

[81]   Ibid.

[82]   Ibid.

[83]   Ibid.

[84]   Mary Louise Pratt. *Imperial Eyes: Travel Writing and Transculturation* (London: Routledge, 2007), 4.

at all. Little cooks … ' as well as 'young doctors'.[85] But the Sunwise Turn was less like a colonising military or commercial venture and more like a missionary venture: Cultural Missionaries in the Capitalist Jungle. Perhaps one in which the missionaries get swallowed up or go bad. When the bookstore moved from 31st Street up to 42nd, right next to Grand Central Station, it was, as it were, moving up river. Mary Mowbray-Clarke is finally a little like Kurtz, wanting to bring light into the heart of darkness and ending by railing at the natives – she stops short of 'exterminate the brutes', but the sentiment is there.

She sneers at booksellers and snarls at the customers: 'Fancy though, serving a public ninety-nine per cent of whom were afraid to buy on our heartiest recommendation … Yet they will swallow volume after volume of Michael Arlen'.[86] So all those long discussions in the shop yielded little – customers still bought bestsellers. That is when they bought at all:

> These amazing people who make the new domestic budgets – yet I have yet to find a budget that includes a sum for books … The same people who exclaim at the price of a book go from our shop to tea at the Biltmore and exclaim not at the cost of a cup, or they go next door and buy a bathing suit for one or two dips or a silk shirt that fades away in a month without a feeling of extravagance. As for candy! I can't be calm when I think of the waste on that expensive injury and the number of profitable distribution centers for it.[87]

Thorstein Veblen could have explained to her about the shirts. He had coined the term 'conspicuous consumption' more than fifteen years earlier in his *Theory of the Leisure Class* (1899), where he declares, 'Conspicuous consumption of valuable goods is a means of reputability to the gentleman of leisure'[88] and insists, 'No class of society, not even the most abjectly poor, foregoes all customary conspicuous consumption … Very much of squalor and discomfort will be endured before the last trinket or the last pretence of pecuniary decency is put away'.[89] Tea … bathing suits … silk shirts … candy. What about philosophy?

> We had a set of Plato with us for four years. Finally it sold before we had quite decided to put it in the inventory of 'furniture and fixtures'. A young assistant said 'don't replace that!' But Plato had to be in our shop with Lao-Tzu and the Mahabharata and Whitman and St Francis. How do people appear so intelligent

---

[85] Mowbray-Clarke, 'The Sunwise-Turn Bookshop – New York', 1706.

[86] Mowbray-Clarke, manuscript, undated, filed with 'Corporation Reports 1923–4', Sunwise Turn Papers, Box 1, HRC.

[87] Ibid.

[88] Thorstein Veblen, *The Theory of the Leisure Class: An Economic Study of Institutions* (New York: Macmillan, 1899; rpt. Dover Publications, 1994), 47.

[89] Ibid., 53.

and read so few books? And does not everyone who does read a good book at once <u>feel</u> enlarged and made more of a civilized creature?[90]

Apparently people do not feel enlarged by reading – at least not enough to buy books:

> The smallness of the sums relative to income spent on books by Americans is appalling ... When we opened the shop we ardently believed that a large number of people would agree to buy at least six books a month. In five years we have found that only a pitiful number have been that rash – as it now appears they think it, and the average annual sum spent with us is only about $18 a year – perhaps less than is spent by each on candy ... [91]

Candy again. Obviously a sore point. Almost worse is the slighting of the fine advice they give in the shop. She tells of a man who consulted her about a project; she worked hard and made up a list of seventy-five books related to it; two weeks later he called and ordered two. 'Astonished, I said, "What about the rest of the list?" He answered quite calmly, "Oh they had all the others at Brentano's."'[92] You can almost hear Mowbray-Clarke gnashing her teeth. Customers should value consultation as they would with a doctor or a lawyer, she writes. And they do not. Publishers too are a problem. Mowbray-Clarke saved an article called 'Few And Better Books', and though she affixed a note at the top, that says 'Loose thinking – vague generalities' she took the trouble to save it and to score certain passages.

What strikes the twenty-first-century reader is how familiar the complaints are. Publishers, we are told, have created 'that class of retail customers who now consider a book that is three or four weeks old behind the times'. The bookseller must

> sell books like Fords' because 'the great requisite for book-reading is leisure, and leisure to-day is an elusive will-o'-the-wisp. With automobiles, movies, radio, weekly magazines, and hourly newspapers, we are living in a hectic age, an age that appeals in many ways to the senses rather than to the mind.

(Curiously, the writer believes 'these so-called obstacles will redound to our advantage, for surely automobiles and radios and movies, yea, even sex magazines, stimulate the mind, and eventually, when the mind is sufficiently stimulated and in the right direction, we have a new book-reader'. Mowbray-Clarke, unconvinced, writes in the margin, 'Why does he go back on his own data?') Even as Mowbray-Clarke was giving her idealistic talk to the booksellers' class at the New York Public Library in January of 1922, the best days of the Sunwise Turn were past.

---

[90]   Mowbray-Clarke, manuscript, undated, filed with 'Corporation Reports 1923–4', Sunwise Turn Papers, Box 1, HRC.

[91]   Ibid.

[92]   Mowbray-Clarke, manuscript, undated, filed with 'Corporation Reports 1923–4', Sunwise Turn Papers, Box 1, HRC.

Madge Jenison had resigned in November of 1920 and was writing her memoir. Loeb had officially resigned in January of 1921 and was already in Europe, founding the little magazine *Broom*. Officially, the Sunwise Turn lasted a full decade, from 1916 to early 1927, but it really peaked after four years. By 1922 the former friends were communicating only through lawyers.

Henri Lefebvre's insights in *The Production of Space* are helpful here. He argues that space is 'produced'; not in the sense that a kilogram of sugar is produced, of course, but space is not simply 'empty ... prior to what ends up filling it'.[93] Space is in part a 'social relationship', but one that is 'inherent to property relationships ... and also closely bound up with the forces of production'. Thus social space is polyvalent: 'its "reality" at once formal and material. Though a *product* to be used, to be consumed, it is also a *means of production*; networks of exchange and flows of raw materials and energy fashion space and are determined by it'.[94] Social spaces are always 'intertwined', overlaid, implicated in various markets – the capital market, the labour market, the market in works, symbols and signs, and, not least, the market in signs themselves. We can see that the Sunwise Turn, conceived as a space that would somehow be within but immune to these forces, was being buffeted and shaped in spite of itself. Social space, says Lefebvre, searching for a metaphor, has a structure more 'reminiscent of flaky *mille-feuille* pastry' than Euclidean space.[95] But then he rejects that metaphor as insufficiently dynamic and settles on an analogy drawn from hydrodynamics. 'Great movements, vast rhythms, immense waves – these all collide and "interfere" with one another; lesser movements on the other hand interpenetrate'.[96] So,

> If we were to follow this model, we would say that any social locus could only be properly understood by taking two kinds of determinations into account: on the one hand, that locus would be mobilized, carried forward and sometimes smashed apart by major tendencies ... on the other hand, it would be penetrated by, and shot through with, the weaker tendencies characteristic of networks and pathways.[97]

He warns that if taken too far the analogy will lead us into error, but applied at its most simplistic we can see modernism as a determination that, from Mowbray-Clarke and Jenison's point of view, mobilises and carries forward but which proved not to be the major tendency the authors of the store thought it was; it was rather a weaker tendency, and the major tendency was capitalism. We can also see the crosscurrents of personal relations (Loeb, Guggenheim, and other women of breeding, lecturers, such as Theodore Dreiser, customers, such as

---

[93]   Henri Lefebvre, *The Production of Space*, trans. Donald Nicholson-Smith (Malden, MA: Blackwell, 1991), 85, 15.
[94]   Ibid., 85.
[95]   Ibid., 86.
[96]   Ibid., 87.
[97]   Ibid.

Thorstein Veblen, inspirational presences, such as Clive Bell) creating, defining, undermining the space of the store. As Lefebvre says, social spaces 'are traversed by myriad currents', are characterised always by 'hypercomplexity'[98] (indeed, class and gender produce and are produced by social spaces). Lefebvre goes on to speak of the 'arrogant verticality of skyscrapers' which, he says, putting it more explicitly than Sullivan, introduce 'a phallic or more precisely a phallocratic element into the visual realm; the purpose of this display, of this need to impress, is to convey an impression of authority to each spectator. Verticality and great height have ever been the spatial expression of potentially violent power'.[99] The towers surrounding Grand Central Station were an apt spatial expression of the powers that would fracture the Sunwise Turn.

A tedious-looking binder in the Ransom Center archives marked 'Board of Directors Minutes' charts the dramatic disintegration of the Sunwise ideal. On 30 June 1920, there were notes about a Special Meeting at which Madge Jenison resigned as Treasurer. The meeting was held at 8:00 p.m. – this was unusual; the others were usually during working hours. Hastily called? Then seven months later (31 January 1921), another Special Meeting was called. Here Harold Loeb and Marjorie resign, their resignations to take effect immediately. Back salaries are owed:

Mowbray-Clarke	$2295.75
H. Loeb	$1127.79
M. Loeb	$1296.94
Miss Jenison	$1346.29[100]

Attention is drawn to the fact that Harold Loeb had paid $1900 to underwrite the publication of *Plays for Merry Andrews*; the Corporation hopes to sell these and refund Mr Loeb; it acknowledges its indebtedness. The immediate resignations suggest strife.

Jumping ahead to 12 January 1922, just two weeks before Mowbray-Clarke's address to the booksellers at the New York Public Library, the minutes of another Board of Directors meeting show the situation becoming worse: 'Various ways and means of economizing were discussed and a reduction of the personnel of the staff and a lowering of salaries and wages was suggested'.[101] Nothing firm at this point. That will come. Then, 'A proposal from the Encyclopaedia Britannica for rental of desk room was considered and approved', and the 'question of meeting the debts of the corporation through a loan from the bank was proposed and left

---

[98]   Ibid., 88.
[99]   Ibid., 98.
[100] 'Board of Directors Minutes', Sunwise Turn Papers, Box 3, HRC.
[101] Ibid.

for further investigation'.[102] So they are looking at cutting staff, renting space, and refinancing. At the Annual Meeting on 27 April 1922, two positions are dispensed with, a part-time basis established for another, and a reduction made in the salaries of the officers. On 15 May the belts were tightened further, with 'Miss Robinson having successfully completed the installation of the card catalogue system, then resigning; and the substitution of a part time book-keeper for the faithful, local services of Miss Pinsky'.[103] Things did not look good: the Britannica proposal was rejected (insufficient reimbursement and too binding a contract – they wanted a seven-year lease), and the Harriman Bank refused to consider a loan. A proposal was made that claimants to back salary relinquish their claim.

Three weeks later, the minutes of 7 June 1922 record that they have transferred their affairs from the Harriman Bank to the Fifth Avenue Bank, which will give them a loan of $5000 at 6 percent interest. That is promising. But the corporation is imploding. On 22 May a letter had been sent to Marjorie Loeb asking her to relinquish her back salary. On 12 June she replied through her brother, lawyer Harold Content of Griffiths, Sarfaty & Content, Attorneys and Counsellors at Law, 120 Broadway. He writes:

> She informs me that her position is exactly this: she has not pressed the Company for the payment of this salary and quite understood that the sum would not be paid until the finances of the Corporation warranted it. The only effect of such cancellation would be to relieve the Company of a debt which was really owed to Mrs Loeb for services which were performed earnestly and diligently.[104]

Harold goes on to say, 'It is not surprising that Mrs Clarke should have acquiesced in the suggestion, because she is still active in the Company and doubtless hopes to derive future benefits from her connection with the Company'. And he concludes, 'While my sister has no desire to be mean or unreasonable, she can see no reason why she should make a present to The Sunwise Turn of the sums actually due her for hard work. Very truly yours … '[105] We can hear the tart tones of Marjorie mixed with the more lofty legal manner, and neither would have sat well with Mowbray-Clarke.

Ten days later (22 June 1922), Madge Jenison writes from Dobbs Ferry, north of Manhattan, not to Mowbray-Clarke but to Ruth McCall, one of the other board members, saying that she will sign off her salary claim

> at the time and in the event that a loan is completed, and if the Loebs do. Otherwise, I would rather hold it over for the time. I am glad that you have weathered another note. I know so well the weariness of spirit that goes along with that element of that very dearly beloved life.[106]

---

[102] Ibid.

[103] Ibid.

[104] Ibid.

[105] Ibid.

[106] Ibid.

The saccharine note of the letter would have brought no consolation – especially since Jenison's *Women's Home Companion* article, 'Bookselling as a Profession for Women', had just appeared on the newsstands. Mowbray-Clarke must have been grinding her teeth. And creditors were becoming restive. A letter of December 1922 from The Diamond Press complains that they have been carrying an account for two years, and 'we have been very lenient with you, but we cannot see our way clear to carry the balance due us indefinitely'.[107] A month later, Mowbray-Clarke is replying to Mr Diamond's lawyers; they work out a deal, it seems, but a month after that the lawyer is writing testily, 'I cannot however agree to your request that the balance will be paid when funds are available'.[108] Clearly Mowbray-Clarke remained resolutely innocent, thinking that earnestness and high ideals would conquer all.

The issue of back salaries dragged on into the new year, when, on 23 January at noon, the Board issued a rebuttal that seems aimed at Marjorie Loeb's claim that Mowbray-Clarke stood to benefit from the proposal:

> The Board of Directors had felt that this request was not unjustified in view of the fact that all the claimants, save Mrs Mowbray-Clarke, the only one to express readiness and even eagerness to give up the back salary, had retired from the Sunwise Turn with monetary recompense far in advance of their investments. The answers, which are incorporated in the records, took no cognizance of this point of view.[109]

So far this was just sabre rattling; no one was making any aggressive moves. Then buried four pages into a report, it emerges that on 16 February 1923, board member and lawyer Charles Alling had discovered 'certain irregularities, certain illegal and invalid acts and improper procedure'. Was the whole corporation invalid?

It appeared that the directors had voted on their own salaries; that salaries had not been approved by stockholders, had not been voted by the board; that it was possible that they might have been voted irrespective of the rights of creditors and that such action might subject the corporation to suit by creditors and stockholders; and that it was possible that an exact inspection of the old books would show that the salaries might be in some cases at variance with the actual facts.

Though couched in the careful language of lawyers ('appeared ... possible ... might ... possible ... might be in some cases'), it looked as though Mowbray-Clarke was in deep trouble. After discussion, the Board had

> RESOLVED that the question of back salaries should be referred to the directors to investigate the old books of the corporation further to see the exact status

---

[107] Ibid.
[108] Ibid.
[109] Ibid.

of such alleged salaries and that the stockholders suggest that all back salaries should be voided and invalidated by reason of the facts stated ... [110]

'Alleged salaries': Mowbray-Clarke and Alling were bringing to bear all possible legal ingenuity to do the Loebs and Jenison out of their salaries. That was not all:

> The question of the accounts of the Mr and Mrs Loeb, two former officers, was brought up by the President who stated that there had been transferred on the books by Harold Loeb who was then Treasurer and had charge of the books, certain accounts owing to the corporation but which accounts were transferred against the amounts alleged to be owing to Mr and Mrs Loeb.

Mowbray-Clarke is going to accuse Loeb of misuse of funds. And the $5000 that Loeb had put in, the half of his remaining patrimony? A Special Meeting of Board 1 March 1923 concluded that Harold Loeb never paid in the $5000 loan, that he used the money 'for his own purposes for a year and that only when it had been ascertained that this money had not been paid over to the corporation did he advise his broker Lauer & Co. to open an account in the name of the corporation for $2000 of this money, crediting that amount with back interest, but stating that checks should be signed by either himself or Mrs Loeb'.[111]

So it was resolved not only that the back salaries to 1 February 1921 were void, but that 'Loeb in taking payments totalling $1,700 before leaving the company (unknown to the President) defrauded the company, and these payments will now be entered as a contingent asset';[112] this will be used to compensate for the money owed to Loeb for the publication of 'Merry Andrews'. Further, Marjorie Loeb's book purchases of $276.46, charged against her back salary, will be considered a contingent asset. However, Mowbray-Clarke's salary is deemed valid: she is entitled to $2421.27 for her services and will consider taking preferred stock.[113] Deftly done. If not illegal, this was at least what used to be called 'sharp practice'. Ironically, the most reluctant capitalist had now become the most aggressive.

Bourdieu's famous opening to his essay 'The Production of Belief' speaks precisely to the situation of the Sunwise Turn, and Mary Mowbray-Clarke in particular: 'The art business, a trade in things that have no price, belongs to the class of practices in which the logic of the pre-capitalist economy lives on'.[114] A pre-capitalist economy for which Mowbray-Clarke, with her dream of guilds, longed. However, says Bourdieu, the logic is more complicated than at first appears: these practices 'can only work by pretending not to be doing what they are doing'.[115] In other words, the challenge for 'economies based on disavowal of the "economic"

---

[110]   Ibid.
[111]   Ibid.
[112]   Ibid.
[113]   Ibid.
[114]   Pierre Bourdieu, *The Field of Cultural Production: Essays on Art and Literature*, edited and introduced by Randal Johnson (Cambridge: Polity Press, 1993), 74.
[115]   Ibid.

is that they can function 'only by virtue of a constant, collective repression of the narrowly "economic" interest' only by a constant 'disavowal'. This makes sense in the art business, an 'economic universe, whose very functioning is defined by a "refusal" of the "commercial" which is in fact a collective disavowal of commercial interests and profits'.[116] The practices 'which in an "economic" universe would be those most ruthlessly condemned, contain a form of economic rationality' in the art business because they lead to the '*accumulation of symbolic capital*' which ultimately guarantees economic profits.[117] Mary Mowbray-Clarke may have been extreme in her zeal, and certainly Harold Loeb felt she was deluded, but she was operating in a space – an 'economic universe' Bourdieu calls it – in which disavowal was the prevailing, indeed necessary, *modus operandi*. However, to be successful, the artist-entrepreneur must exercise a kind of doublethink, or what Tom Wolfe in *The Painted Word* calls 'double-tracking' – a delicate psychological state in which the right hand does not acknowledge what the left hand is doing (taking money).

What Mowbray-Clarke did understand, instinctively, was the importance of symbolic capital; what she did not appreciate was that ultimately, in order to survive, you need to cash in your symbolic capital. Bourdieu goes on to make a distinction that neatly encapsulates the difference between Harold Loeb and Mary Mowbray-Clarke:

> The disavowed economic enterprise of art dealers or publishers, 'cultural bankers' in whom art and business meet in practice … cannot succeed, even in 'economic' terms, unless it is guided by a practical mastery of the laws of the functioning of the field in which cultural goods are produced and circulate, i.e. by an entirely improbable, and in any case rarely achieved, combination of the realism implying minor concessions to 'economic' necessities that are disavowed but not denied and the conviction which excludes them.[118]

Disavowed but not denied. 'Disavowal of the "economy" is placed at the very heart of the field, as the principle governing its functioning and transformation', Bourdieu insists, and 'denunciation of the mercenary compromises or calculating manoeuvres of the adversary' are part of the game.[119] John B. Thompson in *Merchants of Culture* opens with his own concept of the cultural field (borrowed from Bourdieu), which he sees as a 'structured space of social positions … occupied by agents and organizations … linked together in relations of cooperation, competition, and interdependency'; in fact, he insists, the field is not just one field but a 'plurality of fields', a notion which is useful because it 'forces us to think in

---

[116]   Ibid., 75.
[117]   Ibid.
[118]   Ibid., 75–76.
[119]   Ibid., 79.

relational terms'.[120] Harold Loeb, with one foot in business and one in bohemia, understood the dynamics of the cultural field.

Filed with the Corporation Reports for 1923–1924 is a thirty-four-page typescript for a lecture Mowbray-Clarke had given to the Mediaeval Society, at Oxford, back on 21 October 1919, entitled 'Law and Currency in the Middle Ages'. Loeb had said Mowbray Clarke would talk your ear off about guilds, and here she argues that 'the Guilds may be said to symbolize the Mediaeval promise that was never fulfilled'. She contends that currency leads to the breakdown of community and that guilds brought about the institution of the Just Price. After attacking the amorality of Roman law, she ends, 'If therefore I may presume to offer you any advice in your efforts to restore Mediaeval Society it is to make law rather than economics the centre of your enquiries. In so far as you do this you may be assured that you will before long find yourself able to control forces that will lead to a future where the promise of the Middle Ages will be fulfilled'. Ironic, then, that Mowbray-Clarke would wind up trying to manipulate the law to mitigate her economic disaster. Her idealised Middle Ages was not to be fulfilled. The mullioned windows of the Sunwise Turn were a brave symbol, but the skyscrapers defined the space, and the forces of capitalism defined the terms.[121] At a noon Directors' meeting on 9 March 1927, they reported that 'arrangements had been made with Doubleday Page & Co. to sell the physical assets of the corporation at the store and books at warehouse, except plates and including good-will of the business conducted at its address and the list of customers, for the sum of $5000.00 ... ' The Sunwise Turn was finished, sold to Doubleday, who added it to their chain of stores.

In the same box is a letter from John Macramé, Vice-President of E.P. Dutton, 9 May 1923, with a comment on Jenison's book: 'I am pleased that you are satisfied with THE SUNWISE TURN. I think that Miss Madge Jenison has done a good piece of work here, not at all perfect, quite defective, but human withal and carrying certain amount of the attractive personality and impressive enthusiasm of the authoress'. Enthusiastic, but quite defective, a sounder judgement after all than John Tebbel's *History*. The book may indeed have been 'an influential guide to "personal" bookstore operation', but it was one that would lead devotees into a

---

[120]   John B. Thompson, *Merchants of Culture: The Publishing Business in the Twenty-First Century* (Cambridge: Polity Press, 2010), 4.

[121]   One way to approach the contradictions of the Sunwise Turn, separate from yet inextricably bound up with the networks of commerce, is to take the splendid opening paragraph of Stallybrass and White's *Politics & Poetics of Transgression* and replace 'marketplace' with 'bookstore': 'How does one "think" a bookstore? At once a bounded enclosure and a site of open commerce ... A bookstore is the epitome of local identity ... and the unsettling of that identity by the trade and traffic of goods from elsewhere ... [Here] we discover a commingling of categories usually kept separate and opposed: ... stranger and local, commerce and festivity, high and low. In the bookstore pure and simple categories of thought find themselves perplexed and one-sided. Only hybrid notions are appropriate to such a hybrid place'. (27)

swamp of financial disorder. *The Sunwise Turn: A Human Comedy of Bookselling* ends with this fine exhortation: 'When earnest girls asked us if they should open bookshops, we always advised them to do it – find the capital if they did not have it, take the shivering plunge, meet the crises, and take the returns themselves if there were any. I advise every woman in the world to sell books ... '[122] She took the shivering plunge, and then got out of the water. Cheery and unrepentant to the last, in the preface to the new edition, written in 1930 at the Yaddo artists' retreat, Jenison says, 'It is a happy lot to write a book' – but says nothing about the failure of the shop. Ironically, the site today is occupied by a custom shirt shop.

The Sunwise Turn was indeed 'the prototype of the small "personal" bookshop', but not in the sense Tebbel intended. Mowbray-Clarke could not know it, but she was enacting a pattern that would become almost a cliché of Modernism: the idealistic rise of an organisation and its descent into bitterness and bankruptcy – or capitulation to the market (the prime exemplar is Sylvia Beach, but one thinks of Margaret Anderson and the *Little Review*, and Pound and Eliot who went different ways). Yet the unresolvable tensions of the project transcend Modernism. Perhaps the very conception of the project dooms it. Spencer S. Kellogg, Jr. the owner of the Aries Book Shop in Buffalo N.Y. certainly thought so. In June of 1924 he writes to Mowbray-Clarke, 'Your experience simply confirms my judgment of the entire small book shop idea. These shops are simply philanthropic enterprises'.[123] He has only been operating for three years and has come to the conclusion that one can at best cover the rent and make a small profit – and only then by also selling stationary and office supplies. Kellogg considers carrying on as an 'educational feature' in Buffalo, but only if he can 'gather about the shop as a nucleus a group of interested and interesting people. Losing money is then a secondary consideration, because what you get out of it is worth something to you'.[124] It is only as a social space that the bookshop makes sense.

But he doubts that he can sustain such a nucleus – his manager has gone off to work for a more commercial competitor. Kellogg himself is going to take the summer off to paint and write. He could easily afford to do this: his father owned the biggest linseed oil mill in the world, and Spencer Jr had, in addition to a mansion in Buffalo, studios in California, France, and Italy. The next year he would turn to printing and buy, from Frederick Goudy, the hand press that William Morris had used to print the Kelmscott Chaucer. In short, money was not an issue for Kellogg, as it was for Mowbray-Clarke, which makes his final observation to her all the more pointed: 'As to your thought that by putting more cash capital into your business you will be able to make the shop profitable, possibly you are right, but you will then develop into a big book store and your shop will lose its intimacy and flavor of personal contact which it now enjoys'.[125]

---

[122]   Jenison, 153.
[123]   Spencer S. Kellogg, Jr, Sunwise Turn Papers, Box 7, HRC.
[124]   Ibid.
[125]   Ibid.

The space of the Sunwise Turn was folded into another spatial construct, the chain of Doubleday. Lefebvre points out that in urban space we ignore what is obvious in natural space: the aspect of time, a perceptual shift he relates to the modern: 'with the advent of modernity time has vanished from social space ... recorded solely on measuring-instruments, on clocks ... this most essential part of lived experience, this greatest good of all goods, is no longer visible to us'.[126] We see this most clearly with bohemias, that are always in process, from their initial stage ('low rent' in all senses of the word), through middle-class discovery and gentrification, to a space for the bourgeois rich; a space completely commodified, perhaps even a simulacrum of what it once was, as the space moves from subculture to cultural mainstream to cultural parody.

Mary Mowbray-Clarke was all for the natural and the organic; she wanted her store to follow the rhythms of the sun but did not want to acknowledge that the sun also sets. The artists move on, following the (lack of) money, and the space becomes a fictive construct, preserved in art and memoir. Madge Jenison instinctively found the right approach: get out early and write a book about it. If you read carefully, the cautionary note is sounded early: when the shop is still just a gleam in their eyes, Alfred Harcourt sends her to speak to a supplier who tells her, 'But of course you know that you cannot possibly make bookselling pay. The only way any bookshop survives is through stationary'.[127]

A Sense of Mission

The end of the Sunwise Turn marked the end of an era – but it is always the end of an era. John B. Thompson provides a succinct overview of the rise of the chains in the second half of the twentieth century: in 1958 independent booksellers were selling 72 percent of trade books; by 1980 this had dropped to 40 percent; in 1993 the number had been cut nearly in half again, to 23 percent; by 2000 it was 16 percent; and by 2006 booksellers accounted for only about 13 percent of sales.[128] When Doubleday absorbed her small bookshop, Mowbray-Clarke must have felt that chaos had come again, yet even as I was reading of the demise of the Sunwise Turn another idealistic young woman was opening a bookshop on Prince Street in Soho, a twenty-minute walk south of where the first Sunwise had opened.

I interviewed Sarah McNally (daughter of Canadian booksellers Holly and Paul McNally) at a café near the McNally-Jackson bookshop. Tall, slender, with the carriage of a ballet dancer, she's fiercely articulate and passionate about the store, though she laughs easily. She said, 'I feel that I'm creating something ... I care about what's in my window, in fact I feel like what's in my window right now is a little bland and it's like wearing a hideous shirt, it's a reflection of me'. A

---

[126]   Lefebvre, 95.
[127]   Jenison, 6.
[128]   Thompson, 31.

former editor, now she reads, 'everything ... I have to read for my customers, and it's great. I read things I've never read before, like thrillers, because I have to know what the good ones are. People want advice, they want to be told what to read, and they rely on me as a bookseller'.

She told me how they have events every night of the week. This was sounding more and more like the spirit of Sunwise, so I asked her if she had a sense of 'mission'.

> Oh yes. Absolutely. My mission is to sell more international literature in translation. I got the idea of shelving books by country, and then afterward someone told me they do it in France.

> My mission is to have a New York bookstore that is events-driven, where authors can read and that is a place for the community.

> My mission is to have a New York bookstore that is open and welcoming to all who may walk in. If an African-American person walks in, if a Latino person walks in, I want them to see something on the table that will appeal to them.

She paused:

> My mission is also to survive.[129]

---

[129]   Interview, 13 June 2005; the bookstore has survived and thrives.

Chapter 3
Frank Shay's Greenwich Village: Reconstructing the Bookshop at 4 Christopher Street, 1920–1925

Molly Schwartzburg

In 1960, the Humanities Research Center at the University of Texas at Austin – now the Harry Ransom Center – purchased a heavily autographed door that had once hung in a bookshop in Greenwich Village. Covered with approximately 240 signatures of the shop's customers, it was a memento of a vibrant, tiny establishment that operated for less than six years in the early 1920s. The signatures reveal that the shop was a haunt of legendary figures, most of whom were friends of or professional collaborators with Frank Shay, the shop's founder and owner: novelists Upton Sinclair and John Dos Passos; artists John Sloan and James Earle Fraser; poets Edwin Arlington Robinson and Sara Teasdale; publishers Thomas Seltzer, John Farrar, and the Boni brothers; playwright Susan Glaspell and Theatre Guild founder Lawrence Langner; journalists Mary Heaton Vorse and Heywood Broun. As Christopher Morley would later say, 'It was too personal, too enchanting, too Bohemian a bookshop to survive indefinitely, but for five or six years it played a very real part in the creative life of New York'.[1]

Shay or his shop are often mentioned in passing in histories of Greenwich Village and in the biographies and memoirs of the Village's now canonical inhabitants. The shop's relatively brief life, along with Shay's decision to leave bookselling for other pursuits in 1924, are perhaps among the reasons it is virtually absent from histories of American bookselling. A three-page article in 1972[2] comprised the entire history of scholarship on the shop until 2011, when the Harry Ransom Center launched a large online exhibition about the door and the shop, focusing primarily upon the community of customers revealed in the door's signatures.[3] The fifty-year gap

---

[1]   Christopher Morley, 'Wine That Was Spilt In Haste', *Ex Libris Carissimis* (Philadelphia: University of Pennsylvania Press, 1932), 108–09.

[2]   Anna Lou Ashby, 'Juliette's Door', *The Library Chronicle of the University of Texas at Austin*, N.S. 5 (1972), 35–37.

[3]   The exhibition, which is expected to remain online indefinitely, provides a brief history of the shop and an introduction to its place in the Greenwich Village of the day. The vast majority of the exhibition's attention rests upon the door itself, which will, for this reason, receive less attention here. For that project, 199 of the door's 242 signatures were identified, linked with artefacts from the Ransom Center's collections, and tagged with fifty-three categories revealing the social, professional, and creative ties between

between the door's acquisition and its first intensive study might seem surprising, since the door's informational riches are apparent to anyone who looks at it. But for every Bruce Rogers, Ludwig Lewisohn, and Josephine Herbst, the door holds an Alice Willits Donaldson, Christian Leden, Lily Winner, Bar Dar, and Richard S. McCabe.[4] It is likely that just a few years before the project was undertaken, our preliminary efforts to decipher signatures would not have been successful enough to even consider moving forward. However, a critical mass of freely available digitised books, newspapers, and most importantly, magazines, had been reached in Google, Hathi Trust, and commercial newspaper databases. Whereas previously it would have required a lifetime of research to stumble upon the identities of many of the door's more obscure signatories, we uncovered most in a few minutes or hours of intensive, targeted keyword searches. Over the course of the project, we learned to revisit unsuccessful searches; many signatures were identified on a second or third pass because newly digitised texts had just been made available. Digital research, we realised, was what made this project possible, and may be an invaluable tool for the study of bookstores and retail businesses more broadly.

Beyond the door itself, no records of the bookshop's operations appear to survive. Unlike scholars interested in the Sunwise Turn, another bookshop represented in the Ransom Center Collections, we had no published memoir by the shop's owner, and no archival boxes of inventory lists, order slips, cashed checks, legal documents, and so on. The tools for this project were the door itself and tantalisingly fragmentary scraps of information available in other archives, other memoirs, newspaper advertisements, books and periodicals of the period, and in histories of Greenwich Village and biographies of Villagers. It became immediately apparent that these last two sources are replete with inaccuracies, many of which are due to the fact that Shay was associated with two bookstores in Greenwich Village: first, the Washington Square Book Shop, from 1915–1917, and second, the bookshop where the door resided, from 1920–1924. One source had Shay selling *Ulysses* at the Washington Square Book Shop in 1922. In more than one other, Shay's work at one or the other shop is identified as that of Egmont Arens, his friend and a later proprietor of the Washington Square Book Shop.

---

signatories. I offer grateful acknowledgment to the dedicated team at the Ransom Center who helped put this project together, especially Elspeth Healey, who was involved with the project from the beginning. The project concept and the stories told in this article are based in part upon her work and that of Kelsey Harmon, Chelsea Weathers, Bethany Johnson, and Lynne Maphies. The exhibition may be found at http://www.hrc.utexas.edu/bookshopdoor.

[4]   Alice Willits Donaldson was a ceramicist and painter; her massive murals decorated large spaces, such as the Ford Rotunda in Dearborn, Michigan, and the Fairmont Hotel in San Francisco. Christian Leden was a Norwegian explorer and ethnographer who headed several expeditions to the Arctic in the 1910s and 1920s. Bar Dar was the penname of Samuel bar Hammurabi Yaqub, a Jewish Persian-Assyrian poet who, among other things, was E.E. Cummings's favourite typesetter. Lily Winner was a playwright, suffrage activist, and frequent contributor to Margaret Sanger's Birth Control Review in the 1910s. Richard S. McCabe has not yet been identified.

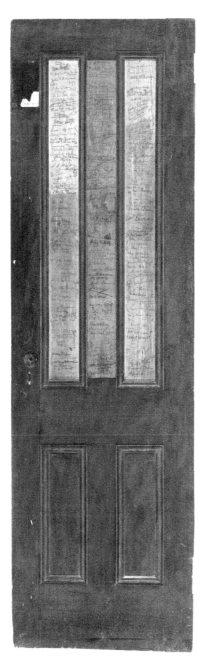

Fig. 3.1   The office door of Frank Shay's Bookshop, 1921–1925. Photograph
by Pete Smith. *Source*: Christopher Morley Collection, The Harry
Ransom Center, The University of Texas at Austin.

This ongoing confusion is curious, since historians of the period invariably emphasise the dramatic differences between the Villages of the 1910s and 1920s. Indeed, some histories of the Village focus on the 1910s to the virtual exclusion of the 1920s. The major Bohemian moment was over and had been displaced by a culture of censorship and prohibition. In the minds of many, the late 1910s were years of 'defeats, fallings-out, defection, expatriations, and retreats'.[5] The war had changed everything, and everyone who was anyone had gone to Paris. Some broader histories of Greenwich Village virtually skip the neighbourhood's culture in the 1920s and 1930s after covering the 1910s in great depth, moving swiftly towards the fresher Bohemianism of the young New York School poets and artists of the 1940s.[6] But as the bookshop door shows, not everyone went to Paris, and those who did often came back to New York. Émigré writers escaping the dangers of the continent in the 1910s, as well as those whose families had immigrated to America within their lifetimes, were not so keen to escape to Europe; it is notable that more than a quarter of the identified signatures on Frank Shay's door were people born in other countries who either lived in or were visiting New York, and more than half of these were immigrants.[7] Young writers and artists continued to come to the neighbourhood to live and work, and even if the Village lacked some of the freedoms it had in the 1910s, it was still a far cry from 'Main Street' America. Notably, only ten percent of the people who signed the bookshop door were born or raised in New York.[8] The rest had come from elsewhere.

The Village of the 1910s was indeed gone, but a differently vibrant, differently creative Village appeared in its place. When Frank Shay's Bookshop is included in the narrative of Greenwich Village's history, the 1920s become a much more interesting site for research into the complex biographies and professional trajectories of major and minor modern writers alike, and the Village of the twenties itself comes alive as a fully formed character in the historical drama of New York.

Frank Shay, Bookman

Frank Shay's Bookshop opened at 4 Christopher Street, just around the corner from the intersection of Greenwich Avenue and Sixth Avenue, in the fall of

---

[5]   Christine Stansell, *American Moderns: Bohemian New York and the Creation of a New Century* (New York: Metropolitan Books/Henry Holt, 2000), 318.

[6]   For instance, Luther Harris in *Around Washington Square: An Illustrated History of Greenwich Village* (Baltimore: Johns Hopkins University Press, 2003) excludes the literary and arts community from his chapter on the Village in the 1920s, focusing almost exclusively on developments in architecture and urban planning in that decade.

[7]   Forty-eight of the identified signatures represent people born in nineteen foreign countries. Twenty-seven represent immigrants.

[8]   Twenty-two signatures represent people born or raised in or near New York City. The American-born signatories came from twenty-nine states.

1920. Shay was already a well-known member of the Village arts community and had been in the book and publishing business for many years. Born Frank Xavier Shea in East Orange, New Jersey, in 1888, he changed the spelling of his last name to 'Shay' in order to associate himself with Shays' Rebellion, an incident in the American Revolution led by a poor farmer.[9] Surviving members of his extended Catholic family remember him as the black sheep, a social rebel like many Villagers.[10] Shay's decision to divorce was likely at the centre of his family's complaint against him. But he found an alternative family in the worlds of books and the theatre. We know little of his childhood, except what he or his wife appear to have submitted to a biographical dictionary in his later years: 'left school at fourteen, but was already a veteran bookseller, having started at the age of twelve in second-hand paper westerns, Nick Carters, and the like'.[11] The article continues, 'In 1912 he was manager of Schulte's Book Store in New York', a fact that is difficult to square with numerous published sources on that store, which indicate variously an opening date of 1914, 1917, or 1918. The only other source of information about Shay's early professional career is a posthumous entry in *Who Was Who in America*: 'In book business, Brooklyn, NY, 1908–1911, and since 1916; book auctioneer, 1911–1912; mgr. book store, lumber jack and at sea until 1916'.[12]

The history becomes richer in about 1915 or 1916, when Shay acquired the Washington Square Book Shop from the Boni Brothers, Albert and Charles.[13] Founded on MacDougal Street by the Bonis in 1912 or 1913, the shop was as close as it got to an epicentre of the Village's political and aesthetic upheavals. The Washington Square Players, which later became the Theatre Guild, was founded in the bookstore's back room. Next door was the Liberal Club, the think tank for left-leaning leaders of the Village community. In 1916 or 1917, presumably while under Shay's ownership, the shop moved to a new location at 27 West Eighth Street, where it was to remain and thrive for many years. In an undated photograph taken at the Eighth Street location, Shay may be seen leaning over a book, accompanied by an unidentified woman.[14]

---

[9]   The ruse worked: his *New York Times* obituary states the Shays association as fact. 'Frank Shay Dies: Wrote About Sea', *New York Times*, 15 January 1954: 19. Proquest Historical Newspapers: New York Times.

[10]   Shay's great-nephew Douglas Barone generously provided this and other information about Frank Shay that had been shared with him by elderly family members.

[11]   'Frank Shay', *Current Biography* (New York: H.W. Wilson, 1952), 536.

[12]   *Who Was Who in America*, 4 vols. (Providence, NJ: Marquis-Who's Who, 1951–1960), 3: 777.

[13]   Inconsistent dates are an ongoing problem in telling Shay's story; according to *Who Was Who*, Shay was 'at sea until 1916', but all other sources seem to agree that he took over the bookshop in 1915.

[14]   Several sources misidentify the man in this photograph as Egmont Arens, perhaps because Arens appears in another Beals photograph of the Washington Square Book Shop, presumably taken some months or years later.

Fig. 3.2   Frank Shay and an unidentified woman, probably Fern Forrester Shay, in the Washington Square Bookshop. Photograph by Jessie Tarbox Beals. *Source*: Jessie Tarbox Beals Photographs, The Schlesinger Library, Radcliffe Institute, Harvard University.

Shay took over the shop at the Village's defining moment: the Provincetown Players were not yet famous, *The Masses* had not yet been censored, the United States was not yet at war. Bohemia is always nostalgic for the moment that has just passed, and 1917 marks the beginning of the end, the 'selling-of-bohemia' or 'faux bohemia', as it was called, the moment when 'bohemianism for bohemianism's sake had triumphed over political and cultural substance'.[15] But Shay was to be present for some of the great moments of the era, and absent for much of the period of change that followed. Allen Churchill describes Shay in these years as 'a breezy giant who dreamed of publishing books and plays'.[16] A tall, thin man with glasses and sandy blond hair, he was known as outgoing and boisterous, with a quick laugh and a temper to match. As the Washington Square Book Shop's new owner, he turned this energy to matching the Boni brothers' investment in the community and in publishing. The brothers had begun to make their mark on the publishing scene during the time they owned the shop, publishing books and Alfred Kreymborg's little magazine *The Glebe*. In 1916, Shay himself published from the shop the slim paperbacks *The Provincetown Plays: Series One, Two* and *Three*. The appearance of these volumes is recognised as a significant event in the

---

    [15]   Gerald W. McFarland, *Inside Greenwich Village: A New York City Neighborhood, 1898–1918* (Amherst: University of Massachusetts Press, 2001), 191.

    [16]   Allen Churchill, *The Improper Bohemians* (New York: Dutton, 1959), 63.

publication history of American theatre. Included were works by Eugene O'Neill, Louise Bryant, Floyd Dell, John Reed, Hutchins Hapgood, Susan Glaspell, Neith Boyce, and Alfred Kreymborg. The nascent Provincetown Players had opened the Playwrights' Theatre at 139 MacDougal, and Shay was involved beyond his publishing work: he played the role of Scotty, a seaman, in the group's first New York production of Eugene O'Neill's *Bound East for Cardiff*, the play that launched O'Neill's career.[17] This early relationship with the Provincetown Players group was to thrive well into the next decade; at least eighteen people associated with the group – including its founders – were to sign the bookshop door on Christopher Street.

The successful move to West Eighth and the publishing efforts that mark this period of Shay's career suggest that had he continued at the Washington Square Book Shop, his career may have paralleled that of his friends the Bonis. His plans appear to have been ambitious. A July 1917 book-trade magazine notes that 'Frank Shay & Company announce for immediate publication Gustavus Myers' "The History of Tammany Hall", Stephen F. Austin's "Principles of Drama-Therapy", and the twenty-fifth thousand of Theodore Dreiser's first novel, "Sister Carrie."'[18] A handful of copies of *Sister Carrie* were produced under the Shay imprint, perhaps as proofs or dummies.[19] But the war intervened: Shay was conscripted in 1917. He fought the draft on the basis of pacifist beliefs, and was quoted in the *New York Times* as stating that he was 'unwilling to engage in any work for the war-making establishment'.[20] As the Times reported, he failed, appealed, and failed again. During the appeal process, he introduced Theodore Dreiser to Horace Liveright, who, with his partners, the Boni brothers, took over the *Sister Carrie* project. It appeared under the Boni and Liveright imprint that year, and Dreiser was to be associated with that firm for many years.[21] Shay remained close with the Boni brothers, who later signed the bookshop door. The bookshop ended up in the hands of another friend and eventual door-signer, Egmont Arens, who ran it at the Eighth Street location for another decade. Arens continued to publish the Provincetown playwrights out of the shop under the series name *Flying Stag Plays*.

---

17   *The Provincetown Plays*, First Series (New York: Frank Shay, 1916), 6.

18   'Items of Interest', *Bookseller, Newsdealer, and Stationer*, 1 July 1917, 31. Myers' book appears to have never been published, and Austin's appeared under the New York imprint 'Sopherim' in 1917.

19   A rare copy of Shay's Sister Carrie edition came up at the Pacific Book Auction in 2012. The auction description notes the planned edition 'may have been made up of sheets from the 1912 Harper edition since our Shay title page is a tipped in cancel'. An inscription on this copy's endpaper states that only five copies were produced. http://www.pacificbook. com (accessed 1 July 2012).

20   'Shay Defies the Draft', *New York Times*, 23 September 1917, 21. ProQuest Historical Newspapers: New York Times.

21   John Tebbel, *A History of Book Publishing in America*, 3 vols. (New York: R.R. Bowker, 1972–1978), 2: 391.

On 2 January 1918, with the shop and his publishing projects now given over to new owners, Shay married artist Fern Forrester and soon after left for France. He served in the Headquarters Company of the 312th Infantry of the 78th Division, United States Army. He managed to continue his literary work in France, serving in 1919 as Managing Editor for the *Flash*, a newspaper published by and for servicemen in the 78th; this experience was to be of great use when he opened his new bookshop two years later. Also in 1919, he published *Barrack Bag Ballads*, a tiny staple-bound collection of soldiers' songs authored by Lloyd Mac Thomas. The fifteen-page collection, under the imprint 'F. Shay', noted two places of publication: Semur, France and New York. It was the first of many Shay publications that demonstrate his passion for popular ballads.

Shay was among the thousands of men and women who flooded back into New York in 1919 after the war was over.[22] He jumped back into his work, editing *The Plays and Books of the Little Theatre* (1919) and co-editing with Pierre Loving *Fifty Contemporary One-Act Plays* (1920) for Stewart Kidd. Also in 1920, Friedman's published Shay's bibliography of the works of Walt Whitman, the first book-length bibliography of the poet. It was based upon the large Whitman collection of Shay's friend Max Breslow; the two men may well have met while working at bookshops on 8th Avenue in their youths in the early 1900s. Shay's interests were piling up fast: theatre, publishing, editing, bookselling, ballad collecting, and bibliography.

In October 1920, notices for Shay's new bookstore began to appear: 'Frank Shay is at it again', said an editorial in the *Greenwich Village Quill*.[23] The shop – so small he preferred to call it a 'stall'[24] – opened at 4 Christopher Street, just around the corner from busy Greenwich Avenue. The large corner building possessed the aura of an earlier Bohemian moment: in a tone approaching awe, the story was often told that in the late 1890s, the English poet and legendary Village resident John Masefield had tended bar in the very spot now occupied by Shay's shop. Occupying another part of 4 Christopher Street was the art studio of Winold Reiss, where artists gathered for life-drawing classes and conversation. Christopher Street was a good strategic choice for a retail establishment: recent infrastructure changes in the immediate neighbourhood meant that this part of Christopher Street was becoming a thriving commercial area.[25] Advertisements from various magazines at the time show the street to be filled with a rich variety of retail businesses: restaurants, gift shops, tea houses, and nightclubs. Just next door was the popular Pirate's Den. The street was also a straight shot to Shay's

---

[22]   Men who served in the war make up at least ten percent of the names on the bookshop door and include such well-known figures as John Dos Passos, William Rose Benét, Achmed Abdullah, Arthur Davison Ficke, and Jonathan Cape.

[23]   Editorial, *Greenwich Village Quill*, October 1920, 5.

[24]   Holland Hudson, 'Progressive Bookselling: One Shop and its Methods', 421–23, *The Publishers' Weekly*, 12 February 1921, 421.

[25]   Christine Boyer, ed., 'Straight Down Christopher Street', *Greenwich Village: Culture and Counterculture*, ed. Rick Beard and Leslie Cohen Berlowitz (New York: Rutgers University Press, 1993), 48–49.

beloved port neighbourhood, not far down Christopher to the west. It was not the most stable of environments – rents shot up by 140 percent between 1920 and 1930 across the village[26] – and many village businesses came and went in months. Shay's five years in business seem, in this context, an impressive run.

Like many Village businesses before and after the war, Shay's shop was equal parts an intellectual, social, and commercial enterprise. It was a meeting place for writers, publishers, theatre producers, and budding filmmakers, and a workspace for Shay's own varied publishing and editing collaborations. From the moment the shop opened, Shay threw himself fully into his work. A 1922 article about the Village in the *Los Angeles Times* called Shay 'the livest wire in the publishing business', and this he certainly seemed to be.[27] He expanded the bookseller-publisher model he had inherited from the Bonis on MacDougal Street. Books began to appear almost immediately under the imprint 'Frank Shay' or 'Frank Shay's Bookshop'. In 1920, he launched the little poetry magazine *The Measure*, edited by a rotating group of writers. He initiated the *Salvo* chapbook series, and by April 1921, four volumes in the series were available: Edna St Vincent Millay's *A Few Figs from Thistles*; Shay's own edited selection of sea chanties, *Iron Men and Wooden Ships*; Hildegard Flanner's *This Morning and Other Poems*; and William McFee's *An Engineer's Notebook*.[28] The first of these, which includes some of Millay's most famous poems, is a landmark in poetry publishing. In 1923 the Pulitzer Prize for Poetry was awarded to an expanded commercial edition of *A Few Figs from Thistles*, published by Harper and Brothers. This expanded edition included another poem first published by Shay as a stand-alone edition, *The Ballad of the Harp-Weaver* (1921), as well as a handful of previously uncollected verses.

The books published from the shop were small, charming volumes that announced their relationship to their publisher, his shop, and the Village itself: *The Ballad of the Harp Weaver* read on its title page, 'printed for Frank Shay and sold by him at 4 Christopher St., in the shadow of old Jefferson Market, 1922'. But Shay was not uninvested in a broad national audience. Of particular note are his commercial drama anthologies aimed at the burgeoning little theatre movement nationwide. *Fifty Contemporary One-Act Plays* (1920) was followed by several more themed anthologies from major publishing houses – Stewart Kidd, Appleton, and Little, Brown – many of which remained in print for decades. Shay's editorial work helped shape the performance canon for community theatres and school and university theatre programs for decades. He also compiled further collections of ballads both during and after his time at the shop; his work in this area was highly regarded and used as a source by later anthologists, including John and Alan

---

[26]   Beard and Berlowitz, eds., *Greenwich Village: Culture and Counterculture*, 19.

[27]   Abby Dune, 'Gotham's Quartier Latin'. *Los Angeles Times Illustrated Magazine*, 7 May 1922, VIII4. ProQuest Historical Newspapers: Los Angeles Times.

[28]   William McFee noted in *Swallowing the Anchor* (Garden City: Doubleday, Page, 1925), xii, that his Salvo volume was printed on the same press as *The Little Review*; whether this applies to the other volumes is not known.

Lomax.[29] Though these editorial projects were not usually published at the shop, they were almost certainly *of* the shop. It was likely the space in which he met with his collaborators. His publishers, co-editors, illustrators, playwrights – and even the sea captains from whom he may have gathered some of his ballads – signed the bookshop door.[30]

Shay was a born marketer: the shop's window displays were often admired and were used to display a range of books, from Shay's own publications to bestsellers. We know of at least two specific books marketed in a remarkably similar manner in his window: Edna St Vincent Millay's *Ballad of the Harp Weaver* and Joseph Hergesheimer's *Cytherea*, both displayed in 1922. The former was, as noted earlier, published by Shay. His wife, the artist Fern Forrester Shay, created the striking cover image and interior illustrations for this spare, elegant chapbook. Millay's bibliographer Karl Yost notes that for the total edition of five hundred copies, Shay printed most of the copies in orange, but also printed a small number each in 'red, dark green, apple green, yellow, and blue' expressly for the purpose of creating striking window displays.[31] The designers at Alfred A. Knopf were of the same mind about their books: *Cytherea*, a novel about a doll of the same name, was likewise printed in variant dust-jackets, and a competition was launched for the best bookstore display featuring an artist's rendition of the doll. Frank Shay's Bookshop, with doll designer Katherine Pierson, won the competition for their display featuring the doll surrounded by multi-coloured dust-jacketed copies of the novel.[32]

Perhaps inspired by his experience in the military, Shay decided to make his shop the source for news about the Village. A newspaper began issuing from the shop sometime in 1921, as *The Bookman* reported:

> 'The Greenwich Villager' is a new weekly newspaper issued from Frank Shay's Bookshop. It's a vivid little sheet – at least the first three numbers have been so. We called on the sandy-haired friend of Masefield and McFee last night, to find him, as usual, excited over the words of Edna St Vincent Millay. He is to publish a book a month this year – at least a book a month! And his window displays continue to be original and entertaining.[33]

---

[29]   Shay's *Drawn From the Wood* (New York: The Macauley Company, 1929) is cited as the source of the ballad 'Snagtoothed Sal' in the Lomax collection *American Folk Songs and Ballads* (New York: Macmillan, 1934). Shay's contributions to the literature on sea chanties were featured prominently in his *New York Times* obituary, whose full headline read 'Frank Shay Dies; Wrote About Sea: Expert on Chanties was 65 – Helped O'Neill and Millay as "Village' Publisher'.

[30]   Some of these signers include Shay's publisher John G. Kidd, co-editor Pierre Loving, illustrator Edward Wilson, and sea captain and ship-owner David William Bone.

[31]   Karl Yost, *A Bibliography of the Works of Edna St. Vincent Millay* (New York: Harper, 1937), 28.

[32]   'The Cytherea Prize Doll', *The Publishers' Weekly*, 1 April 1922, 973.

[33]   'The Gossip Shop', *The Bookman* 14.1 (September 1921), 93.

A single issue of the now very rare newspaper, preserved by Christopher Morley and held in his voluminous archive at the Ransom Center, is chock full of information for insiders: gossip columns, book reviews, and advertisements for nearby businesses. It contains mention of no fewer than thirty-two people who signed the bookshop's door.[34] A 1922 article about Village publications notes that Shay's paper, which was printed for about a year, was 'filled to the brim with scandals and the latest doings of the villagers'.[35]

Shay clearly thrived personally in his little 'stall', surrounding himself with friends and customers and experimenting with various forms of publishing and publicity. However, financial success was less straightforward. He sustained his community by expanding his business – first, into a larger space, and second, by taking it on the road. In a 7 September 1921 journal entry, Shay's close friend Christopher Morley noted Shay's decision to expand the shop:

> Up to Frank Shay's at lunch time: we had spaghetti and spumoni ice cream at Ugobono's on 6th Ave: Frank is going to enlarge his shop by building back into Winold Reiss's studio: Frank says money is very scarce just now: God knows that's the truth as regards CDM [Christopher Darlington Morley].[36]

A 21 October entry in the same journal indicates the expansion's completion. Yet with expansion seems to have come further financial difficulty. On 16 January 1922, Morley noted, 'WRB [William Rose Benét] and I lunched with Frank Shay at Ugobono's. Frank said business so bad he had not been able to pay his employees their full wages'.[37]

Despite (or perhaps because of) this precarious situation, Shay invested that summer in a custom-built automobile that would allow him to take the shop with him to Provincetown, Massachusetts, the long-time summer haven of the Bohemian crowd and his own eventual permanent home. Inspired by Morley's fictional travelling bookshop in the 1917 novel *Parnassus on Wheels*, Shay filled a real-life version, in the form of a souped-up Ford, with books and escaped the city's blistering heat, selling his stock along the sandy streets. In a charming, upbeat article on this project, written for the *New York Times Book Review*, Shay offers some insight into his bookselling philosophy and experience, as well as some helpful details of the nature of his stock:

> All about the truck are shelves. On the right there are five seventy-two inch shelves filled with the latest fiction. At the back are eight shelves filled with selections from the popular libraries: Everyman's, Modern and the World's Classics. The left side has but four shelves and is divided into thirds: on each

---

[34]   *The Greenwich Villager*, 9 June 1921.

[35]   'Magazines are published by Greenwich Artists', *The Oregonian*, 26 March 1922, 5. NewsBank Readex Database: America's Historical Newspapers.

[36]   Christopher Morley, Journal (1921–1922), Works: Journals, Christopher Morley Collection, Harry Ransom Center, University of Texas at Austin.

[37]   Ibid.

for essays and biography, juveniles and miscellaneous. The best sellers are all here, the freshest of non-fiction, the latest plays from Broadway and the presses, poems on which the ink has hardly dried. Freshness and lateness are desirable, for this book wagon is designed to meet the needs, not of the country people, but of the customers who have left the shop's locality.[38]

A Bohemian, of course, likes reading a bestseller on the beach as much as the next person, as unlikely as he or she might be to admit it to one less forgiving than his neighbourhood bookseller.

Despite Shay's energetic leadership of the shop – or perhaps due to burnout – the shop began petering out by the middle of 1923. Morley's journals make repeated mention of his friend's financial difficulties over the years, but we do not know that this was the reason for the shop's closure. Shay published books as a steady clip through 1922. He continued in 1923, but the Frank Shay imprint begins to show 'Summit, New Jersey' as its location, rather than New York. Soon after, Shay ceased publishing under his own imprint for good.[39] It seems that at the end of the summer of 1924, the Shays simply did not return from their annual Provincetown trip.

Shay appears to have sold the shop to a man named Robert A. Hicks, who reissued at least one of the shop's 1921 publications from the 4 Christopher Street address in 1924, but the record is cloudy.[40] After Shay left the shop, the name was changed, and in advertisements from the time it appears variously as 'The Greenwich Village Bookshop' and 'The Village Bookshop'. We know that the shop's circulating library, which began in Frank Shay's day, continued after he left, because Christopher Morley, who remained a loyal customer of the store, never returned a copy of Virginia Woolf's *Jacob's Room* with the circulating library slip in the back. The shop finally closed in June 1925, less than a year after Shay left. The shop was managed, or perhaps owned, at the time by a woman named Juliette Koenig, but little further evidence of its final year appears to survive.

The New Village: Professionals, Personalities, and Celebrities

It is telling that the bookshop did not survive long after its title lost the personal name of 'Frank Shay' and became generic, for Shay's personality – and the quality of personality itself – was arguably the shop's very soul. The shop was a social hub from the start, thanks to Shay's entwined talents of friendship and self-promotion.

---

[38] Frank Shay, 'Bookselling on the Broad Highroad', *New York Times Book Review*, 11 May 1924, 2. Proquest Historical Newspapers: New York Times.

[39] Norman Lee Swartout had been publishing plays for several years in Summit, in a vein similar to Shay; is possible that Shay eventually gave Swartout his lingering projects.

[40] Some copies exist of William McFee's *An Engineer's Notebook* (New York: Frank Shay, 1921) with a new imprint tipped into the title page: New York: Robert A. Hicks, 1924, with the address '4 Christopher Street'. I have been unable to find further evidence of Hick's identity or association with the shop.

Fig. 3.3   Henrik Willem Van Loon's illustration for Holland Hudson's 'Progressive Bookselling: Guaranteed Bookselling – One Shop and its Methods' in *The Publishers' Weekly* (January, 1921). Source: Image courtesy of the Perry Castaneda Library, The University of Texas at Austin.

In January 1921, just months after the shop opened, *The Publishers' Weekly* published a three-page feature article on the shop, its famous customers, and its innovative marketing techniques (the door was not mentioned because it had not yet been installed). Written by Holland Hudson, the article was illustrated with a Hendrik Willem Van Loon cartoon of America's most famous writer, Sinclair Lewis, browsing the shop's sidewalk bins. Lewis signed the cartoon, literally endorsing the shop. He, Van Loon, and Hudson all later signed the bookshop door.

Donald Ogden Stewart wrote in his memoir that if you wanted to meet another writer, you would do well to seek him out at Frank Shay's. He recalled the time when, in 1922, a friend 'took me to a cellar on MacDougal Street where the Provincetown Players were putting on The Hairy Ape for the first time. I thought it was terrific and met [Eugene] O'Neill in Frank Shay's bookshop'.[41] Shay's friend Bobby Edwards implicitly encouraged literary celebrity hunters to visit the shop when he included this description in the gossip pages of his *Quill* magazine:

> Dropping in at Frank Shay's Book Shop we were introduced to William McFee, and Christopher Morley. Before we left we noted the following customers, Floyd Dell, Mary Austin, William Rose Benet, Captain David Bone, Henry G. Aikman, Sherwood Anderson, Tod Robbins, Gordon Stiles, Jeanne Judson, Susan Glaspell, and about steen[42] others whose names make up the honor roll of contemporary American Literature. It begins to look as if Frank would have to change the name of his shop to the Author's Bookshop. Note – Frank wrote this.[43]

All but two of the names listed here (Robbins and Aikman) are to be found on the bookshop door.

It was apt that the Ransom Center project began with our attempts to decipher signatures and identify signers, because beyond its eponymous title, Frank Shay's Bookshop was very much about specific people: the famous customers and the famous bookseller himself. The signatures on the door are, in a way, an appropriate emblem for the often, but not always, commercial celebrity that was an important feature of Village culture in the 1920s. Indeed, the bookseller himself depended on the concept of celebrity – his own unique, immediately recognisable personality – for survival. It was, importantly, not 'Shay's Bookshop' but '*Frank Shay's Bookshop*'. Shay was not alone among booksellers of the time who sought to identify his bookstore with his personality, tastes, and his friends.[44] But the

---

[41]   Donald Ogden Stewart, *By a Stroke of Luck* (New York: Paddington Press, 1975), 102.

[42]   Period slang for 'lots of'.

[43]   News item, *The Greenwich Village Quill*, June 1921, 29.

[44]   Notably, at least two people who signed the door imitated Shay's style the year after his shop opened: Hector MacQuarrie opened Hector MacQuarrie's Bookshop in 1921, and publishers' traveller Dorothy Grant likewise opened Dorothy Grant's Bookshop around the same time.

survival of the shop's door, with its list of names, emphasises the fact that a great deal of the shop's success depended upon personality.

Shay emphasised his own role perhaps more than many other booksellers of the time, using a marketing gimmick often found in bookstores today: the personal recommendation flag. Shay's was a printed strip wrapped around selected volumes, which read 'FRANK SHAY RECOMMENDS THIS BOOK / It is sold with the guarantee that if it does not measure up to our statements we will exchange it for another book or refund the purchase price'. The idea was novel enough to be described in an advice column in the advertising-industry magazine *Printers' Ink*, entitled 'The Little Schoolmaster's Classroom'.[45] Other observers were ambivalent about the scheme, such as one who wrote, 'He wants to be the Dr. Samuel Johnson of the village and tell everybody just what to read and look at – and sell it to them'.[46]

Individuality and personality had certainly been essential to economic survival in the Village in the 1910s but seem to have become even more important in the 1920s, when shop owners were among the Bohemian celebrities who drew tourists and their wallets to the neighbourhood. Even with this influx of customers, the fast-rising cost of living in the increasingly 'gentrified' Village pushed out many businesses that had been more suited to the more self-contained community of the 1910s. Travel journalists from around the country wrote features about the Village and its quirky characters, suggesting that the draw was as much the Village's individuals as its overall charm. A 1922 article in the *Miami Herald* captures the personality-driven popular image of Shay's neighbourhood, and the major role Shay played in the drama of the Village at the time:

> Evening has come to the village streets. Claude McKay, the negro poet, is walking homeward with Max Eastman, radical writer, and Mike Gold, editor of the *Liberator*. Frank Shay, in shirt sleeves and puffing a cigarette, is standing in front of his bookshop.
>
> His shop is a rendezvous for the young intellectuals – John Farrar, Burton Rascoe, Scott Fitzgerald and John Weaver … It is the hour when the village really begins to work. Tony Sarg is working on his marionettes at his attic window. Romany Marie's back yard restaurant is ready to cater to curiosity and lean purse …
>
> A knotted group waits for Harry Kemp's alley playhouse to open and reveal the futility of life. Smudgy-faced Italian children are hanging about the entrance of MacDougal alley waiting for 'Lady Bountiful' – Mrs Harry Payne Whitney – to arrive in her motor car. In a half-filled coffee shop sit Michio Itow, Fania Marinoff, Djuna Barnes and Edna St Vincent Millay.[47]

---

[45]   'The Little Schoolmaster's Classroom', *Printers' Ink*, 14 April 1921, 200. Google Books.

[46]   'Magazines are Published by Greenwich Artists', 5.

[47]   'New York Day by Day', *The Miami Herald*, 23 November 1922, 8N1. NewsBank Readex Database: America's Historical Newspapers.

The bookseller, his customers, and other business owners seem like characters in a play, the opening scene set for a rapt audience.

Indeed, by the 1920s the Village had, in the eyes of many long-term residents, begun to seem like a caricatured version of itself. Tour buses of out-of-towners gawked at the Villagers, and visitors from uptown came to drink at speakeasies, browse in quirky shops, and watch shocking plays in little theatres once attended mainly by the friends of the players. Allan Churchill eloquently narrates the changes to the village in the late 1910s and early 1920s, particularly in a chapter entitled 'Half-Bohemians', in which he describes how the Village's transgressive Bohemianism was watered down by insiders and outsiders alike. By the mid-1920s, even Robert Edwards, a self-promoter who often included a map of hot spots for tourists in his *Greenwich Village Quill* magazine, had had enough of the 'poseurs', ending the magazine's decade-long Village run in a huff in 1926.

Histories of the Village often imply that the long-time inhabitants of the Village were split into two groups in the 1920s: those who despaired of the loss of the 'authentic' village, and those who saw an opportunity and profited from it by becoming caricatures of themselves. But these two vocal groups tend to drown out the third, largest category: those residents for whom the Village simply remained a space for creative people to meet, not necessarily ideologically laden or self-consciously subversive of the rest of 'American culture'. Daniel Aaron's description of the new generation of young Villagers is instructive for how we consider this third group of existing Villagers. He notes that new arrivals like E.E. Cummings might have looked to the 1910s not as a lost moment of vitality but a moment of naiveté: 'Cummings (and the same could be said of the new Villagers of comparable age and background) was more sophisticated, hard-boiled, sardonic, and scatological than the prewar Village pacifist', hardened by the war into a perspective not of 'anger and bitterness' but 'impotence'.[48] The war had made them simply incapable of comprehending the old Village's model of an aesthetics that was closely tied to direct social activism. Instead, they focused inward:

> He and his circle took their writing very seriously. They were professionals who scrabbled for their livings, took on editorial jobs, wrote novels and plays and poems, sold pieces to *The Dial*, *Vanity Fair*, *The New Republic*, or *The Freeman*. They worked to perfect their skills and were more concerned with self-expression than social redemption.[49]

Of course, this description could apply to the careers of the vast majority of long-term Bohemians too. Just a few years older than Cummings and his friends, they published in the same magazines, worked similar editorial jobs, or moved up

---

[48] Daniel Aaron, 'Disturbers of the Peace: Radicals in Greenwich Village, 1920–1930', 276–300, *Greenwich Village: Culture and Counterculture*, 279.

[49] Aaron, 280.

to positions of greater responsibility in publishing. Viewed from another angle, the new Village's focus upon celebrity was, in fact, more of a turn away from communal rebellion and towards literary professionalism.

Holland Hudson expressed a similar weariness with the dichotomy of 'bohemia' and 'pseudo-bohemia' from the bookseller's perspective as he (somewhat archly) dismissed both at once in favour simply of books themselves, and of bookselling as represented by Frank Shay's bookshop in particular:

> In many small book-shops we escape one kind of rubbish only to be affronted with another. We escape flapper fiction, and vellum editions of the Hoosier poet only to encounter propaganda for one queer cult after another – for anarchism, Bolshevism, Cubism, Egoism, Dada-ism, Ferrerism, and so thru the alphabet ... I find something refreshing in a little book-shop like Frank Shay's where the Great Cause is simply selling books.[50]

From the perspective of a bookseller, Shay's focus on personality would likely have been seen not as a crass attempt to build his own celebrity but as a celebration of intimate, personal bookselling. Shay was one of four lecturers on the topic of 'The Intimate Bookshop' at the New York Library Club in January 1922.[51] These shops were part of the much-discussed trend in small bookstores that Murray Hill called a 'remarkable phenomenon':

> About ten years ago there were three kinds of book stores in this country. The large, handsomely appointed, exhaustively stocked book stores in the centre of the city ... the dealers handling exclusively rare book, choice items, fine bindings, first editions, association volumes, and such things ... then, the second hand bookstores. Yes, there were, of course, too, some few bookshops confined to their special subjects ... But the bright little specialty bookshop which now has come into vogue hardly existed.[52]

Hill goes on to point out the emphasis on close, personal relationships in these shops: 'The owner of a little bookshop ... usually wants his shop to stay a small bookshop. He wins his customers' confidence; they put themselves into his hands, and are grateful to him'.[53]

---

[50] Hudson, 423.

[51] 'Talks on Bookshops', *The Publishers' Weekly*, 28 January 1922, 212. The two other speakers were 'Mrs Mowbray-Clarke of the Sunwise Turn Bookshop' and 'Miss Marion Cutter of The Children's Bookshop'. No transcript of Shay's talk appears to have survived.

[52] Murray Hill, 'Murray Hill on Little Bookshops', 528–33, *The Bookman* 54.6 (February 1922), 530–31.

[53] Ibid., 533.

The Bookshop Door

The autographed door, installed sometime not long after the shop's expansion in the fall of 1921, is symbolic both of the intimacy of Shay's shop and of the dramatic changes being experienced in the Village. Before it hung in Shay's office, it was an interior door in a flat down the block at 11 Christopher Street. Coincidentally (or not, perhaps), the flat had once been occupied by Floyd Dell, a friend of Shay's and fellow member of the Provincetown Players. Dell was, of course, an icon, one of the Village's most prominent figures in the 1910s (and one of the most vocally nostalgic for that era's loss). In late 1920 or 1921, the flat and its building were demolished to make room for new construction, a common fate of many small buildings as modern apartment buildings began to be built to support the growing population. Before the demolition, Shay removed the interior door, carried it across the street, and hung it between the shop and the office. In his memoir *Homecoming* (1933), Dell tells the story of the door's 'rescue':

> In 1925, at Antibes, where I was severely ill with gastritis and was very homesick, I heard from some fellow-American that the little house at 11 Christopher Street had been torn down. The red-painted door of my upstairs apartment, I was told, had been piously rescued by Frank Shay, and was being kept in his book-shop across the street; he was using it as an autograph-'album', on which all the authors who came into his place were asked to write their names ... so 11 Christopher Street was gone! And being gone it lived again more vividly in my memory.[54]

The provenance, as described here, is credible: bits of red paint can still be seen around the door's latch where the later, vibrant blue paint has chipped away. The door was literally transported to a new era, from the old Village to the new.

The door's new life began in earnest when, one day, according to Morley, Shay's good friend Hendrik Willem Van Loon spontaneously signed his name, accompanied by a drawing of a ship with full sails, right in the middle of the door.[55] Soon after, others followed. Several signatures are dated 1921, but we do not know when the tradition began, or when it ended. We do not know who was invited to sign the door or why. The vast majority of signers were well known, while others were local businesspeople, and more than forty remain unidentified or illegible. We do not know which way the more heavily signed side faced; its layer of grime suggests that it may have faced into the office, where tobacco smoke would likely have filled the air. Perhaps signatures were added after a visitor had joined Shay in the back office for a drink and some literary conversation. It is impossible to know what percentage of the shop's customers signed the door; one assumes that

---

[54]   Floyd Dell, *Homecoming* (New York: Farrar, Rinehart, 1933), 360. Dell likely heard the story from a friend at a much earlier date, since he himself signed the door at Frank Shay's shop well before 1925, when he claimed to have first learned of it.

[55]   Morley, 110.

hundreds, even thousands, of further visitors came through the store's front door over the years. But one also imagines many repeat visitors; perhaps the shop was an unofficial headquarters for this particular creative set and the door indeed represents the vast majority of customers.

Research into the names on the door reveals a number of important facts about the signers. First, they included members of dozens of mutually influential communities. If a poet's signature appears on the door, one might also find that of her book publisher, the editor of a magazine where one of her poems was first printed, a novelist whose short stories appeared in the same issue of that magazine, and the screenwriter who brought the novelist's work to the screen. Also remarkable are the number of signers whose careers took multiple paths. Many worked in more than one creative industry, wrote or made art in many genres, or lived in many different creative communities. The largest shared profession of the signers is journalism, a field in which, it seems, anyone who wished to succeed in the literary community need to work at some point. The magazines and newspapers represented a range from the largest to the smallest, the highbrow to the lowbrow, the commercial to the avant-garde.

Common social groups, political beliefs, and personal interests become apparent. World War I veterans pepper the door's surface, as do seafarers and scholars of Walt Whitman. Liberal activists, from socialist publishers to suffragettes, are likewise well represented. The Provincetown Players is perhaps the single most important group on the door, represented by its founders, ten of its playwrights, and several more people involved in this innovative group. Christopher Morley's friends, and members of his Three Hours for Lunch Club, are virtually all represented (except club member Frank Shay, who did not sign his own door). Of particular note are the many people associated with the periodical *The Bookman*, including editors Robert Cortes Holliday and John Farrar, owner Seward B. Collins, and any number of writers whose articles it published and whose books it reviewed.

Also significant are the names and communities missing from the door. Eugene O'Neill and Edna St Vincent Millay did not sign the door, though we know that O'Neill visited the shop, and it is hard to imagine that Millay did not come by to discuss Shay's latest editions of her work. No African-American writers signed the door, despite the burgeoning Harlem scene and various intersections between the Village and Harlem communities. The author rosters of entire magazines published in the Village at this time are entirely lacking from the door – one among many intriguing facts that I hope will spur research by other scholars into other seemingly distinct sub-communities within the Village at this time.

By the time the shop had been open just over a year, the door had become a destination for Greenwich Village visitors in the know. In far-off Portland, Oregon, a literary columnist reporting on a visit to Greenwich Village in 1922 wrote: 'Most everyone visits his shop to have a look at his queer door whose panels are white pine strips on which are the signatures of many of the best known artists, sculptors, writers and actors in America. He is going to have the door taken down and the panels framed when they are all covered, which won't be long now'.[56] Shay likely added the door's striking blue 'frame' before he sold the shop in 1924. At some point, varnish was added, protecting most of the signatures, though some had already smudged or faded beyond recognition. In 1925, an advertisement for the shop in the *Quill* used the door as a marketing tool, stating, 'Come in and see our door' under the address. When the shop closed, Koenig moved the door to her New York apartment, where it remained for more than thirty years. Some sources claim that the door passed into Christopher Morley's possession at some point, but this is not the case. In 1960, a notice of Mrs Frank Leon Smith's intention to sell the door appeared in the 'Trade Winds' gossip column of the Saturday Review,[57] and it was soon added to the Christopher Morley Collection at Texas, no longer a personal memento, but an artefact of the Modernist past.

The Modern Bookshop

If this rediscovered physical artefact of the door prompted the project, a rediscovered digital artefact found more than eighteen months into the project transformed it and provides complementary information about the shop that will conclude my narrative. In May 2011, after all the research for the online and gallery exhibitions had been concluded, a routine Google search produced an unexpected result: a photograph of the interior of the bookshop from a recently digitised 1922 issue of a business-to-business magazine, *Bookseller and Stationer*. The photograph was one of many single images of bookstores and stationers that served as filler between articles, accompanied only by simple identifying captions. It appears to be the only existing photograph of the shop's interior and shows the shop as it appeared in 1922, after the expansion.

The photograph is a remarkable artefact, especially when viewed in comparison with the interior image of the Washington Square Book Shop taken six years earlier. The Washington Square Book Shop looks little different from a residence, except for its large quantity of books. Furniture that may have been used for other purposes in the past appears to be repurposed for display purposes, and much of the space does not include books; a large sculpture appears to dominate the back room. Most of the books visible in the photograph appear to be stocked in only one copy, with a handful displayed in sets of three. Only a few are displayed so their covers may be seen.

The photograph of Shay's shop at 4 Christopher Street looks like a contemporary bookshop (to be more precise, it differs little from two independent bookstores where I worked in the 1990s, one in Oakland, California, and one in Boulder, Colorado). Three freestanding, purpose-built display cabinets each showcase the

---

56   'Magazines are Published by Greenwich Artists', 5.
57   'Trade Winds', *Saturday Review* 43.1 (1960), 11.

FRANK SHAY'S BOOKSHOP.

Fig. 3.4 'Frank Shay's Bookshop' in *Bookseller and Stationer* 57.2 (July 15, 1922). *Source*: Image courtesy of Princeton University Libraries.

front covers of about forty different books, while also displaying fourteen stacks of multiple copies (or perhaps multi-volume sets) with shelves of further books beneath. Dust jackets dominate the entering visitor's view. Shelves line the walls, holding spine-out volumes, and a special rack on the left showcases face-out pamphlets and little magazines. In the far back left corner, the door may be seen, ajar. A curious visitor walking to the back of the shop to look at it would pass by about ninety face-out book covers on the free-standing tables alone.

Holland Hudson, describing the shop before the expansion, noted the shop's differences from other bookshops, suggesting that the difference between the Washington Square Bookshop and Frank Shay's is not just a matter of six years' progress, but of mindset:

> The center of the room contains an article we have never seen outside department stores (where aisle space is at a premium), altho it seems designed especially for the small book-shop – a patented table which displays several hundred titles in such a way that each jacket is entirely and enticingly visible. The shop is not cluttered up with terribly artistic furniture and fire-irons and

pottery and lampshades and futuristic sculptures; it is simply arranged to display and sell books.[58]

The photograph confirms what we know from newspaper and magazine advertisements and from Shay's own description of his 'Parnassus on Wheels' travelling shop. He sold a wide variety of books: fiction, non-fiction, little magazines, poetry chapbooks, children's books, and even some rare books. In April 1922, Christopher Morley noted in his journal that he had stopped by the shop and seen his first copy of the famous blue-covered first edition of James Joyce's *Ulysses*, fresh from Shakespeare and Company in Paris.

To describe the diversity of the shop's offerings is not to say that Shay's personal tastes did not dominate to at least some extent: he likely displayed the works of virtually all his literary friends, and a particularly rich selection of his two favourite writers, Joseph Conrad and Walt Whitman; Conrad's portrait has pride of place on the upper right-hand wall of the front part of the shop in the photograph. But the shop was pointedly not 'terribly artistic' like other shops of the time: whereas those shops shouted their distinctiveness, Shay's shouted inclusiveness. Murray Hill might well have been describing Shay's shop when he described the changing face of bookstores past and present in the famously 'bizarre business activity' of Greenwich Village in the late 1910s and into the 1920s:

> As in the innumerable tea rooms that sprouted up, the bookshop scheme of decoration was sometimes of delirious post-futurist design. And the displays were of 'The Liberator', and 'The Birth Control Review', and everything going on psycho-this and psycho-that. Also a magazine for 'endaemonists'. They? Why, neo-Epicureans, ultra-Hedonists, and beings of that sort. But the Village has lately changed more than many people know. A Greenwich Village little bookshop today has very much the same stock as a little bookshop anywhere.[59]

It is a compelling description, for it suggests that the shop that thrived on the reputations of its charismatic owner, famous customers, and even the aura of the previous decade, strove at the same time to achieve a generic modern business model – just another shop on Sinclair Lewis's Main Street.

So much had changed from 1916, when Shay inherited the physical and social capital of the Washington Square Book Shop. If that shop was dominated by the shared radical ventures that dominated the Village in the 1910s – the Liberal Club, *The Masses*, the Provincetown Players, and so on – Frank Shay's Bookshop might be said to be dominated by intimate interactions and individual careers: it was where specific people shopped, individual collaborators began projects, professional partnerships were built.

Though both of Shay's shops are associated with famous names, the nature of that fame changed from 1915 to 1924. A remarkable number of the people who

---

[58]   Hudson, 421.

[59]   Hill, 531.

signed the bookshop door were born in the late 1880s. They had been in their twenties during the creative and political surge of the 1910s and were now in their thirties. To some of the younger generation, they seemed worn out, surviving on the fumes of their past glories. When the young Malcolm Cowley arrived in the Village in 1919, he felt surrounded by 'a pervading atmosphere of middle-agedness.'[60] But the careers of those who signed the bookshop door show no loss of vitality; indeed, the Village of the 1920s was to have, arguably, a more profound influence on American culture than that of the 1910s. No longer unknown upstarts, some remained proud radicals or amateurs, but many were becoming widely known. Some pursued successful careers as nationally recognised writers and artists, while a great number became influential editors, publishers, film producers, newspaper owners, and other leaders of creative industries. Many, like Frank Shay himself, never became household names but made tangible contributions to the literary culture of the decade.

Shay's bookstore, like the Village itself in those years, is not easy to pin down. Equal parts nostalgic, innovative, Bohemian, intellectual, middlebrow, commercial, and impossible to understand apart from the personalities of its proprietor and customers, it reveals the rich possibilities inherent in further study of the shop's community, and more broadly, the future study of bookselling in this period.

---

[60]   Stansell, 336.

Chapter 4
'Lady Midwest':
Fanny Butcher – Books

Celia Hilliard

In the aftershock of the Great War came a long struggle, resonating across all the arts, to reinterpret a changed and fragmented world. In those uncertain years, the most stirring new voices in the field of literature seemed to emerge in America. Bold, awkward, and disquieting stories and poems, born of fresh energy and irreverent sympathies, suggested a contemporary sensibility in the making. At the same time, a new generation of publishers gambled that, despite the conventional reading habits of the public at large, these more inventive works could attract a broad and enthusiastic audience. As one critic observed in 1919, the victories of American arts and letters would now be built upon 'the battlefields of modern life'.[1]

That critic was Fanny Butcher (1888–1987) of the *Chicago Tribune*, then arguably the most powerful newspaper in the Midwest – the region that nurtured such quintessentially American masters as Sherwood Anderson, Willa Cather, Theodore Dreiser, and Edgar Lee Masters. A book editor at the *Tribune* for almost fifty years (1914–1962), Butcher would be a sympathetic advocate for the many writers she came to know and admire. During the 1920s, she was also proprietor of a small and distinctive bookshop on Michigan Boulevard – the only one in the country, she claimed, to be owned and operated by a literary critic. The power of her popular column drew a stream of customers to that shop – not only the curious public, but also a spectacular coterie of literary and theatrical celebrities in search of her professional approval. In turn, the personal acquaintance she cultivated there informed her critical impressions and, over a long period of years, influenced the public perception of many authors whose works were essential to the modern project.

Breaking into Print

Fanny Amanda Butcher was born in Fredonia, Kansas, in 1888, the only child of Hattie and Oliver Butcher.[2] When she was just a few years old, the family moved

---

[1]   Fanny Butcher, 'Literary Lions Roar Tribute to English Tongue', *Chicago Tribune*, 21 February 1919, 5.

[2]   See Butcher's autobiography, *Many Lives – One Love* (New York: Harper & Row, 1972), for an extensive account of her childhood and early career. A similar but abbreviated version appears in Ishbel Ross, *Ladies of the Press* (New York: Harper & Brothers, 1936),

to Chicago so that her father, a commercial artist, could attend night classes at the Art Institute. Some careless dental surgery resulted in a long illness that ruined his health and wrecked his larger ambitions. Growing up in an atmosphere of frustration and disappointment, Butcher nevertheless managed to secure a sturdy education at the University of Chicago. She earned part of the money to pay for it by reading aloud accomplished works of history and biography to a blind woman who had graduated in the first class at Mt Holyoke.

Following college, Butcher taught high school and extension classes for a few years, but she was first of all 'crazy about books',[3] and her earliest ambition was to be a writer herself. To make a beginning she submitted features to a couple of short-lived magazines. One of these articles involved an interview with 25-year-old Edna Ferber, who had just published her first novel, *Dawn O'Hara*, a meeting which fired her own literary hopes.[4] Probably the most consequential association of Butcher's young years was with the Little Theatre and Maurice Browne, who founded that enterprise and inspired the idealistic movement that spread across the country. Browne called on many leading English and American actors to work with his troupe, which performed in a ninety-nine-seat playhouse in Chicago's Fine Arts Building. Butcher was employed by the fledgling company, first as a volunteer and then as a modestly paid staff member. Diligent and determined, she took firm charge of tickets, travel arrangements, publicity, and ushers and even appeared onstage herself in minor roles. She met major theatrical personalities and many Chicago society people who supported the venture.[5]

Also hanging about the Fine Arts Building were vociferous members of the local bohemia, who included Butcher in their picnics, debates, and excursions to radical bookstores and cafes. Cocktails were served. Young Fanny was encouraged to smoke. Floyd Dell, who would shortly depart for New York to work on the revolutionary magazine *The Masses*, was often one of the party. Eager and ever watchful, Butcher got the courage to ask Dell, who was then editor of the *Friday Literary Review*, if she might write something for him. She would not expect payment, of course, or a byline. He gave her a stack of books to review. Among them was *Alexander's Bridge*, a first novel by an unknown named Willa Cather. Butcher read it carefully, recalling later that she 'almost prayed for light'.[6] Some months after her review appeared, Floyd Dell got a letter from Cather stating that,

407–08. Related materials are also found throughout the Fanny Butcher Papers (hereafter Butcher Papers), a large collection of correspondence, clippings, notes, diaries, records, and photographs at the Newberry Library, Chicago.

   [3]   Fanny Butcher, interview with the author, 10 January 1983.

   [4]   Julie Goldsmith Gilbert, *Ferber: A Biography* (New York: Doubleday, 1978), 418–19.

   [5]   For a thorough discussion of Chicago's Little Theatre, with notes on the 'heroic girls' who served as volunteers and staff, see Maurice Browne, *Too Late to Lament* (Bloomington: Indiana University Press, 1956). Butcher is mentioned by name on p. 146.

   [6]   For an account of Butcher's first assignment for Dell, see *Eye Witness*, 'Medillians Told Some Things on Book Reviewing', *Chicago Tribune*, 17 March 1922, 11.

in contrast to most notices the book had received, the writer signed only as 'F.B.' had understood precisely what she was trying to accomplish.[7]

In 1913, Butcher was hired by the women's editor at the *Chicago Tribune* to write service features about love, beauty, clubs, parties, earning money at home, and bright sayings of children. Occasionally, she served as special correspondent at political events, and once she covered a murder trial. Her real intent in taking the job was to find an opportunity to write about books. During those years, book news in the Chicago papers was dominated by a remarkable group of literary cowboys – well informed, fierce in their opinions, giddy over new ideas, impatient, noisy, and sometimes spiteful. Among reporters who covered the subject they were held in generally higher esteem than their New York counterparts. The *Tribune*'s book editor was Robert Burns Peattie, once described as 'a little exotic for Chicago',[8] a would-be boulevardier who owned a tailcoat and could read French. His wife Elia wrote educated but mostly genteel commentary for a Saturday page titled 'In the Field of Literary Endeavor'. She was not sure, for example, if Carl Sandburg's 'whap-bang style' was really poetry or just another instance of that old trick called 'shocking the bourgeoisie'. Her vehemence was reserved for things sexual and sordid. She condemned Theodore Dreiser as 'the tomcat of literature'.[9]

Fanny Butcher proposed compiling a series of book notes to run on Sundays (which she later described as 'a sneaky toe in the door'),[10] and after a few tries, her idea was adopted as the Tabloid Book Review. Her first signed column appeared on 27 December 1914. 'The Tabloid' contained intelligent talk about serious new fiction and poetry and sometime later included commentary on published plays. Best sellers were listed. Popular genre fiction was noted, with reading recommendations for uncles at Christmas and girls headed to camp. Butcher made mention of little magazines, limited editions, and some private press publications. She expressed opinion on censorship and copyright issues. There were announcements of literary prizes and new books available at the public library.

By now she had established a firm friendship with Edna Ferber and begun a tender (if platonic) alliance with Sinclair Lewis, then just a red-haired, red-faced young editor at the George H. Doran Company.[11] Carl Sandburg was reciting

---

[7] Willa Sibert Cather to 'Literary Editor, Chicago Evening Post', 16 October 1912, box 2, folder 90, Butcher Papers.

[8] For observations of Robert Burns Peattie and his wife Elia, see Burton Rascoe, *Before I Forget* (New York: Literary Guild of America, 1937), 324–26.

[9] Ibid.

[10] Fanny Butcher, *Many Lives – One Love*, 114.

[11] In 1915 Butcher began a close and well-documented friendship with Lewis, which lasted until his death in 1951 (box 5, folder 324, Butcher Papers). She was enthusiastic about his early work but gave his later books mixed reviews, and her diary entries reveal conflicted feelings about Lewis the man. On 6 November 1930, the day he was awarded the Nobel Prize for Literature, she wrote in her diary, 'I very violently think he doesn't rank it'.

his poems to her on the elevated.[12] Wytter Bynner, another aspiring poet, wore a ceremonial kimono when he received her for tea and interviews.[13] Her column was laced with gossip of all these authors and many others. Occasionally, she ran photos and sketches of well-known names with little-seen faces.

In short, Butcher covered the literary landscape in a language and format that had wide appeal – to both readers and writers. Her voice was trusted, and in a surprisingly few span of years she developed a large following and a measurable ability to influence book sales and even move manuscripts toward publication. The poet Vachel Lindsay wrote to his friend Harriet Moody: 'Is the mayor of Chicago well? And how is Fanny Butcher?'[14]

The New Butcher Shop

In 1919, the French consul in Chicago, Antonin Barthelemy, assembled a group of the city's cultural elite to help organise a gallery to show the art of the French avant-garde, with proceeds to benefit the families of artists killed or wounded in the war. The prominent architect Ernest Graham offered to lease a large space for it in the Pullman Building, to be decorated by Rue Winterbotham Carpenter, a devoted Modernist and president of the influential Arts Club. At some point, Fanny Butcher suggested the gallery might include a small corner devoted to notable art books and catalogues from Paris. She was asked to take charge of such a corner. The pictures for exhibition never arrived, caught in a tangle of bureaucratic red tape, but preparations for Butcher's little store went ahead and it opened for business early in February 1920. A week or so later, on her 32nd birthday, Barthelemy walked in with a lordly visitor who signed his name in the new guestbook with a great flourish–'Maeterlinck'.[15]

At that time, the retail book trade was prospering in Chicago. In addition to large, elaborately-stocked stores like Brentano's and A. Kroch, there were cavernous secondhand outlets, book sections in big department stores, and a multitude of specialty and antiquarian shops. Some of them hosted lectures, mounted shows, and even published books and periodicals themselves. A few had acquired a slightly bawdy reputation, as did the shop of Covici-McGee, whose basement quarters were said to be 'written by Balzac'.[16]

---

[12]   In his poem *Improvisation* Sandburg recalls his times with Butcher 'in midnight streetcars/in owl cars on the I.C … ' (n.d., box 7, folder 459, Butcher Papers). For memories of the young Sandburg, see also Manuscript 8, box 11, folder 670, Butcher Papers.

[13]   Fanny Butcher to Louis Sudler, [1972], box 7, folder 525, Butcher Papers.

[14]   Vachel Lindsay to Harriet Moody, 19 November 1923, *Letters of Vachel Lindsay*, ed. Marc Chenetier (New York: Burt Franklin, 1979), 308–10.

[15]   Fanny Butcher – Books Guestbook (1920–1927), entry dated 13 February 1920, box 36, folder 1565, Butcher Papers.

[16]   Vincent Starrett, 'A Gossip on Chicago Bookshops', *The Publishers' Weekly* 105, 26 (28 June 1924), 2007–11.

Conceived to complement a showcase for the artistic vanguard, Fanny Butcher's store sounded a new note of urbanity in a city longing to shed its image as a provincial hinterland. It was well situated on the south stretch of Michigan Boulevard, across the street from the Art Institute, next door to Orchestra Hall, and down the avenue from several major hotels. The Pullman Building itself was a tall granite fortress, embellished with turrets and corbels and a wealth of ornamental detail. Once the most important office building in Chicago, with three floors of grand apartments as well, it still retained some of its most romantic features – massive fireplaces, handsome iron balustrades, and ornate bronze locks and knobs. Louis Tiffany had designed the restaurant in the 9th floor penthouse, which was now frequented by a mix of actors, reporters, and downtown business people.[17]

The little bookshop was located in a corner of the main floor. Rue Carpenter, who designed its interior, was justly called Chicago's leading advocate of the modern. Married to the composer John Alden Carpenter, whose work wove jazz motifs with classical forms, she exhibited, in the galleries of the Arts Club, the work of Brancusi, Braque, Kandinsky, Miro, Picasso, and others.[18] As a decorator, she seemed to specialise in transforming bare and unlikely spaces into settings for dramatic occasions or refined pursuits, and her arrangements typically imparted a sense of aristocratic ease. She also had a fondness for the unpredictable touch – odd, inexpensive objects or materials she could paint over or refashion. In the bookshop, Carpenter built floor-to-ceiling shelves made of the cheapest available pine, which were then stained dark brown to look like walnut. Their edges were decorated with gold stencilling in a delightful rolling wave design. Some shelves had glass panels, others were left open. A desk was also stencilled with gilt and some plain kitchen chairs as well, after they had been coated a bright regal blue. A small book ladder was tucked in a corner. An added note of warmth was achieved through the unusual lighting system Carpenter installed. A series of geometric V-shaped fixtures such as were usually seen in art galleries cast a soft downward glow and also reflected light back onto the shelves, showcasing the vivid colours and titles of books lined up there. Everyone agreed the result was captivating.[19]

Butcher was also fortunate in the assistance of Antonin Barthelemy, whose spectacular imports from Paris enabled the store to open with an immediate splash. Barthelemy, who first visited Chicago as secretary to the French commissioner of fine arts at the World's Columbian Exposition, had returned to the city in 1916 to

---

[17]   For an extended description of the Pullman Building, see *The Autobiography of Irving K. Pond*, ed. David Swan and Terry Tatum (Oak Park, IL: Hyoogen Press, 2009). Pond was an architect hired to design some of its exterior and interior appointments. He and his brother Allen shared an apartment there until 1916. The building was demolished in 1956.

[18]   For more on Carpenter's work to advance the cause of modern art in Chicago, see James M. Wells, *Portrait of an Era: Rue Winterbotham Carpenter and the Arts Club of Chicago 1916–1931* (Chicago: Arts Club of Chicago, 1986).

[19]   'Six New Middle Western Bookshops: IV Fannie Butcher, Books – Chicago', *The Publishers' Weekly*, 97, 14 (3 April 1920), 1102.

build support for the Allied cause. Small, frail, and quiet, he was a man of rare humanity and erudition, and even for a professional diplomat, he was exceptionally deft. Butcher recalled years later that he had introduced her to modern French literature, sharing stories and revelations about European writers and artists, among whom he had many friends.[20] When the first shipment of books arrived, the crates contained not only magnificently illustrated tomes on art but also choice pamphlets and periodicals, yellow-covered paperbacks, and first editions, many of them signed. To these Butcher added a selection of difficult-to-obtain English imprints and many volumes of poetry. In fact, although she was cautioned against it, she put poetry to the fore in her shop, right alongside the art books, and made an attempt to carry at least one copy of all the new poets receiving local or national attention.

Her initial stock also included many titles by leading authors of the day, ancient and modern classics, and a selection of staple sellers, which was important because very soon it became apparent that the shop would have to stand or fall as an independent business. The empty art gallery was given up, but as Ernest Graham had prepaid a year's rental charges, he told Butcher that if she wished to continue, she could have her space for free until the lease expired. From this almost accidental genesis was born 'Fanny Butcher – Books'. As soon as her name was painted in gold letters on the door, her colleagues at the Tribune were crowing in print about the new 'Butcher shop', gently ribbing readers that they would now know where to find their 'Lamb, Hogg, and Bacon'.[21]

In Person: Writers and Readers on Parade

For almost a decade the store served as an extension of Fanny Butcher's critical platform in Chicago and her ambition to be counted a player herself in the cultural landscape. Its legacy as a Modernist enterprise, while now beyond question, was perhaps not a clear imperative at the start (despite its origin as appendage to an avant-garde art gallery). Certainly some other Chicago shops were more deliberately positioned as 'progressive'. When Butcher worked in the Fine Arts Building she was a frequent visitor to Francis Fisher Browne's seventh-floor bookstore. Its startling interior, designed by Frank Lloyd Wright, was revolutionary in appearance, but its stock was actually devoted mostly to rare books, fine bindings, and the work of the nineteenth-century New England writers Browne revered in his prestigious magazine *The Dial*. (Its conservative pages even made fun of Harriet Monroe's ground-breaking *Poetry* – dismissing it as 'a futile little periodical described as a Magazine of Verse'). Opened in 1907, the Browne

---

    [20]   In addition to Butcher's tribute to Barthelemy in *Many Lives – One Love*, a good account of his diplomatic skills and connections is also found in *Traveling Through Life: Being the Autobiography of Clara E. Laughlin* (New York: Houghton Mifflin, 1934), 190–92, 201.
    [21]   W.L.N., 'A Line O' Type or Two', *Chicago Tribune*, 25 February 1920, 8.

store moved to more conventional space in 1911 and closed in 1912, for want of sufficient business. The Walden Shop, a successor to the celebrated Radical Bookstore where Floyd Dell had held court, also drew much attention for its décor (*a la* Greenwich Village) and its striking Modernist logo (a black crane poised on a tree limb). Its stated policy was to carry 'only really good things'. The Walden Shops later incorporated under new management and added two branches, one of them in the new Art Deco Diana Court building on North Michigan Boulevard. The interior there featured chromium and glass furnishings by Donald Deskey and allotted almost as much space to prints, watercolours, and ceramics as it did to books. For all its streamlined verve, however, it probably had more impact as notable design than literary resource. On still another note, the nearby Aquarius, advertised as 'The Book Shop of Tomorrow' and sporting a sky-blue façade and lemon yellow walls, was expressly dedicated to works promoting the cause of brotherhood across the spectrum of modern thought. Its owner, Mima Porter, was the wife of a wealthy Chicago landowner and a follower of Jiddu Krishnamurti. In Porter's honour, Krishnamurti came to town with his Theosophist colleague Annie Besant, and a party was held among the shelves which had been packed with interesting and unusual volumes spanning all the arts and sciences. The store enjoyed a brief celebrity, but following the death of her husband just months after the opening, Porter closed it and moved to New York.

It remains the case that over a crucial period of years 'Fanny Butcher – Books' was a prominent, reliable, go-to source for new and thought-provoking literature. It was accompanied by Butcher's narration, so to speak – in print and in person. Further, Rue Carpenter's rendition of 'modern' was comfortable and relaxed. The décor of the shop was sophisticated but never intimidating. Thus 'the new' was made accessible to customers representing a wide range of the reading public, who responded with an eagerness to experiment, a willingness to engage upon those 'battlefields of modern life'.

Above all, Butcher's store was a place of encounter, a literary conversation that went both ways. In fact, many years later, Butcher acknowledged that her time in the shop had been a fundamental education about readers. Her fellow critic Harry Hansen once declared that anyone who aspired to a place in publishing should spend a season in a store. 'When you sell books', he said, 'you feel the pulse of the public'.[22]

On account of the shop's beginnings as a charitable enterprise, Butcher could depend on the loyalty of the carriage trade. They had set the shop on its feet financially when they purchased the treasure in that first exciting shipment from France, most of it quite expensive. For a while they even seemed to treat the place as a club where they could meet friends and leave messages. However, the shop also drew a broader clientele, in spite of the fact that Butcher could not afford to advertise. Friendly columnists did make mention of it, and publishers sometimes listed it in their own newspaper ads, but the real lesson for Butcher

---

[22] Harry Hansen, 'Ben Huebsch, Man of Causes', *Chicago Tribune*, 23 August 1964, K8.

was the importance of the personal equation in the job of building a customer base and attempting to shape public taste. She discovered that 'No work in the world is more satisfying than giving the right book to the right person at the right time'.[23] To accomplish that, the seller had to be supremely aware of his stock and the customer had to reveal something of his inner thought and desire.

Of course, as in all bookstores, not every visitor arrived in search of an intimate transaction. Some were interested only in the work of one or two authors, and quite a number wanted just to get their hands on the latest Tarzan novel the day it came out. Others might make a curt request: 'I want three books you yourself have read and liked'.[24] Some browsers pulled all the books off a shelf, so carefully arranged in alphabetical order, and then walked away without buying any. A few customers liked to hide in the back and 'steal a read', like the young woman who came in on her lunch hours and left a hairpin in the book to mark her place.[25]

However, Butcher found that people typically wanted to talk. Some of them surprised her with unsuspected depths or salacious tastes. Many more were uncertain about their preferences and hesitant in their selections. Butcher reportedly had great influence with women. A male colleague once wrote, 'At the Public Library it has been said: "When Fanny Butcher recommends a book we get many inquiries for it from shop girls"'.[26] (Some of those shop girls patronised the store too, and in any case Butcher later stated that her customers were about equally divided between men and women.) They all trusted her to say exactly what she thought without an eye to the cash register and to intuit what they might most like to read. Her friend Edna Ferber may have stated it best in her tart testimonial for the store: 'Fanny Butcher knows what you're talking about, even if you don't'.[27]

If there is something Butcher could be said to have adamantly promoted, however, it was modern poetry.[28] She continued to maintain a very good selection of it, with many hard-to-find volumes and ephemeral little sheaves of verse. In addition to the Chicago-based *Poetry* magazine, she carried runs of the English *Poetry Review* and also imported earlier publications of the Poetry Bookshop in Bloomsbury, London. (These latter were by then collector's items, and so fragile they proved unsalable after even a week of curious handling. She eventually

---

[23]   Fanny Butcher, 'Tabloid Book Review', *Chicago Tribune*, 19 October 1919, Pt 7, p. 7. Butcher added that a bookseller is 'a sort of combination of doctor, minister, theatrical manager, and social service job'.

[24]   Katherine Sproehnle, 'The Decay of the Customer', *The Bookman*, 56, 5 (January 1923), 588–90. This account of daily life at a small, unnamed bookstore was written by Butcher's recently departed clerk, who moved to New York City and a job at George H. Doran & Company, which published *The Bookman*.

[25]   Fanny Butcher, autobiographical manuscript, box 17, folder 874, Butcher Papers.

[26]   Harry Hansen, *Midwest Portraits* (New York: Harcourt Brace, 1923), 199.

[27]   Edna Ferber, signed testimonial dated 8 April 1925, composed for use at Butcher's booth at the first Woman's World's Fair in Chicago, box 3, folder 175, Butcher Papers.

[28]   Fanny Butcher, 'You Never Can Sell Poetry', *The Publishers' Weekly*, 106, 13 (27 September 1924), 1154–55.

discontinued them.) She stocked Edna St Vincent Millay before she was popular and likely carried *Harlem Shadows* by the young black poet Claude McKay, whose work she discussed (along with other emerging 'Negro voices') in the pages of the Tabloid.[29] She was also happy to report to her readers that Robert Frost's important collection *North of Boston*, published in 1915, was still in demand.[30] Carl Sandburg she touted to customers simply as 'the factory whistle' of the modern movement.[31] (In an interesting aside, though mystery novels could be found in her store, Butcher seldom reviewed them, complaining they 'usually give away the secret on page four line three'.[32] She later made an exception, however, for *The Rumble Murders* because it was written by T.S. Eliot's older brother.[33])

Butcher said that whenever she observed someone surveying the poetry shelves, she would promptly engage them in conversation. They often knew no one later than Keats and Shelley ('possibly Rupert Brooke or Robert Service'). She was dumbfounded that 'only one person out of a hundred knew "A Shropshire Lad"'. She would quickly open a book the customer might find appealing and put it in his hands. A thing that amazed her was how many businessmen were at first sceptical, then eager. She concluded that poetry was too often treated 'as a sort of secret sin by the red-blooded American nation. The public has to be coaxed with the utmost discretion to admit that it wants poetry'.[34]

Butcher quite purposely stocked collections of plays and short stories as well, though neither category sold even as much as poetry. She agreed with Sherwood Anderson that the story form was eminently suited to contemporary life. (He was a customer at the store too, gratified by the high praise she had given his book *Winesburg, Ohio*.) 'Really wonderful things might be done with the short story', he observed to her, 'once we dismiss the notion that it has to end with a trick turn that entirely wipes out the mood that the story has tried to induce'.[35]

Fanny Butcher's passion for books was matched only by her passion for writers. Her frank cultivation of the brightest stars in the literary and theatrical firmament, together with the power of her weekly column, drew a parade of the famous and celebrated to her Chicago store. More even than her superbly chosen stock or her presence as advisor and guide, it was this guise of the shop as informal salon that gave the place its singular cachet. Further, the eclectic and varied nature of her Tabloid reviewing undoubtedly had a permanent impact on

---

[29] Fanny Butcher, 'Tabloid Book Review', *Chicago Tribune*, 4 June 1922, Pt 8, p. 14. McKay is now considered a seminal figure of the Harlem Renaissance.

[30] Eleanor Jewett, 'Art and Artists', *Chicago Tribune*, 10 September 1922, E10.

[31] Advertising flyer for 'Fanny Butcher – Books', n.d., box 36, folder 1564, Butcher Papers.

[32] Fanny Butcher, 'Ben Hecht's Latest', *Chicago Tribune*, 18 August 1923, 10.

[33] Fanny Butcher, 'Critic Reads Just One Book for Pleasure', *Chicago Tribune*, 19 April 1932, 19.

[34] Butcher's attempts to promote poetry were recounted in her article 'You Never Can Sell Poetry', ibid.

[35] Sherwood Anderson to Fanny Butcher, [1919], box 1, folder 15, Butcher Papers.

Butcher's critical approach and, consequently, on her relationships with writers. She seldom attempted thoroughgoing analysis. Her aim was, rather, to introduce readers to a multitude of authors and to make some estimate of how well they had fulfilled their own intentions. Her reviews were not without an edge, and she had a sharp eye for the trite, repetitious, and sentimental. She connected with some writers immediately, admiring Eugene O'Neill's 'sheer grinding power',[36] Fitzgerald's anguished searchlight 'on the flapper in the back seat',[37] and Ring Lardner's distinctive use of the American language, predicting he would still be read when the musings of other humorists had been forgotten.[38] She could even appreciate Fannie Hurst, with the caveat that her 'mushy' back-alley tales were probably best 'eaten hot off the pan'.[39] Butcher could also stumble badly, as when she condemned Ernest Hemingway's novel *The Sun Also Rises* as a story about 'a group of rotters' which 'leaves you feeling that an artist has just done something to be smart'.[40] Her misjudgement was compounded when her review was innocently reprinted in the Paris edition of the *Herald Tribune*, fuelling Hemingway's rage. He lambasted her as 'Veal Brains'.[41] (They later developed a cordial entente. He inscribed a copy of *Death in the Afternoon* 'To Miss Fanny Butcher, whether she likes it or not'.[42])

What never wavered was Butcher's instinctive sympathy for struggle and her visceral perception of the fear and uncertainty that plagued every author – the great ones as well as the ordinary. She knew that a sustained career demanded above all courage and persistence. She told her readers once, 'Writers … are in their own lives often much more intriguing heroes than any fictional creations'.[43] She saw herself as a compatriot, a fellow traveller bringing encouragement and support, in print and in person, to an arduous journey.

The guestbook of 'Fanny Butcher – Books' is a testament to the extraordinary range of her associations and of their appreciation and reliance on her critical generosity. Simple and inexpensive, probably purchased in haste, the book contains 114 signatures, most with addresses and many with messages, poems, or flighty little sketches and portraits. Butcher's correspondence reveals in addition

---

[36]   Fanny Butcher, 'Tabloid Book Review', *Chicago Tribune*, 9 May 1920, Pt 1, p. 9.

[37]   Fanny Butcher, 'New Fitzgerald Book Proves He's Really a Writer', *Chicago Tribune*, 19 April 1925, 11.

[38]   Fanny Butcher, 'Tabloid Book Review', *Chicago Tribune*, 8 January 1922, Pt 8, p. 10.

[39]   Fanny Butcher, 'Tabloid Book Review', *Chicago Tribune*, 7 May 1922, F14.

[40]   Fanny Butcher, 'Hemingway Seems Out of Focus in "The Sun Also Rises," *Chicago Tribune*, 27 November 1926, 13.

[41]   Ernest Hemingway to F. Scott Fitzgerald, 15 September 1927, *Ernest Hemingway: Selected Letters 1917–1961*, ed. Carlos Baker (New York: Charles Scribner's Sons, 1981), 260–61.

[42]   Inscription, box 35, folder 1558, Butcher Papers.

[43]   Fanny Butcher, 'Christmas Books in Review', *Chicago Tribune*, 15 December 1934, 13.

that every prominent author who stopped in the store did not sign the book and many of those who signed once made multiple visits. She mostly had no idea who might walk in on any given day and surprise her.

The poets, of course, were much in evidence. Edgar Lee Masters arrived early on, and Carl Sandburg too, who jotted the question, 'Next to a real restaurant/ What is more holy than a real/Bookshop?'[44] The popular poets were there – Edgar Guest, Edmund Vance Cooke (dubbed 'the poet laureate of childhood'), and Joyce Kilmer's widow Aline, who had just published her own volume of verse, the sonorous *Candles That Burn*. Stephen Vincent Benet stopped by, Butcher reported, 'safely sheltered behind large glasses and a beautiful young lady'.[45] The most loyal contingent was the *Poetry* magazine crowd. Its editor Harriet Monroe (whom Butcher found prickly but brilliant) came in, as did the reclusive Henry Blake Fuller, then working at the magazine as an honorary editor. He signed his name but was one of the few too shy, Butcher recalled, to note an address. In an odd but fortuitous coincidence, the nineteen-year-old Glenway Wescott was then working as an office boy at *Poetry*. Though his signature does not appear in the guestbook (nor would he then have had the stature to claim a place in it), he and Butcher made a real friendship. Subsequently, his 1927 novel *The Grandmothers*, which won the prestigious Harper Prize, contained a character written directly, as he acknowledged, from Butcher's own memories and with her 'helping hand'.[46]

These American poets actually followed three eminent Irishmen, who were among the first to sign in the guestbook – all of them associated with the Abbey Theatre in Dublin. Padraic Colum, whose work borrowed abundantly from themes and characters in faery lore, came in to wish that the 'Olden/One Fair/Women nurtures' might bring young Fanny 'seven/Waves of Fortune!'[47] The only greeting William Butler Yeats could manage was 'Sputtery pen!' Butcher was able, nevertheless, to give her readers a vivid impression of the great man in person – a lock of hair falling over one brow, with eyes that looked straight through her and beyond. He read his own verses to her in the chant he said all poets had used since Homer and opined that Thoreau's *Walden* was the greatest piece of prose ever written by an American.[48]

John Galsworthy, whom Fanny had met on his American travels in 1919, had directed these two Irishmen and a third one to the shop as well – St John

---

[44]   Guestbook entry, 8 March 1920, box 36, folder 1565, Butcher papers.

[45]   Fanny Butcher, 'Tabloid Book Review', *Chicago Tribune*, 23 October 1921, Pt 8, p. 1.

[46]   Inscription, box 35, folder 1558, Butcher Papers. Wescott inscribed to Fanny Butcher a later edition of *The Grandmothers*, 'a book to which she lent her helping hand – in which, on pages 179–89, underneath the fiction, she may note traces of her youth and mine, devotedly, Glenway'.

[47]   Guestbook entry, 12 February 1920, box 36, 1565, Butcher Papers.

[48]   Butcher spoke of Yeats' memorable visit to Chicago and her shop multiple times, the first in her 'Tabloid Book Review' of 7 March 1920, 9. She also expanded upon her impressions of the great poet in *Many Lives – One Love*.

Ervine. A Protestant from Northern Ireland, Ervine had written some plays already considered minor classics and was then serving as drama critic of *The London Observer*. He spent hours in the store and gave it invaluable international publicity when he subsequently praised Chicago in his column, making special mention of 'a charming girl, Fanny Butcher, who keeps a bookshop and lets me, when I drop in, read all her books for nothing'.[49]

Yeats and Ervine were both among the many Irish and Anglo writers then embarked on cross-country lecture tours in America. Accompanied by his wife Georgie, Yeats was on an expedition to earn enough money to fix up the half-ruined tower he had acquired for a country retreat. Similarly, Ervine reported that he had given more than thirty speeches in twenty towns in eleven weeks.[50] Everywhere, they and other literary travellers were lionised by hostesses and applauded by crowds many times the size of their audiences at home. Yeats drew up to $1000 a reading. (One Irish woman declared, 'Just to look at him is worth the money'.)[51] Their book sales soared. In Chicago, a stop at Butcher's store was *de rigueur*, a part of the program.

These authors from abroad could be self-conscious of their role as entertainers, sometimes adopting extravagant dress or pompous talk. John Drinkwater, whose *Abraham Lincoln* was a Broadway hit, always wore a stand-up collar and a monocle on a cord. He autographed countless copies of his play on his several trips to Chicago. Butcher never forgot that when she asked the playwright J.B. Priestly what was happening in England, he answered, 'I am'.[52] As for John Cowper Powys, a British novelist Butcher had met years before at the Little Theatre, he sometimes lectured on Thomas Hardy for as long as two hours, garbed in a voluminous black gown. Butcher found him verbose and ingratiating, though they must have had some literate talk because he noted in her guestbook, 'Nearly all my favorite modern writers have been introduced to me by people in book shops'.[53] Almost all these visitors from across the ocean carried some lasting marks of the war, whether physical or emotional, hidden perhaps by affected manners. Ervine had lost a leg in combat. The novelist Hugh Walpole told Butcher that a sadness was all over England now, with the realisation that the world, which was supposed be redeemed by the sacrifice of all their young men, 'is not finer at all'.[54]

---

[49]   St. John Ervine, 'At the Play', *The [London] Observer*, 28 October 1923, 11.

[50]   'What America Thinks', an interview with Mr St John Ervine, *The [London] Observer*, 18 April 1920, 15.

[51]   Cecil Roberts, *The Bright Twenties* (London: Hodder and Stoughton, 1970), 34.

[52]   Fanny Butcher, *Many Lives – One Love*, 295.

[53]   Though Powys was a highly acclaimed speaker, Butcher did not favour his florid, verbose style. She wrote in her diary on 18 January 1930, 'I never did really like him', noting with disapproval the way he 'wangled a free book' out of Marshall Field's at a luncheon the store hosted in his honour.

[54]   Fanny Butcher, 'England is Sad, U.S. Gay, British Novelist Finds', *Chicago Tribune*, 13 October 1919, 13.

The cosmopolitan character of the store was also evident in the great variety of its visitors. It seemed every historian, scientist, wit, philosopher, and true believer was writing a book. Signers in the guestbook include prominent explorers, clergymen, boxers, missionaries, actors, and New York men about town, all clamouring to be heard. The conservationist Enos Mills, who had hosted Butcher at his rarified camp at Long's Peak, Colorado, appeared to promote his book, *The Adventures of a Nature Guide*. A fish from another kettle was Rupert Hughes, who had just published a novelised version of his popular Pullman-car farce, 'Excuse Me' (later adapted for Broadway, with music by Jerome Kern). Butcher lamented that Hughes (the uncle of Howard) had already given his heart and soul to the movies.[55] He was shortly recognised as the highest paid screenwriter in Hollywood.

Authors in every category wrote generous inscriptions to Butcher, autographed copies, praised the store, joked, flirted, and, subtly or not, pressed the hope that Butcher might give their work special attention. It might be, however, that Butcher got the better of this interchange overall. As these writers strove to make themselves vivid, she had every opportunity to take their measure as people and use her observations and reactions to animate her newspaper columns. Moreover, the visitors talked to her not only of themselves but of their friends and rivals. This had begun almost at once, when Maurice Maeterlinck had spent the afternoon in her shop musing on writers he knew in Paris. After the death of Joseph Conrad in 1924, Butcher heard from different sources interesting personal stories of Conrad the man, some of which she shared with the public.[56] Carl Van Vechten, that ardent advocate of the Harlem Renaissance, was in the store many times. It would appear that the day he signed the book he was accompanied by Maurice Browne and the actress Lynn Fontanne, then playing in *Dulcy*, her first starring role. Van Vechten was a font of gossip, a conversational charmer who also alerted Butcher to authors she should know, such as Ronald Firbank, Henry Handel Richardson, and Wallace Stevens. For her stock file of author images, Van Vechten sent her, unbidden, a photograph of a recent picture of himself by Florine Stettheimer whom he said was 'the most interesting painter in America now'.[57] Butcher did not rave over all of Van Vechten's books, but she always gave them immediate notice. His novel *The Tattooed Countess* was published on 15 August 1924, 'and in two days', he boasted, 'I was the best seller in Chicago'.[58]

A memorable exception to this near-universal craving for publicity was W. Somerset Maugham. He had scheduled a fortnight's stop in the city on a long

[55]   Fanny Butcher, 'Tabloid Book Review', *Chicago Tribune*, 26 September 1920, Pt 1, p. 9.

[56]   For one such story see Butcher's column 'Literary Visitors', *Chicago Tribune*, 15 November 1924, 10. Cecil Roberts dismissed notions of Conrad as a gruff nautical type, describing him instead as a meticulous craftsman and sophisticate who 'always looked as if he had just been turned out by a fashionable tailor'.

[57]   Carl Van Vechten to Fanny Butcher, 30 January 1923, box 8, folder 566, Butcher Papers.

[58]   Carl Van Vechten to Arthur Davison Ficke, 30 August 1924, *Letters of Carl Van Vechten*, ed. Bruce Kellner (New Haven: Yale University Press, 1987), 68.

journey westward to Indonesia and the Banda Sea. He made an appearance at the Chicago Book Fair, sponsored by Marshall Field's department store, where he signed copies of *The Moon and Sixpence* for a full day – after which, he said, the South Seas held a new allure.[59] The remainder of his visit was spent quietly in Butcher's store – browsing, chatting, and slipping into the back aisles whenever another customer walked in the door.[60]

Later in life, Butcher always recalled the Twenties as a 'yeasty' time,[61] and it is clear that the most important literary associations of her long career were made during this period. Two friends stand out, who by their example and in their affectionate support served to open her sensibilities, broaden her vision, and lift her taste. These bonds, moreover, went far beyond their doubtless commercial value to the parties concerned.

H. L. Mencken: Mephistopheles Advises

One of these friends was H.L. Mencken, the reporter, critic, and satirist whose merciless attacks on the American middle class ('the booboisie')[62] and all its attendant shams were legendary. He bemoaned the genteel tradition in American letters – the Uplifters, Faithful Husbands, and tin-horn Messiahs, the Bad Against the Good, as he put it – and championed an appreciation of life as 'the gaudiest and most gorgeous of spectacles'.[63] He called out bunk wherever he saw it and flayed enemies and friends alike with his coldblooded verdicts. Butcher knew him at first only by reputation and thought him amusing as well as brilliant, but by her own admission she was afraid of him.

One June day in 1920, not many months after she had opened the store, Butcher arrived to find a stocky man in a rumpled suit and Panama hat sitting in a chair, holding court – Mencken himself.[64] Edna Ferber was in the shop too, engaging

---

[59]   Harry F. Hansen, 'The Marshall Field Book Fair', *The Publishers' Weekly*, 98, 17 (23 October 1920), 1251–52.

[60]   Butcher maintained a casual friendship with Maugham over many years. When his wife Syrie opened a decorating establishment in Chicago, he wrote asking Butcher to send her some good reading (W. Somerset Maugham to Fanny Butcher, [1928], box 5, folder 351, Butcher Papers), but by that time Butcher had given up the bookstore.

[61]   Fanny Butcher to Louis Sudler, [1972], box 7, folder 525, Butcher Papers.

[62]   A term coined by Mencken in 1922 to describe an ignorant and complacent public. His infamous article published in the American supplement to the 17 April 1920 issue of *The Nation of London* dismissed the literature of the East Coast as conformist and senile and proclaimed Chicago to be the 'literary capital of the United States'.

[63]   H.L. Mencken, 'The Last of the Victorians', *Prejudices: First Series* (New York: Alfred A. Knopf, 1919), 139–45.

[64]   Butcher recounted this scene in *Many Lives – One Love*, 402–03. Another version is found in a letter from Harry Hansen, who was also present that day (Harry Hansen to Fanny Butcher, 19 May 1972, box 3, folder 224, Butcher Papers). See also Butcher's diary entries starting 7 June 1920.

him in friendly banter, much to the enjoyment of other customers. Just as the two of them were trading written barbs in the guestbook, in strolled William Allen White of the *Emporia Gazette*. Probably the most renowned small-town editor in America, he had come to deliver an autographed copy of his latest novel for Fanny Butcher, who had already given it a warm review. These three visitors were friends with each other, and they were all in town to cover the Republican Convention at the Coliseum.

A spirited discussion in the shop that day led Mencken and Butcher to a late date the following evening, when they had what Butcher said was 'a lovely long talk' over a plate of Shrimps Newburg. She promptly reported to her readers that without his 'Mephistopheles makeup' this Mencken was just an ordinary man, kind and straightforward to boot.[65] She told her diary that he was 'really a peach'.[66] She saw him several more times during the convention, and he returned to town again a few weeks later. He teased her that he was in love for the first time in ten years.

Mencken floated similar chimerical romances with a series of women and for the next several years wooed Butcher with lightly amorous correspondence. There was nothing imaginary, however, about the sturdiness of his efforts to enhance her shop and buttress her column. He liked her page, he said, finding it 'interesting and civilized',[67] but he often contested her opinions. He seemed to urge her toward a greater appreciation of human difference and eccentricity. At the same time, he warned her to be firmly on guard against the scourge of bohemian mountebanks (all that 'batik and Havelock Ellis').[68]

Mencken always asked after the store ('your warehouse', he called it)[69] and sent her signed books and ephemera 'for the select trade'.[70] He worried over her long work day, concluding that if worst came to worst, he might have to summon his friends Dreiser and Cabell and Huneker and 'we'll take turns waiting on trade'.[71] He had plenty to say about the photographs she hung on the walls. 'Already you flout my advice. Don't begaud your shop', he warned, with framed pictures of 'second and third-raters', which 'give your place a Greenwichy look, and that is precisely what you ought to avoid. If I remember rightly, you display Holliday. Haul him down. I believe that you could get a view of Anatole France by simply asking him for it. And Arnold Bennett'.[72] He sent her a photo of Conrad and, at her request, some views of himself, though noted that the one 'with the sad, beery

---

[65]   Fanny Butcher, 'Tabloid Book Review', *Chicago Tribune*, 13 June 1920, Pt 1, p. 9.
[66]   Fanny Butcher diary entry, 22 June 1920, Butcher Papers.
[67]   H.L. Mencken to Fanny Butcher, 20 February [1921], box 5, folder 372, Butcher Papers.
[68]   H.L. Mencken to Fanny Butcher, 2 December 1921, ibid.
[69]   H.L. Mencken to Fanny Butcher, 5 September [1921], ibid.
[70]   H.L. Mencken to Fanny Butcher, 5 October 1920, ibid.
[71]   H.L. Mencken to Fanny Butcher, 1 October 1920, ibid.
[72]   On 27 August 1920, ibid., Mencken wrote Butcher a letter replete with suggestions about how to run a bookshop of the better sort.

eyes is for your back room only'.[73] He also noted that her window 'shows too many books' and recommended 'concentrating on one or two at a time, or on the works of one author'. He offered to send original manuscripts and memorabilia for display, not all of it his own. Mencken encouraged Butcher to understand her store as a stage, where she ought to in effect dramatise fine literature and the new authors most worthy of attention.

Willa Cather's Oasis

Equally vivid but in a much different key was her friendship with Willa Cather, whom she called her 'lady Buddha',[74] whose serenity of soul and elemental love of writing impressed her deeply. In sharp contrast with the continual publicity-seeking that factored into Butcher's relations with almost every author of her acquaintance, Cather had to be coaxed to promote herself and preferred intimate talk and time alone. Cather was glad to hear about the new bookshop, she wrote. Perhaps Butcher could figure out now what was the problem with that business.[75]

Their friendship, of course, grew out of that first anxious review of *Alexander's Bridge*. As Cather shifted the focus of her novels to the lives of nineteenth-century pioneers on the great Midwestern plains, Butcher enthusiastically followed her career in the Tabloid, continuing the same perceptive analysis of Cather's writerly intentions. Cather told her once that it was worth the effort of composing a novel just to have Butcher understand it so completely.[76] She was annoyed that Butcher along with others labelled her a 'woman novelist'. Otherwise, over many personal conversations she gave Butcher revealing glimpses into her working habits and literary creed and then allowed Butcher to share those thoughts in her newspaper column. In one such reported conversation discussing Cather's 1925 novel *The Professor's House*, Cather said that she 'wanted to show that most of the really important events in our lives come to us through some entirely accidental contact'.[77] At the same time, she added, she wanted to show not just the picture but the design of life. 'I've always been much too interested in the way characters conquered fate', she confessed, 'to realize that, after all, fate conquers them ... '.[78]

Cather lived in New York but came through Chicago frequently on her journeys west. Even when she had only a few hours between trains, the two women tried

---

[73]   H.L. Mencken to Fanny Butcher, 4 September 1920, ibid.

[74]   Fanny Butcher, 'Tabloid Book Review', *Chicago Tribune*, 4 September 1921, D1.

[75]   Willa Cather to Fanny Butcher, 16 February [1920], box 2, folder 90, Butcher Papers. In this letter Cather offers to help mind the shop and talk to the customers.

[76]   Willa Cather to Fanny Butcher, 27 October [1926], ibid.

[77]   Both observations were made in an interview Butcher reported in 'Willa Cather Tells Purpose of New Novel', Chicago Tribune, 12 September 1925, 9. On the same occasion, Cather admonished her that the term 'woman novelist' was out of date, adding that 'very soon the critics will have to begin talking about prominent male novelists'.

[78]   Ibid.

to manage a visit. The usually sensitive and reticent Cather insisted the two of them must be on a first-name basis, and she wrote her letters to Butcher by hand, in spite of her weak penmanship. She made a warm inscription on the portrait photo she sent for the wall of the store.[79] Like Mencken, Cather worried Butcher was working too hard. If business got too rushed, she said, she would come and help tie up packages. Some day she might even give a talk to the customers. She found the store to be something truly apart, an oasis.[80] Apparently Cather at one time considered moving to Chicago. She once allowed Butcher to drag her around town to meet local booksellers, an exhausting foray she said would never be repeated. In a rare moment of deference, she bent to the opinion of Butcher (and Alfred Knopf) and renamed her novel *One of Ours* on the theory that under its original title (*Claude*) the book would never sell.[81] (Ironically, though *One of Ours* won a Pulitzer Prize, it was one of the few Cather works which Butcher found intermittently 'unreal', a reservation echoed by others at the time.)[82]

It seems likely that Butcher occupied a larger place in Cather's imagination than the author's biographers have previously recognised. Cather was apparently stunned when Butcher suddenly married in 1935 a man of whom she was completely unaware. Though Cather gamely wished her joy, thereafter her letters to Butcher were typewritten, and she never included a greeting or reference to this husband again. In 1936, she asked Butcher to stop quoting her private observations in the newspaper. Their mutual affection endured, however, and in times of stress, Cather told her, when she lay awake at night unable to sleep, she liked to dwell on Fanny Butcher and other faces, though she might not always stay otherwise in touch.[83]

The Queen of Sheba in New York

Butcher maintained important ties to publishers and editors as well as writers, and a good number stopped by the shop on visits to Chicago. Most of her business with them, however, transpired in New York and Boston, where she travelled two or

---

[79] The portrait is dated 16 February 1920 and is inscribed, 'For Fannie Butcher, who wrote the first discriminating review of my first novel. (In this case my interest in the reviewer has outlasted my interest in this novel, for I don't think much of that book now!)'

[80] In a letter to Butcher dated 8 November 1927, box 2, folder 91, Butcher Papers, Cather lamented the closing of Butcher's shop.

[81] Butcher's autobiographical account of this incident is confirmed in James Woodress, *Willa Cather: A Literary Life* (Lincoln and London: University of Nebraska Press, 1987), 323.

[82] Fanny Butcher, 'News and Views of Books', *Chicago Tribune*, 10 September 1922, E24. Ernest Hemingway implied that Cather's battlefield scenes were cribbed from D.W. Griffith's film Birth of a Nation (see *Selected Letters*, 105).

[83] Willa Cather to Fanny Butcher, 4 February 1937, box 2, folder 92, Butcher Papers.

three times a year, on behalf of both newspaper and store, to renew relationships, study the spring and fall lists, and buy books.

The idea of publishing as a 'gentleman's profession' was under revision even then, though a surprisingly large number of the participants were indeed products of elite eastern schooling, with some mavericks and snake oil merchants into the mix. A strong back list was still useful, but the old houses were recombining, new firms were organised, and talented editors moved around, stealing established authors and courting new ones.[84] It was a very good time for young, untried voices. Publishers actively sought out the unorthodox, and they were willing to battle censors of any stripe. Always an enigmatic coalescence of the romantic and the commercial, the trade now adopted more obvious marketing and distribution techniques. Prominent among these was the introduction of the Book of the Month Club and the Literary Guild ('The Box of Candy a Week Club' to their critics).[85] These innovations, schemes, and gimmicks – some of them crass and none of them 'highbrow' – actually worked to the benefit of many important authors, multiplying sales across the board.[86]

In this atmosphere of literary hustle, the attention of Fanny Butcher, with her powerful column and busy shop, was prized. When she arrived at the Doubleday offices in Garden City, she was greeted, she said, 'as if I were Queen of Sheba',[87] treated to luncheon with the Doubledays themselves and chauffeured about in Nelson's powerful Rolls Royce. In Manhattan, she made the rounds of the publishing houses all day, garnering the same excited reception everywhere, till four o'clock in the afternoon. Then it was time to set off for a series of literary 'teas', where the publishers auditioned the writers, the serious mixed with the frivolous, and the flamboyant bewildered the timid – while they all, Butcher noted, tried to 'make a life work of alcohol'.[88] Among her souvenirs is a sly and sexy invitation to an 'inspirational orgy for the spiritual benefit of Rockwell Kent', hosted by Random House and held very probably the year the artist designed their famous logo (Kent designed the ribald invitation as well).[89] Butcher remembered another afternoon party at the home of the humorist Irvin Cobb. He plied her with refills of his famous Kentucky White Mule cocktail and took her round the fractious crowd, even introducing her to gate-crashers he did not know himself.

---

[84]   For an interesting discussion of publishing in the 1920s, see Cass Canfield, *Up and Down and Around* (Harper's Magazine Press, 1971). Canfield was long-time head of Harper & Row, where he served in many roles from 1924 to 1985.

[85]   Anonymous, 'Has America A Literary Dictatorship?' *The Bookman*, 65, 2 (April 1927), 191–99.

[86]   Along with lists of leading authors and titles, throughout the 1920s *The Publishers' Weekly* featured up-to-date advice on how to market books of all kinds successfully, together with profiles of distinctive shops and their owners.

[87]   Fanny Butcher diary entry, 17 March 1927, Butcher Papers.

[88]   Fanny Butcher, 'Books', *Chicago Tribune*, 16 August 1930, 4.

[89]   Invitation from Bennett Cerf and Donald Klopfer to a party at Random House, box 4, folder 285, Butcher Papers.

Next day she spied him moving down Fifth Avenue 'like a sloop in a heavy sea'. When they happened to meet at the traffic light, his face lit up. 'Well, if it isn't little Fanny Butcher from Chicago', he said. 'I haven't seen you in a month of Sundays'.[90]

In spite of her advantageous standing, Butcher, mostly a teetotaller, was never quite at ease at these showy and brittle gatherings, often collapsing in her hotel room afterward into a slough of nausea and nerves. There were people who interpreted her abstinence and discomfort as backwardness or prudery. (Her fellow critic Harry Hansen wrote to Carl Van Vechten that Butcher 'always stands for Correct Behaviour'.)[91] Butcher could down a glass of port when she wanted and bandy repartee with anyone, but there is no doubt she was on more confident footing in her hometown. She paid close attention to the distinguished books published by Alfred Knopf, for instance, who entertained her frequently at his apartment in New York. She impressed him most, however, when he encountered her as chatelaine of her bookshop in Chicago. After one such trip Mencken wrote Butcher, 'Noff delivered an harangue on your virtues. It appears that you are not only a pretty gal and very hospitable to visiting literati and publicati, but also that you buy shrewdly, keep accurate books and pay on the nail. This last virtue made Alfred eloquent'.[92]

Butcher's store did maintain a satisfactory profit margin, partly by adopting some of the merchandising techniques abroad in the larger publishing world.[93] She offered book certificates and related merchandise such as bookplates, bookends, holiday cards, and stylish Valentines. All her packages were wrapped in a distinctive lemon yellow paper and tied with orange tape. She established a Christmas shopping service and also a book subscription program, along with an inventive variation, whereby a customer could regularly 'Add-A-Book' to a series of volumes by one author (say, Robert Louis Stevenson or Herman Melville) in modern bindings. In the wake of Mencken's advice, her display windows were notable for their verve and imagination. When the first volume of Carl Sandburg's acclaimed biography of Abraham Lincoln was published, she showed not only multiple copies of the book (which sold out quickly in Chicago) but also many relics borrowed from her friend Oliver Barrett, the great Lincoln collector. During one holiday season, she featured early editions of classics that had never gone out of print – *Tom Sawyer*, *Le Morte D'Arthur*, *The Swiss Family Robinson* – reminding shoppers of childhood favourites they might like to buy again as gifts for a new generation.

---

[90]　Fanny Butcher, 'The Literary Spotlight', *Chicago Tribune*, 26 March 1944, E13.
[91]　Carl Van Vechten to Edna Kenton, [August 1924], *Letters of Carl Van Vechten*, ed. Bruce Kellner (Yale University Press, 1987), 69.
[92]　H.L. Mencken to Fanny Butcher, 9 May 1921, box 5, folder 372, Butcher Papers.
[93]　For scattered business records and information about Butcher's marketing efforts, see box 36, folder 1564, Butcher papers.

Shop Worn: The Final Years

In 1922, sometime after Burton Rascoe, the pugnacious critic who followed Robert Burns Peattie as chief editor of the *Tribune*'s book pages, was fired for one too many nasty innuendos, Fanny Butcher was finally named to the top post. She would now write the lead reviews of major books and oversee a section which had grown considerably in size and scope. At this time, she tried to cut back her hours at the shop to Wednesday, Thursday, and Friday afternoons.

In the first few years, Butcher had had the peripatetic clerical assistance of a young University of Chicago graduate named Kate Sproehnle, a cousin of the famous columnist Franklin P. Adams and something of a dry wit herself. A startling beauty, she attracted the notice of many of the bookshop's illustrious customers (one of them could not decide whether she was a Rossetti or a Renoir)[94] and stole a boyfriend from Edna Ferber, who thenceforth referred to Sproehnle as 'goddess girl'.[95] Eventually, Sproehnle departed for New York, where she became part of the Algonquin Round Table crowd, subletting Alexander Woollcott's apartment and contributing articles to *The New Yorker* and other prominent magazines.[96]

After Butcher was promoted at the *Tribune*, she hired another young woman, Margery Barker, whom she later designated manager of the store. With Butcher's encouragement, Barker involved herself with all facets of the enterprise and assumed authority over day-to-day matters. She was especially interested in the rare book trade, which Butcher had already established with the assistance of New York dealer Gabriel Wells. A few years later, Butcher opened branch operations in the suburbs of Geneva and also Lake Forest (where she supplied new and standard titles to the Cake Box, a tea shop run by the Junior League). Yet another outlet was her book booth at the Woman's World's Fair, an annual exposition where she showcased the work of women writers.

With this expanded effort, the shop was increasingly successful, but it also meant that what had begun as a literary adventure was now a serious business in need of additional capital and constant fiscal attention. By her own admission, Butcher was not at all adept with balance sheets and audit reports. In the winter of 1927, following the onerous job of taking yearly inventory, Butcher regretfully

---

[94]   Robert Cortes Holliday, *Men and Books and Cities* (New York: George H. Doran, 1920), 204–05.

[95]   Julie Goldsmith Gilbert, *Ferber: A Biography* (New York: Doubleday, 1978), 419.

[96]   Butcher and Sproehnle maintained lifelong ties. In New York, Sproehnle made a close friendship with Jane Grant, then wife of New Yorker publisher Harold Ross. Over a period of years Sproehnle's cool, acerbic articles on fashionable city life appeared in *The New Yorker* and also *Saturday Evening Post*, *Collier's*, and *Vogue*. In the 1940s, she served for a time as theatre critic of *Mademoiselle*. She married the builder Alfred Rheinstein, who was first chairman of Mayor Fiorello LaGuardia's City Housing Authority. Butcher visited Sproehnle and Rheinstein often at their sixteen-room house on E. 71st St, where she made many valuable professional and personal contacts. In 1960, Sproehnle sold the house to *My Fair Lady* lyricist Alan Jay Lerner.

began to consider a sale of the store. In later years, Margery Barker, with whom she developed a contentious relationship, implied that the *Tribune* management had at last forced Butcher to choose between two conflicting roles.[97] There is no other available evidence to support that opinion. Rather, it seems the press of two demanding jobs, held concurrently, simply took too great a toll on Butcher's time and energy. 'Came home dead tired tonight', was a refrain repeated over and over in her diary. 'Couldn't do anything but go straight to bed'. Her doctor suggested she was 'too highly strung, with too many people twanging the wires'.[98]

To lighten the workload and with Butcher's agreement, Margery Barker had hired a friend, Frances Hamill, to help out in the shop. These two became partners in business and in life. They would eventually establish themselves as the preeminent dealers in 'Bloomsburiana', departing England every summer with trunks full of important letters and notebooks, their greatest acquisition being the diaries of Virginia Woolf, purchased from her husband Leonard.[99] But in 1927 they were two young women in their mid-twenties trying to work out some way, should Butcher's store go on the market, to buy it themselves. Probably they could not have managed that, except over time and at a somewhat discounted price. Butcher sold the shop instead in October of that year to Doubleday-Page & Co. for $10,000 cash and the right to use her name for a year.[100]

The Literary Spotlight

The sale of the store freed Butcher to explore other avenues of influence in the literary world. She travelled twice to Europe where she connected with many expatriate writers she had known only on paper, visiting Sylvia Beach and even spending a painfully stilted hour with James Joyce. She was appointed to the faculty of Bread Loaf, the summertime writers' conference in the mountains of Vermont, and for a year she hosted a 15-minute radio program on books and authors. Most important, she had more time to cultivate friendships with such figures as Gertrude Stein and Alice B. Toklas, when they came to America on tour, and most rewarding of all, with the playwright Thornton Wilder, who arrived at the University of Chicago in 1930 to teach literature to undergraduates.

---

[97]   Ruth B. Hutchison interview with Terry Tanner, 9 October 1990, box 1, folder 14, Hamill & Barker, Inc. Archive, Charles Deering McCormick Library of Special Collections, Northwestern University Library (Evanston).

[98]   See Fanny Butcher diary 1927 entries for 28 March, 11 April, and 14 July, Butcher Papers.

[99]   For an excellent account of Barker and Hamills' joint career in the rare book trade, see Ruth B. Hutchison, *Women Building Chicago 1790–1990: A Biographical Dictionary*, ed. Rima Lunin Schultz and Adele Hast (Bloomington: Indiana University Press, 2001), 62–63.

[100]   Sales contract dated 29 September 1927, box 36, folder 1564, Butcher Papers.

Fig. 4.1   Fanny at a dinner party during Gertrude Stein's 1934 visit to Chicago. From left to right, Bobsy Goodspeed, hostess and President of the Arts Club; Gertrude Stein; Fanny Butcher; Richard Bokum, the man Fanny will marry the following year; Alice Roullier, art dealer; Alice B. Toklas; Thornton Wilder. *Source*: Photo courtesy of The Newbery Library, Chicago. Call # Midwest MS Butcher, Box 44.1847.

During and after the war years, the *Tribune*'s book pages were reorganised several times. Fording the vicissitudes of internal politics at the paper, Butcher found herself, once again and rather unhappily, just one among a group of book editors. Her consolation prize was a new weekly column called 'The Literary Spotlight'. She held on, continuing to amplify her now classic byline. Over the years, she was the recipient of many awards for her efforts to promote the cause of books and reading. Perhaps the most important of these was a city-wide tribute organised by the Chicago Public Library, for which Carl Sandburg wrote a courtly homage, hailing Butcher as 'Miss Chicago, Lady Midwest'.[101]

Doubleday operated the shop in the same location till its lease expired in 1931, at which time the stock was transferred to create a new book section at Mandel Brothers department store. 'Fanny Butcher – Books' was much missed, not least

---

[101]   Carl Sandburg, 'Homage to Fanny Butcher', 3 May 1953, box 7, folder 459, Butcher Papers. His tribute reads in part, 'Fanny is Miss Chicago, Lady Midwest, and has still other titles … '.

by its international clientele. St John Ervine told London readers at length of his crushing disappointment when, after braving high winds and slushy streets on a winter afternoon, he reached the Pullman Building, only to find the shop gone.

The store did not entirely disappear, however, its ghost living on in the pages of 'The Literary Spotlight'. Butcher made of the column an extended reminiscence of those seminal years of the Twenties. Week after week, she contemplated one modern author and then another, often sadly, in conjunction with a related obituary. Her word portraits, tempered by time and shot through with personal remembrance, drew much of their impact from conversations and impressions formed in the bookshop. At last, better able to appraise the whole crowd of literary aspirants, she was no longer reluctant to make judgements about which of their works might endure. For many years, some readers turned to her column before they looked at anything else in the paper. She was abidingly influential.

Today, the worn and fragile guestbook of 'Fanny Butcher – Books' lies safely in archival hands, a souvenir of what is now counted beyond doubt as the greatest decade in American literature. It is, further, a testament to a time when such a shop might be an exciting destination and an opportunity to stand with its owner at a vital crossroads in the flow of culture and ideas.

Chapter 5
'A Place Known to the World as Devonshire Street': Modernism, Commercialism, and the Poetry Bookshop

Bartholomew Brinkman

To the regret of bibliophiles and poetry lovers on both sides of the Atlantic, on 22 June 1935, Alida Monro announced the closing of the Poetry Bookshop:

> I need hardly say with what deep regret I have come to this decision and I want to thank you most warmly for the manner in which you have supported us, and to tell you what great joy my husband and I had in conducting it. We never felt that any effort was too great if by it we were able to stimulate interest in poetry. It is indeed some consolation to look back and to realize that when Harold Monro opened the Poetry Bookshop in Devonshire Street, Theobald's Road, in January 1913 modern poetry was hardly known. Now, more than twenty one years later there is hardly a bookseller who is not forced to keep more poetry on his shelves than he would have thought possible all those years ago. Perhaps the Bookshop has not lived in vain![1]

The outpouring of responses confirmed that the Poetry Bookshop indeed had a significant role in the making of poetic modernism. Humbert Wolfe wrote to Alida:

> you are more than entitled to the claim which you make at the end of your letter. There is no doubt that the Poetry Bookshop was the most substantial single influence in re-establishing the poetry of our period. Its continued existence in the present stage of transition would have formed a rallying point, and its disappearance is therefore a loss to all who care for verse.[2]

Michael F. Cullis registered his appreciation for the Poetry Bookshop as well, explaining that 'as far as the P.B. had a mission, it has been entirely successful – more accurately, insofar as it partook in a general, if struggling movement to rehabilitate modern poetry (genuine poetry), that movement has won'.[3]

---

[1]   Form letter, Poetry Bookshop Papers: 145. British Library, hereafter BL.
[2]   Humbert Wolfe to Alida Monro, 18 July 1935, Poetry Bookshop Papers: 158, BL.
[3]   Michael F. Cullis to Alida Monro, Poetry Bookshop Papers: 152–53, BL.

Conrad Aiken, writing for the *New Yorker* under the pseudonym Samuel Jeake Jr, noted that for many, Alida's letter 'must be the announcement of an end of an era'.[4] Aiken explained that people came to the Bookshop

> literally from the ends of the earth; it became a meeting place and a battle ground. A history of it, of the poets who lived there, or met there, and of the ideas and tendencies which first shaped themselves there, all the way from the prewar period of Rupert Brooke and Vorticism and *Blast* through the successive waves of Georgianism to the crystallization of the *Criterion* group around its later quarters in Great Russell Street, would be the history of a generation.[5]

Such lavish praise underscores the often overlooked role of bookshops on the development of literary modernism in general and on transatlantic poetic modernism in particular. While scholars have increasingly recognised the importance of modern print culture, investigating various nodes of authorship, publication/printing, and reception, along what Robert Darnton has famously identified as the 'communication circuit' of the book, they have mostly neglected points of access and distribution.[6] As such, with some notable exceptions, such as Lawrence Rainey's study of the publication of James Joyce's *Ulysses*, the bookshop has largely been ignored as a modern print institution.[7]

A thorough study of the bookshop is integral, however, to any comprehensive sense of modernism. It is necessary, for instance, to consider the ways in which those bookshops that doubled as publishing establishments not only complicate our understandings of little magazines and small presses but also require us to reassess how publications from those bookshops should be read alongside modern mass magazines and books from the bigger publishers. It is also important to understand the bookshop as a privileged site for the access and distribution of literary modernism – the arena where differing and often competing modernisms meet face to face. True, many magazines were taken on subscription, and books were often purchased directly from the publisher or borrowed from a library or friend. But the bookshop afforded a special opportunity, where publications of various schools and stripes could come together in new and unpredictable formations to challenge and mutually influence one another as they lay together on a table or were arrayed along a shelf. These material juxtapositions could then lead to new associations in the mind of the bookshop visitor, who was herself not infrequently an author. As a forum for browsing, informal conversation, and more structured activities, such as lectures and readings, the bookshop could also bring

---

[4]   Samuel Jeake Jr, *The New Yorker* (10 August 1935), 39.

[5]   Ibid.

[6]   Robert Darnton, 'What Is the History of Books?', *Daedalus* 111, no. 3 (Fall 1982), 65–83.

[7]   Lawrence Rainey. *Institutions of Modernism* (New Haven: Yale University Press, 1998), 42–76. Even here, Rainey focuses more on the printing and collecting of *Ulysses* than on other dimensions of Beach's famous bookshop.

these various and often competing modernisms into frequent, immediate dialogue with one another.

Such was the case with the Poetry Bookshop. While (at least initially) restricting its purview to the genre of poetry, Harold Monro and the Poetry Bookshop sought to popularise a capacious verse – marked by both tradition and an emerging avant-garde – through the encouragement of visiting and browsing, through public poetry readings, and through the publication and distribution of many well-known Modernist texts. Despite its key role in the formation of poetic modernism, however, the Poetry Bookshop would, after two tumultuous decades, come to an end – a casualty of the Great Depression that neither financial restructuring as a limited liability company nor a return to an old system of literary patronage could save. As such, in its strained negotiation of the coterie and the commercial, the Poetry Bookshop indexes the more general relationship between literary modernism and its means of production, distribution, and consumption that were marked by the social and economic conditions of modernity.[8]

Beginning the Bookshop

In the September 1912 issue of *Poetry Review* (1912–1915) – a journal that was itself scarcely half a year old – Harold Monro announced the opening that following January, 'in the heart of old London, five minutes' walk from the British Museum, a Bookshop for the sale of poetry, and of all books, pamphlets and periodicals connected directly or indirectly with poetry'.[9] As the universalising 'all' suggests, from the beginning, Monro saw the mission of the Poetry Bookshop (as it would come to be known) to be the advancement of modern poetry in all its forms, rather than the championing of one particular school or movement. This meant that the Bookshop, like many other modern literary institutions, straddled the traditional and the progressive. Monro's hope to reclaim something of poetry's traditional role is made clear in his lament that

> the old-fashioned bookseller has almost disappeared from London, replaced by the Universal Provider in literature, and the Newsagent. The secondhand bookseller alone remains as a relic. Let us hope that we shall succeed in reviving, at least, the best traits and qualities of so estimable an institution as the pleasant and intimate bookshop of the past.[10]

---

[8] Much of this discussion will necessarily cover ground that has been worked over in Joy Grant's still indispensable 1967 study, *Harold Monro and the Poetry Bookshop*, though my focus is different and I view many of her conclusions in the context of more recent discussions of print culture and the institutional networks of modernism. Joy Grant, *Harold Monro and the Poetry Bookshop* (Berkeley: University of California Press, 1967).

[9] Harold Monro, 'The Bookshop', *Poetry Review*, no. 1 (November 1912), 498.

[10] Ibid.

This is symbolised by, among other things, the choice to lease for the Poetry Bookshop and the offices of the *Poetry Review* 'the whole of an eighteenth century house' in the heart of old London.[11] At the same time he acknowledged the importance of the past, however, Monro also recognised that, inevitably, 'we find ourselves compelled to pass beyond tradition; unavoidably in this new and wonderful world of the twentieth century we must throw in our lot with those who are endeavouring to stretch, force, and even wrench form to meet the exigencies of expression'.[12] This intermingling of the old and the new – in both literary and business strategies – would continue throughout the life of the Bookshop, embodied in such features as the 'futuristic shop-sign' that portrayed an illuminated book and a lyre.[13]

As Monro suggests, a common denominator among the various schools and movements was the recognition that poetry was not being well represented at the larger London bookshops – what Amy Lowell would characterise as

> one of those large and flourishing establishments where every sort of book is sold that you do not want to read; where rows and rows of the classics you wish you could read again for the first time flaunt from the shelves in gaudy leather bindings, and a whole counter labours to support the newest and dullest novels, and another is covered with monographs which instruct you minutely as to how to grow fruit trees, catch salmon, handle golf clubs, or bicycle through the home counties.[14]

Not unlike the small press or the little magazine, the Poetry Bookshop sought to define itself against this mass commercialisation of the book. As Monro explained, 'we are merely undertaking to supply the class of literature which [the recognised booksellers of London], with a few exceptions, apparently have long since found themselves obliged to consider unmarketable'.[15] He would echo the point in a 1913 draft of the prospectus for the Poetry Bookshop:

> With the commercialization of the book-trade, the advent of lending-libraries, + the wide exploitation of the poetaster by unscrupulous publishers, the confidence of the public has been so shaken, the fortunes of the publisher + bookseller so increased by enormous roles in the more popularized branches of literature, that current poetry (except such as is published in the periodicals) with its failure to be a source of income to publishers + booksellers, has indeed almost dropped out of the literary market.[16]

---

[11] Ibid., 499.

[12] Ibid.

[13] Noted in the *Daily Chronicle*. Quoted in Grant, 164.

[14] Amy Lowell, 'The Poetry Bookshop', *Little Review*, no. 2 (May 1915), 19.

[15] Monro, 'The Bookshop', 498.

[16] 'Prospectus', Poetry Bookshop Papers, 1–11, BL.

The importance of the Poetry Bookshop to stand against the marginalisation of poetry in the modern literary marketplace was recognised not only by the poets it served but also by the public at large, as evidenced in a number of reviews that Monro clipped and pasted into his scrapbook.[17] A review in the January 1913 *Pall Mall Gazette*, for example, recognised that to 'take a shop in a typical London street and fill it full of poetry for sale is an enterprise that surely comes nigh to the heroic'.[18] The success of the Poetry Bookshop, however, could also be read as collusion with the commercial. As the *Southampton Times* remarked, 'the fact that a commercial success has recently been made of such a seemingly "unbusiness-like" thing as poetry is being freely commented upon. For in Bloomsbury there is actually a "Poetry Bookshop", where nothing is sold but volumes of verse and drama', concluding triumphantly that 'poetry is now casting off her academic gown and clasping hands with commerce'.[19] Just as the little magazine and the small press that sought to define themselves against mass commercialisation through the formation of 'counterpublic spheres' also frequently relied upon marketing strategies it supposedly rejected, Monro was able to turn the marginalisation of poetry to his economic advantage through the Poetry Bookshop's setting, its use of physical space, and its encouragement of browsing that promised a place for poetry apart from the bigger bookshops.

A Place Known to the World

Among the many poets who celebrated the physical setting of the Poetry Bookshop, Raymond Bell dwells on the Bookshop's relationship to its immediate surroundings in his 1919 poem 'A Humble Offering to the Poetry Bookshop from a Stranger':

> There is a place where happy spirits meet
> A place known to the world as Devonshire Street.
> In vain the 'Bookshop' tries its skill to raise
> The tone of its surroundings: e'en the Bays
> Of Poets do not serve to overcome
> The drab and dirty greyness of this slum.
> Its name recalls sweet smelling hay and cream
> And all things fitting for a poet's dream.
> 'Tis true there is a sign whereof an arm
> Of purest gold stands out as if to charm.
> But how can even Gold light up a place
> When Poetry herself cannot add grace
> To such a street.
>   And yet perchance someday

---

[17] Harold Monro, Scrapbook, British Library Manuscripts Collection, 57766, BL.
[18] 'Poems and Profit', *Pall Mall Gazette*, January 1913. Monro Scrapbook, 135, BL.
[19] *Southampton Times*, 5 April 1913. Monro Scrapbook, 135, BL.

> When I am old and creeping down that way,
> The subtle influence which the Muse exerts
> May have induced the People washing shirts
> To hang them in a less conspicuous Place:
>> And I may see the street wear a new face
>> And slumdom ended, and the air as sweet
>> As one could e'er expect in 'Devonshire Street'.[20]

Bell's poem, already steeped in nostalgia, emphasises the importance of the Bookshop's location and the potential that this had for cultural transformation. Monro's decision to place the Bookshop on the seedy Devonshire Street – a decision largely made through economic necessity – kept it apart from the commercial bookshops in the more culturally pronounced areas of London. As such, the Poetry Bookshop existed not only generically, but also quite literally, on the cultural and commercial margins of London. It was not a place that the casual book buyer was likely to come across; it had to be sought out like gossip. This marginality did not, unfortunately, end slumdom, as Bell suggests it might (though Bell himself recognises the limits of such a proposition in claiming that the air would only be as sweet as 'one could e'er expect' on such a soured street), but it did mean that the Bookshop had the potential to function outside of established literary norms, making it a potent site for a renaissance of poetry and for an emerging avant-garde that tried to keep its distance from the commercial.

The interior of the Poetry Bookshop contrasted starkly with its surroundings. It was warm and friendly inside, populated by Harold's cat and later Alida's dogs. Romney Green made furniture and bookshelves in the Arts and Crafts tradition, giving the shop the intimacy of a private library. As Amy Lowell remembered,

> It was a room rather than a shop, for there was a smart fire burning in the grate, and there were chairs and settles, and a big table covered with the latest publications. The walls were lined with shelves, and under the window was a little ledge entirely filled with reviews from all over the world.[21]

Lowell confirms Monro's attention to both the present and the past, noting that

> I turned to the shelves and my surprise was even greater. There were a lot of shelves, all round the room and even over the chimney-breast. Every volume of poetry recently published was there. That I had expected, but what I had not expected was that all the classics were there too. Not bound in to mausoleums, 'handsome editions in handsome bindings, which no gentleman's library should be without', but readable volumes, for the reader who wants to read.[22]

---

20   Raymond Bell, 'A Humble Offering to the Poetry Bookshop from a Stranger', 31 October 1919. Poetry Bookshop Papers, 59, BL.

21   Lowell, 'Poetry Bookshop', 20.

22   Ibid.

Poems of the past were not simply to be admired from afar as fetishised cultural objects but were to be read and used to further current verse. In this same vein, Lowell notes, there 'was not one bit of glass in the shop, all was open and touchable. Of course I touched, and opened, and browsed'.[23] Harriet Monroe echoed Lowell's sentiment, noting that in her London quest for poets,

> under cold storms I sought out the Poetry Bookshop, where Harold Monro has flown the Georgian flag through the winds of war and the no less difficult draughts of peace. There was a certain still warmth to the place, despite the temperature, especially when a little flame was lit in one of those microscopic grates which tease the growl out of winter in England. It was a warmth of austere withdrawal; the doors opened, but not too widely, to whatever venturesome stranger might drift in, as to an island port from a gray indifferent sea; for Mr Monro has a dread of drifting poets, and a remotely hidden room to retire into until their credentials have led them past the secretarial barrier.[24]

The lengthy and careful descriptions by Lowell, writing for the *Little Review*, and Monroe, writing for *Poetry*, suggest the importance that the Poetry Bookshop had for modern poets on both sides of the Atlantic. It had become part of a pilgrimage for American poets visiting London and a key site for fostering transatlantic networks of modern poetry.

The Poetry Bookshop had become an important modern institution not only because it housed poetry for purchase but also because it did not immediately demand that one make a purchase. Monro explains that

> the accommodation of the shop itself is arrayed for the conscience of visitors who may desire to have prolonged visits for the personal examination of all recent publications. Those in charge of the shop, being personally acquainted with the wares, are in a position to give, when requested, information either of a general or of a technical nature, and under no circumstances are those visitors who are unable to select any volume of personal interest expected to pay for some volume they do not require, out of an unnecessary sense of obligation to buy something.[25]

This last point affirmed Monro's earlier recognition that

> our invitation is a direct encouragement of loiterers, and further, indeed, that it is open to the suspicion of being bad business; but, since we esteem the circulation of poetry a spiritual, or at least, an artistic, rather than an economic enterprise, we shall endeavour to tolerate a limited amount of loitering.[26]

---

[23] Ibid.
[24] Harriet Monroe, 'Comment: The Editor in England', *Poetry: A Magazine of Verse* 23, no. 1 (October 1923), 34.
[25] Monro, 'Prospectus'.
[26] Monro, 'The Bookshop', 498.

While this loitering was merely 'tolerated', and it was hoped that some purchase would eventually be made, the effect of this policy was that the Poetry Bookshop was more than just a distribution point. It was itself a site of literary production and reception, helping to create new writers and readers who might soon supply material. The openness of the shop also meant that various books and journals could be juxtaposed in the mind of the browser – the flaneur or flaneuse of the shelves – so that poets were necessarily and immediately read in relation to their contemporaries and predecessors. Beyond this vicarious intercourse, the Bookshop allowed for the meeting of those poets and writers themselves, who could directly debate issues of aesthetics and politics. The poet David McCord, for example, recalled that he learned of the work of Charlotte Mew because of something Monro said as he scanned the shelves, and related that on another visit:

> I was talking with Mr Monro when he excused himself to greet a customer, as I supposed, carrying a manuscript wrapped in old brown paper. I remember that they stood together by what must have been a schoolmaster's desk. The visitor was a slender man with dark glasses, graying hair, totally absorbed in what he was discussing. I glanced at him several times simply out of curiosity. When he departed, Mr Monro asked me if I knew the name of the visitor. I knew hardly anyone in London. 'That was James Joyce'.[27]

As this incident makes clear, the Poetry Bookshop was not only a venue for associating with likeminded writers but also an early place for literary sightings in what Aaron Jaffe points to as an emerging modern culture of literary celebrity.[28]

Some acts of 'loitering' were more permanent than others. Among the poets who at some point took advantage of the shop's cheap attic accommodations were Jacob Epstein, Wilfred Gibson, John Alford, Lascelles Abercrombie, Eric Gillett, M. Willson Disher, and Robert Frost – the last of whom John Cournos recalled as 'sitting on a table, his feet dangling, his voice smiling, while addressing a group of young poets (more than a dozen I think), the American poet and his listeners all chuckling'.[29]

Resuscitation through Recitation

In addition to facilitating informal get-togethers, the Poetry Bookshop presented formal lectures and recitations by both established and emerging poets, in an effort to help bring poetry into the public sphere. Among those who came to read were T. S. Eliot, Ezra Pound, Edith Sitwell, Robert Graves, Roy Campbell, Harriet Monroe,

---

[27]   David McCord to Joy Grant, 8 January 1962, Series 1, Box 1, folder 2, J. Howard Woolmer Poetry Bookshop Collection. McFarlin Library, University of Tulsa, hereafter ML.

[28]   Aaron Jaffe, *Modernism and the Culture of Celebrity* (Cambridge: Cambridge University Press, 2005).

[29]   Grant, 67. John Cournos to Grant, 2 December 1961, Series 1, Box 1 Folder 1, ML.

Francis Meynell, Margaret L. Woods, Emile Verhaeren, Humbert Wolfe, and Anna Wickham.[30] Amy Lowell had hoped to read as well but was unable to make the trip due to surgery.[31] Though today some of these figures are better known than others, this list represents a fairly good cross-section of poetry in the first decades of the twentieth century and suggests the wide-ranging aesthetic commitments of the Bookshop. Many poets and writers recalled the readings fondly, though some, like Leonard Woolf, the husband of Virginia Woolf, remarked, 'I think we went to some of the readings but not many as neither my wife nor I really liked this kind of readings'.[32] Inevitably, not all readings were equally well received. Lowell had offended Monro with a scathing critique of a reading by Van Wyck Brooks, to which her essay on the Poetry Bookshop was intended to make some amends.[33]

Monroe, in contrast, described the readings as if they were weekly temple rites, explaining that

> if the venturesome stranger is persistent enough to return toward six o'clock any Thursday afternoon, he may be blessed, if sensitive to impressions, with a real emotion. For the attic chamber, in which someone, for half an hour or more, is reading poetry, centralizes – I had almost said sanctifies – the spirit of heroic isolation one feels even in the shop downstairs. The room is a temple used for no other purpose, a temple entered by a tiny rickety winding stair and lit only from the sky – a gray sky that falls on gray-curtained walls and fifty or sixty seats arranged in rows. For seven days and nights, it gathers a faintly perfumed atmosphere for the weekly rite.[34]

Just as the shelves downstairs facilitated browsing and conversation, the secluded attic space encouraged a kind of spiritual awakening that was voiced in the readings themselves. Monroe recalled hearing 'Mr. Monro read there a few poems by Rupert Brooke, the beauty of his voice and the priestly authority of his presence made a ritual – a ritual enriched by overtones from the voices of many other poets who had stood on the little platform, some of them never to be heard again'.[35] This ethereal quality, in which the poetic past would reverberate through a new vocalisation, was something that Monro consciously strove for in his own poetry. As Alida recalled, Monro's poems needed 'to be heard. They were written with that in mind + I had always to read a poem out to him to make sure that the speech rhythm was obvious – if I stumbled over it then it was tackled again to get it right'.[36]

---

[30]   Grant, 83.

[31]   Lowell to Monro, 16 December 1924, Box 3, 'Amy Lowell' folder. Harold Monro Papers. Charles E. Young Research Library, UCLA. Lowell to Monro, 15 April 1925, Box 3, 'Amy Lowell' folder.

[32]   Leonard Woolf to Grant, 20 June 1962, Series 1, Box 1, folder 3, ML.

[33]   Lowell to Monro, 2 November 1914. Poetry Bookshop Papers, 81–83, BL.

[34]   Monroe, 34.

[35]   Ibid., 34–35.

[36]   Alida Monro to Grant, 15 May 1967, Series 1, Box 1, folder 2, Woolmer.

These readings were instrumental in legitimating and popularising modern poetry. As Mark S. Morrisson has argued,

> Monro created the Poetry Bookshop as a center for the oral performance of poetry by poets ranging from the most conservative to the most avant-garde [...] the Poetry Bookshop brought poetry readings out of the Victorian parlor and in front of the public. Monro and others attempted to restore to poetry through oral performance the stature it had attained in prebourgeois, preprint societies.[37]

The readings of the Poetry Bookshop, Morrisson argues, staged the poetic voice against the visual tendency of the modern poem, evident in such movements as Imagism, and in this way was 'able to appropriate the logic of the pure voice as a marker of distinction in order to change the field of production and reception of literary culture, and thus helped effect a transformation of the relationship of poet to public'.[38]

It is important, however, to consider the degree to which this mark of distinction carried valences of region, class, and nationality. As Monroe recalls, 'when I offered to this small London audience a group of the most middle-western poems I could find, beginning with Carl Sandburg's *Chicago*, I wondered whether the Georgian overtones would shatter into discord, and the gray curtains tremble with rebellious reverberations during their seven-days' meditation'.[39] Monroe's speculation (which she never answers) is rooted in the variations of the voice itself, with accent being one of its most noticeable markers. Her concern is not just over the subject matter of poems like 'Chicago' but also over how the recitation of such poems – delivered in her flat midwestern accent – could itself disrupt crimped Georgian verse. While there are national variations, such as spelling, that are noticeable only in print, these would seem to be less pronounced and less affectively stirring than when national and regional differences are voiced.

As important as poetic performance was for the Poetry Bookshop's efforts to popularise poetry, it was still largely mediated through networks of print distribution that Morrisson only partly acknowledges. For example, in arguing for the importance of verse recitation, Morrisson quotes from Monro in *Poetry and Drama*:

> We make a regular practice of reading poetry aloud, and any one who wishes to stroll in and listen may do so ... We are absolutely certain that the proper values of poetry can only be conveyed through its vocal interpretation by a sympathetic and qualified reader. Indeed so obvious does this appear that we regard the books on sale in the shop merely as printed scores for the convenience of refreshing the memory in hours of study or indolence.[40]

---

[37] Mark S. Morrisson, *The Public Face of Modernism: Little Magazines, Audiences, and Reception, 1905–1920* (Madison: University of Wisconsin Press, 2001), 56–57.

[38] Ibid., 82.

[39] Monro, 'Poetry Bookshop', 35.

[40] Morrisson, 72.

The sentence that Morrisson excises, however, requires close attention: 'The second time he comes to listen he is merely asked to buy a copy of this periodical [*Poetry and Drama*] if he has not already got one'.[41] This seemingly offhanded remark is made more explicit in Monro's prospectus:

> Since it is the belief of the founders that the recent transplantation of poetry out of common ways of life into the study is an abuse in no sense to be tolerated, + that the true nature of its propagation, the inherent aspect indeed of its existence, be delivery aloud by the voice of a sympathetic + qualified speaker, or rhapsodist, readings of poetry are given twice a week in a large room behind the Bookshop, admittance to which is absolutely free on a first occasion, + on successive occasions by the purchase of a copy of <u>Poetry and Drama</u> in which a slip will be found entitling the holder to apply at the Bookshop for a card of entrance on all the remaining Tuesdays and Saturdays of the current quarter'.[42]

It may be that printed journals and volumes merely provide the score for the oral performance, but they also are necessary to keep the Bookshop humming. After all, browsing and listening does not pay the bills. While the Poetry Bookshop downplays its commercial aspects, it nevertheless depends on them to forward its other, perhaps more altruistic, activities. Moreover, the printed journals and volumes stand proxy for those not privy to the weekly recitations, thus becoming a print extension of the Poetry Bookshop itself, as well as an invitation to visit.

Publishing Poetry

On the front cover of Monro's *Poetry and Drama* (1913–1914) is an engraved picture of the Poetry Bookshop, and on the back cover is a map with directions for how to get there.[43] These images help make explicit the symbiotic relationship between the Poetry Bookshop and its publications: the Bookshop was a means of distributing periodicals and books printed by Monro, and these periodicals in turn helped advertise the Bookshop where they could be found. This was a planned symbiosis. As Monro recognised in the *Poetry Review*, it is 'hardly necessary to point out the great advantages of maintaining a periodical in conjunction with a Bookshop. In *The Poetry Review* we shall recommend the public what to read: in the Bookshop we shall sell them what we have recommended'.[44]

The periodicals and anthologies published by the Poetry Bookshop did not only promote various books and schools of poetry in its critical reviews but also, in providing examples from poets and playwrights whose volumes could be found in

---

[41]   Monro, *Poetry and Drama* 1, no. 4 (December 1913), 387.

[42]   Monro, 'Prospectus'.

[43]   This image is not available in such reproductions as the Kraus reprint edition (New York: Kraus Reprint Corporation, 1967) or in the bound volumes available to many scholars, reminding us of the holes in the archive of little magazines.

[44]   Monro, 'The Bookshop', 498.

the shop, they became metonymic of the Poetry Bookshop itself. The relationship between these publications and the Poetry Bookshop is both centrifugal and centripetal: publications carried ideas and expressions beyond the lectures and readings of the Bookshop into a wider public sphere, while these same publications (marked, like other modern bookstore-publishers, such as Shakespeare and Company in Paris, with an imprint that could be traced to a visitable location) often brought readers into the Bookshop to experience the lectures and readings. Having a larger circumference than London word-of-mouth, these publications were of particular importance for forging transatlantic and international modernisms that were characteristic of the shop conversations and readings, attracting such poets as Lowell, who had read of the Poetry Bookshop 'in a stray number of *The Poetry Review* that had drifted my way'.[45]

This relationship was mediated through other Poetry Bookshop publications as well, such as the popular Georgian anthologies edited by Edward Marsh. As Grant argues, the

> association between the Poetry Bookshop and the popular Georgian Poetry series was pointed out in many of the reviews of the volumes as they appeared – in 1912, 1915, 1917, 1919 and 1922 – and it was due to this, far more than to any other single publication, that the Bookshop's name was made familiar to the poetry-reading public.[46]

Monro pasted several of these newspaper and magazine reviews in his scrapbook and underlined select passages (to be used, perhaps, for promotional purposes). Reviewing the first *Georgian Anthology* (1911–1912), the *Sunday Times* notes that 'a perusal of the small book's contents will surprise those who had imagined that poetry was languishing in the twentieth century', the *Contemporary Review* remarks that 'in some ways it may prove important as a forerunner of the revival in poetry for which all critics are waiting', and the author/journalist Arthur Ransome exclaims that there 'is poetry being written to-day that in twenty years' time, in fifty years' time, it will be a disgrace not to have read. Ours is the opportunity'.[47] Reviews in such relatively wide-circulating newspapers and magazines point to the impact that the Poetry Bookshop and its publications were beginning to make on the larger London cultural scene.

Publicity continued and widened through subsequent volumes, as when the *New York Times* wrote of the 1913–1915 volume: 'In "Georgian Poetry" we have a phenomenon – a volume of verse written in wartime, yet breathing no hint of war. The editor has shown good judgment; he has built an ivory tower wherein no sound of alurum enters, and each of whose chambers is, in its kind and degree,

---

45　　Lowell, 'Poetry Bookshop', 19.

46　　Grant, 65.

47　　'Georgian Poetry', *Sunday Times*, 23 February 1913. Monro Scrapbook, 13. *Contemporary Review* (March 1913). Monro Scrapbook, 14. Arthur Ransome, 'Georgian Poetry'. Monro Scrapbook, 12.

beautiful'.[48] Although for Monro, who was deeply invested in the war, the volume's perceived aesthetic isolation was not necessarily a good thing, the success of the Georgian poetry series was nevertheless instrumental in bringing patrons to the Bookshop. As Dominic Hibberd has noted, 'it was perhaps inevitable that the shop became thought of as some kind of Georgian headquarters. Despite everything Monro could do to counter this misapprehension, the myth persists to this day, partly because Pound liked to repeat it'.[49] Although Monro may not have held literary allegiance to the Georgian poetry series, the Poetry Bookshop depended in great part on its widespread commercial success, underscoring the often complex negotiation between aesthetic and commercial modernism. As Hibberd and others have noted, however, the Poetry Bookshop publications were not at all restricted to the Georgian aesthetic. Monro published Pound's *Des Imagistes* anthology in 1914, which was to some degree intended, as Grant puts it, to 'cock a snook' at the more popular and aesthetically less daring *Georgian Poetry* series.[50] Monro did see true merit in the movement, however, as evidenced by his later publication of Richard Aldington's *Images* and F. S. Flint's *Cadences* in chapbook form. But Monro also recognised the ephemerality and self-parodic potential of such movements as well. In the May 1921 issue of the *Monthly Chapbook* (1919–1925), the journal that succeeded *Poetry and Drama*, for example, Monro published a four-page parody of the Imagistes, 'Pathology Des Dommagistes'.[51] Monro's willingness to poke fun at one of his most significant literary interventions suggests once again the extent to which no particular school or movement was sacred. The main thing was the cause of modern poetry as a whole.

This desire to promote modern poetry in all its forms meant that when Monro's activities as poet, critic, and editor/publisher did at times conflict with his ownership of the Bookshop, the Bookshop took precedence. As Monro told John Drinkwater, who had complained to him about his books not selling as well as he would have liked,

> Personally, I have always endeavoured in my capacity of Proprietor of the Poetry Bookshop to represent it as a public institution independent of my private views and judgments. As shopkeeper, I always try to show the utmost impartiality and recommend to each individual person the authors or books which seem most adapted to the tastes of that person, and those who work with me do the same.

---

[48]   *New York Times*, 14 September 1916. Monro Scrapbook, 23.

[49]   Dominic Hibberd, 'The New Poetry, Georgians and Others: *The Open Window* (1910–11), *The Poetry Review* (1912–15), *Poetry and Drama* (1913–14), and *New Numbers* (1914)', *The Oxford Critical and Cultural History of Modernist Magazines, Volume I, Britain and Ireland, 1880–1955*, ed. Peter Brooker and Andrew Thacker (Oxford: Oxford University Press, 2009), 189.

[50]   Grant, 100.

[51]   'Pathology des Dommagistes: Being Specimens for a Projected Anthology to be Issued in the U.S.A)', *Monthly Chapbook (A Monthly Miscellany)*, no. 23 (May 1921), 21–24. I would like to thank Robert Scholes for directing me to this issue.

Incidentally of course, we have sold hundreds and hundreds of your books. The question has been brought rather forcibly before me several times as to whether my various remarks in writing about my contemporaries were compatible with my activities in the shop, but I have decided that the two capacities could remain independent, though I believe others have decided differently about the matter.[52]

Similarly, although Monro had passed on the chance to publish both T. S. Eliot's 'The Love Song of J. Alfred Prufrock' and 'La Figlia Che Piange', and did not seem to care much for him, he kept Eliot's review, the *Criterion* (1922–1939), in his shop. Acting as go-between, Aldington inquired of Monro as to whether 'your magnanimity will stretch to the extent of helping the Criterion not only by contributing (which you have already done) but by displaying the magazine conspicuously in your shop and by mentioning it to possible subscribers?'[53] Monro replied that, 'I do not think THE CRITERION and THE CHAPBOOK overlap much and I certainly want to support THE CRITERION in any way that might not interfere with THE CHAPBOOK. We keep a set of back numbers in the shop conspicuously displayed'.[54] While they had their poetic and personal differences, both Eliot and Monro no doubt recognised the mutual benefit of having the *Criterion* displayed in the Poetry Bookshop – a benefit to commercial viability as much as aesthetic autonomy.

Similarly, Wilfrid Gibson wrote to Monro in 1927 of his *Collected Poems* that

> Macmillan is printing a circular, reprinting some of the generous reviews the book has received. I wonder if you would object to enclosing copies of it in parcels of books you send out? I do not know if doing so would be against your principles! I, for my part, would much rather think the Poetry Bookshop was making something out of the sale of the book, than that other bookshops were getting what little profit there may be![55]

Monro replied, 'I certainly have been responsible for the sale of several copies of your Collected Poems, although generally speaking I find the Collected Works of living authors are more difficult to sell than occasional volumes. We always find it rather difficult to make any point of enclosing prospectuses with parcels as they are more apt to be overlooked than included', but agreed to do so nonetheless.[56] One the one hand, Monro hesitates to promote a bibliographical form that itself signals a shift from the coterie to an institutionalised modernism that threatens an eclipsing commercialism; on the other hand, the *Collected Poems* is simply a bad bet in being too difficult to sell. Such economic contradictions often put the Poetry Bookshop in a vexed position and ultimately contributed to its collapse.

---

[52]   Monro to John Drinkwater, 30 January 1924, Box 1, folder D, Harold Monro Papers, BL.

[53]   Aldington to Monro, 6 June 1923, Box 1, folder 4, Harold Monro Papers, BL.

[54]   Monro to Aldington, 21 June 1923, Box 1, folder 4, Harold Monro Papers, BL.

[55]   Wilfrid Gibson to Monro, 5 January 1927, Box 1, folder G, Harold Monro Papers, BL.

[56]   Monro to Gibson, 21 February 1927, Box 1, folder G, Harold Monro Papers, BL.

Closing Up Shop

Although Monro attempted to run the Poetry Bookshop with an eye to both aesthetic and commercial interests, it was, nevertheless, often in dire financial straits. In 1926, after the lease on the original premises expired, the Bookshop moved from the 'drab and dirty greyness' of Devonshire Street to the heart of Bloomsbury at 38, Great Russell Street – within spitting distance of the British Museum. With the move would come other big changes: the lecture hall space would be doubled, holding up to 100 people, and the Bookshop widened its ken to include all branches of literature and art. Ostensibly, this was to 'take a position among the foremost ranks of intelligent General Booksellers', but it also indicated the difficulty Monro had in getting poetry alone to turn a profit or to even be self-sustaining, and necessarily undermined the Bookshop's initial central focus.[57]

To help fund the move, Monro distributed a 'Scheme for the Conversion of the Poetry Bookshop into a Limited Liability Company'.[58] He invited investments of five to ten shares at £1 a share, explaining enthusiastically that, 'the turnover of the business for the last six years has been an average £3,238 per annum. It is confidently expected that, with the increased facilities for trading and for renewing publishing activities at the new premises, this turnover can be doubled or trebled'.[59] His potential investors were not so confident. While some friends made token contributions, many saw the Bookshop as a bad investment.[60] Accounts were poorly managed, and much of the staff had to be let go.[61] The decision to form a limited liability company, while spurred on by the move to a new location, was a bandage on a long-festering wound that had plagued the Bookshop since

---

[57] Circular, 1926, Harold Monro Letters, 58–59, BL.

[58] Ibid.

[59] Ibid.

[60] A card recording shares purchased gives the following numbers: Humbert Wolfe 10 shares @ 1 pound each; John Bailey: 10; Major H.C. Brodie 20; F. E. Halliday: 5 or 10 (*sic*); Mrs M. F. Ball: 10; Albert Rutherson: 5; Richard Aldington: 5; Arnold Bennett 25; E. McNight Kauffer 5. The card also notes that 'the scheme apparently didn't attract enough interest and no shares seem to have actually been sold'. Series 2, Box 1, folder 3, ML.

[61] A letter from Monro's accountants shows a trading loss in 1920 of £527. 6. 11 ½ and explained that 'the expenses appear to us to be out of all proportion to the business done, and the amount of stock carried, too large. In view of the result shewn for 1920 and the state of trade generally throughout the country it appears to us to be imperative that drastic measures of economy be taken at once'. Goddard, Dunkley, Davie & Fryer, Chartered Accountants to Monro, 26 May 1921, Poetry Bookshop Papers, 73. Monro would reply that 'the Trading & Profit and Loss account which you sent me has thrown much light on my present position. I have been obliged to dismiss nearly all of the staff and work the business on much more economical lines. […] We are daily gaining ground through the large reduction effected in wages, and various other economies. But business is still so very bad, and we have made a few promises to pay certain other accounts, which we must meet before the end of July'. Monro to Goddard, Dunkley, Davie & Fryer, Chartered Accountants, 18 June 1921, Poetry Bookshop Papers, 75, BL.

its beginning and stood as an early indicator of how an investment in literary modernism was unlikely to be economically self-sustaining.

Finding such a restructuring unsuccessful, Monro was by 1931 attempting to return to an earlier system of literary patronage, appealing to rich friends for help. He wrote to Lady Keeble in January that 'if you thought of making use of the Bookshop in the future, and of recommending any of your friends to do so, it would be a great help to us in our struggle to keep our heads above water, and incidentally it would be of assistance to the poets themselves, because the more books we sell the better for them'.[62] By June of that year, Monro's pleas became much more desperate. He lamented to Keeble that unless something extraordinary happens,

> there will be no Poetry Bookshop left to be discussed in that connection at all, for, during the past weeks, a hideous slump has settled down on the book trade (as on most other trades) and it has now become impossible to know from week to week what may not happen unless some improvement takes place. We are, in fact, in a very serious situation, and, after these two decades of effort, there may be a sudden collapse unless someone comes to the rescue.[63]

By mid-August, Monro wrote to John Helston, requesting funds (and receiving £120, about one-third of what was needed to keep the Bookshop afloat). He reminded Helston that the Bookshop

> is entirely an idealistic institution and its eighteen years of life have been fraught with great anxiety. It was reared with difficulty as the Great War coincided with the first few years of its life. It struggled through the next ten years. Then its house was sold over its head and it had to seek new and more expensive quarters. We were just thinking that at least it would emerge triumphant when it was struck a second time by the Great Slump which now threatens to murder it.[64]

The Great Slump, from which the Bookshop would never recover, was clearly related to poor financial management, but it also marks a more general shift away from a coterie modernism that the Poetry Bookshop had helped to forge and subsequently depended upon. In this respect, the end of the Poetry Bookshop is a salient example of Rainey's observation that 'the Great Depression effectively eliminated the structures of private patronage that had sustained modernism's growth and its emergence as a significant idiom within the family of twentieth-century languages'.[65] Having previously tested the Bookshop's potential as a limited liability company, and finding that unsuccessful as well, it is fair to ask

---

[62]   Monro to Keeble, 8 January 1931, Poetry Bookshop Papers, 126, BL.

[63]   Monro to Keeble, 12 June 1931, Poetry Bookshop Papers, 139, BL.

[64]   Monro to John Helston Esq., 18 August18, 1931. Poetry Bookshop Papers, 149, BL.

[65]   Lawrence Rainey, *Revisiting The Waste Land* (New Haven: Yale University Press, 2005), 100.

whether anything would have worked to save the economic viability of poetry in the throes of the Great Depression.

One of the great ironies here, though, is that the Poetry Bookshop itself had helped to prove poetry's commercial viability in a wider field of cultural production and distribution that transcended its own privileged space. The Bookshop helped to popularise modern poetry, and once this poetry reached a wide enough audience it was attractive to larger publishers who could use it to turn a profit. Monro's prescient worries over this poetic reproduction are evident in an exchange of letters with the UK-based Macmillan Publishing Company over the work of W. B. Yeats, one of the first modern poets to attract a large and profitable readership. Monro wrote to Macmillan & Company in December 1921, explaining his distress that they had let several of Yeats's volumes go out of print and remarking that 'it is most unfortunate that the works of the poet of the importance of Mr Yeats should, for so long a period, be entirely unobtainable: whereas, no doubt, a firm of less standing than yours, would be only too proud to be in a position to issue them to the public'.[66] Macmillan replied that plans were underway for a collected edition of Yeats's poems and plays.[67] To this Monro lamented,

> I am sorry to learn that Mr Yeats' Poems and Dramas are to be published in a Collected Edition, and not in their original volumes; as collected editions, whilst the Poet is still living, are always unsatisfactory. As we have many enquiries for his books I should be much obliged if you would tell me whether the volumes will be saleable separately? I very much hope that they will be as otherwise the sale will become extremely limited.[68]

Monro's enquiry underscores his hesitation over the publishing and selling of a collected edition of poems. He likely felt that a Collected Poems suggested the culmination of a career and the streamlining of a poet's corpus that, for Yeats in particular, would prove to be short-sighted. But there was also the sense that a Collected Poems would gloss over the aims and achievements of the individual volumes as self-contained *books*. Not only is the integrity of the individual poetry book compromised, but also there is potentially a very real loss of money for the Bookshop when several previous books can be found under one cover.

Only certain poets were given Selected and Collected Poems, however, so that these forms acted as aesthetic and commercial gatekeepers, helping to distinguish those poets deemed most worthy of reproduction and purchase. This not only had the effect of streamlining a canon of poets to be studied in university settings and elsewhere, as Rainey suggests; it also reduced the risk of carrying poetry for the larger bookshops. If the larger London bookshops felt that modern poetry had

---

[66]   Poetry Bookshop to Macmillan, 21 December 1921, Poetry Bookshop Papers, 164, BL.

[67]   Macmillan to Poetry Bookshop, 28 December 1921, Poetry Bookshop Papers, 165, BL.

[68]   Poetry Bookshop to Macmillan, January 1922. Bookshop Papers, 166, BL.

reached a critical mass of readers so that it was worth keeping on the shelves, it could still make the safe bet of only carrying those volumes that would potentially have the widest appeal, thereby attracting an audience that would have previously sought out the Poetry Bookshop or not looked for poetry at all. Not only did the Poetry Bookshop have a big hand in popularising modern poetry; it also succeeded in singling out and popularising particular poets to its own detriment.

Monro died in March 1932, not living to see the fullest effects of an institutionalised modernism that he had helped create. Alida Monro continued to run the Poetry Bookshop for three more years before finally ending it in 1935. While the material shop ceased to exist (a point starkly depicted by Alida's recollection that 'a lot of stuff had to be pulped after the basement of the P.B.S. premises was flooded as a result of bombing in '41'), and its books and periodicals would no longer be published, it has left an indelible imprint on poetic modernism.[69] As he began the Poetry Bookshop, Monro recognised that 'there can be scarcely a hundred first-class readers of poetry in England, the demand for them having almost ceased. But we are on the way to altering all this. We hope that Poetry Bookshops will eventually be established in all the principal towns of England – not as institutions, but as houses of enjoyment'.[70]

As Grant notes, not many bookshops followed the Poetry Bookshop's example.[71] But the legacy of the Poetry Bookshop extends beyond its few direct followers. In a complex negotiation of genre and market, the Poetry Bookshop galvanised the cause of modern poetry in the first decades of the twentieth century, bringing together in person and in print many of its most formidable practitioners. It was a central, if often critically neglected, institution of transatlantic poetic modernism, illuminating both for modern literary critics and for historians of modern print culture the important work of proprietors like Monro, and of the deep and lasting legacy of the Modernist bookshop.

---

[69]   Alida Monro to George Sims, quoted in George Sims, 'Alida Monro and the Poetry Bookshop', *ABMR: A Monthly Magazine of International Antiquarian Bookselling, Collecting and Bibliography* 9, no. 7 (July 1982), 264.

[70]   *Poetry and Drama*, no. 1 (December 1913), 387.

[71]   There was at least one direct imitator, the Poetry Shop, which existed on Pryme Street, Hull, between 1919 and 1937, drawing such readers as Walter de la Mare and Monro himself. Grant, 75.

Chapter 6
Counter-Space in Charles Lahr's Progressive Bookshop

Huw Osborne

O'Connor: You don't very much like selling books, do you?

Lahr: Well, I like selling books to people who can appreciate them, but I hate selling books to people who try to make money out of them ... Those people who speculate in books ... I hate those people. I cannot give him a book if he ... if he can't appreciate it.

O'Connor: You love books.

Lahr: Oh my God yes.

O'Connor: Why?

Lahr: I don't know ... books have been my downfall.[1]

Introduction

When Charles Lahr, the proprietor of The Progressive Bookshop at 68 Red Lion Street in London, died in 1971 at the age of 86, his obituary in *The Times* was written by Rhys Davies, the prolific Anglo-Welsh novelist whose career Lahr was instrumental in establishing. Davies remembers Lahr as a wandering spirit and romantic figure of perseverance, a kind of patron saint of literary London:

> Lahr seldom failed to track down a rare book for a favoured habitué. When he could no longer afford the rent of the Little Newport Street shop, he functioned from his remote suburban home, cycling back to the street stalls and obscure shops, carpet bag dangling, his jaunty beret, old raincoat and sandaled bare feet well known in such haunts. In the shabby bag might be Winston Churchill's novel, picked up for a shilling, together with a bunch of flowers from his back garden, to be left beside the milk bottle on some old friend's doorstep. He kept

---

[1]   Transcript of a BBC Interview of Lahr by Philip O'Connor, 'London Characters no 6 – Charles Lahr, Bookseller', 5 May, 1965, Philip O'Connor Papers, Harry Ransom Center at University of Texas, Austin Texas, hereafter HRC.

cycling on such pilgrimages until he was 80. Perhaps he was one of the last of his unworldly kind.[2]

This portrait of Lahr as a friendly sprite of the London book world is an apt one; he is not only 'unworldly' but almost otherworldly as well, and the description captures the elusiveness that has since characterised his role in literary culture. This unworldliness is 'immaterial' in other ways: Lahr was not only elusive but also generously uncommercial and ultimately unimportant in terms of conventional definitions of literary success. By the time Davies wrote the obituary, he had been a solidly selling author in Heinemann's lists for the past thirty years; when he describes Lahr cycling through 1960s London at the age of 80, he also dreams of the literary world in which he met Lahr in the 1920s, when ascetic gestures to artistic sacrifice seemed possible. Davies's obituary celebrates and laments not only the death of one man but also the death of a way of imagining literature as a defence against and resistance to the grinding, reductive forces of consumer culture.

However, as many have pointed out, such idealised oppositions of the commercial and the aesthetic tempt us away from the more complex operations of literary culture and literary markets. Figures like Lahr are interesting not because they are removed from literary institutions but because they constitute them. Lahr is one of those figures who remind us of the ways in which books are produced and literary careers negotiated.[3]

Despite the prominent role that many writers attribute to Lahr, we know very little about him and the nature of his contribution to modern literature. He peeks out at us from other people's autobiographies, from memoirs, from letters, from the footnotes of a literary culture that has largely forgotten him.[4] We get one amusing

---

[2]   Rhys Davies, 'Charles Lahr', *The Times*, 18 August 1971, 14: H.

[3]   He is one of what Robert Darnton calls the 'forgotten middlemen of literature'. In his numerous roles, Lahr occupied an important site of literary production and negotiation in the 'crucial area where supply [meets] demand'. Robert Darnton, *The Kiss of L'Amourette: Reflections in Cultural History* (New York: Norton, 1990), 128.

[4]   The best focused treatment of his life is David Goodway's 'Charles Lahr: Anarchist, bookseller, publisher', *London Magazine* (June/July, 1977), 47–55. A very informative bibliographic essay is George Jefferson's 'Charles Lahr, Publisher of D.H. Lawrence, Liam O'Flaherty, and H.E. Bates', *The Book Collector* 113 (August 1993), 66–78. More recently, Christopher Hilliard's article 'The Literary Underground of 1920s London', *Social History* 33.2 (May 2008), 154–82, offers an excellent discussion of Lahr's place in his leftist, Grub Street community and his role in publishing and disseminating 'obscene' material. Also see Chris Gostick's short study *T.F. Powys's Favourite Bookseller, The Story of Charles Lahr*, Powys Society Monographs, 2009. Other places where Lahr makes significant appearances are R.M. Fox's *Smoky Crusade* (London: Hogarth, 1938); Kenneth Hopkins's *Corruption of a Poet* (London: James Barrie, 1954); O.F. Snelling's *Rare Books and Rarer People: Some Personal Reminiscences of 'The Trade'* (London: Werner Shaw, 1982); H.E. Bates's *The Blossoming World* (London: Michael Joseph, 1971); Rupert Croft-Cooke's *The Numbers Came* (London: Putnam, 1963); Rhys Davies's *Print of a Hare's Foot: An*

glimpse of Lahr within his friendly community of culture-producers from the end notes or 'Ex Cathedra' of the second number of *The London Aphrodite* (1928), a periodical published and edited by P.R. Stephensen and Jack Lindsay, two Progressive Bookshop regulars. The piece begins by summarising and apparently enjoying the generally negative reception of the periodical, then continues to describe a party celebrating *The London Aphrodite*'s inception:

> However, several minor reviewers welcomed the rash venture, kind friends did not hesitate to backslap, and for instance Charley Lars [*sic*] sold sixty copies in his sentry-box bookshop in Red Lion Street. Whereupon the Editors and Liam [O'Flaherty] and Charley Lars got drunk in a cellar kept by Louis XVII, other guests being Rhys Davies, who couldn't find the cellar at all; Tommy Earp [one of *The New Coterie* editors], who tried to sing 'Rule Britannia' at 3 a.m. on a beer barrel (empty), but overbalanced and broke Louis [Golding]'s collarbone; a calm German scholar who had to go early; an Oxford Don who passed out; an ex-member of the I.W.W. with good intentions but a too-small stomach; a bald and cheerful Australian cartoonist; two roaring Irish bhoys covered in tap-room sawdust; two great policemen; and other Bloomsbury intellectuals. At dawn Charley Lars and the Editors took Liam home, where he irrationally began swallowing raw eggs. Then Charley vanished in a mist, and the editors sat down in the gutter, together with a pint of (salvaged) whiskey to reflect upon the Universe.[5]

The editors present themselves and their contributors as a house of misrule appropriate to their iconoclastic treatment of the mouthpieces of both 'high' and 'mass' culture. I particularly like the description of Lahr 'vanishing in a mist' at the end of the evening, for it seems an apt illustration of his intangible, elusive, and largely forgotten influence in this eclectic and active community of writers, editors, printers, and publishers.

Despite this obscurity, Lahr was instrumental in the careers of a large group of international writers. He worked very closely with D.H. Lawrence during the final years of Lawrence's life. C.L.R. James credits him as a source of information and inspiration for *World Revolution* (1937), and George Woodcock acknowledges Lahr as an important early influence and the publisher of his first collection of poetry in 1937. In the 1920s, Lahr published the little magazine *The New Coterie* (1925–1926), which was the printed extension of the community of his shop. It included works by D.H. Lawrence, William Roberts, Liam O'Flaherty, T.F.

Autobiographical Beginning (Bridgend: Seren, 1996), Bonar Tompson's *Hyde Park Orator* (London: Jarrolds, 1936); Hugh MacDiarmid's *Lucky Poet* (Manchester: Carcanet, 1994); and in fictional form in H.E. Bates' short stories, 'No Country', *Something Short and Sweet* (London: Jonathan Cape, 1937), 'A German Idyll', *The Woman Who Had Imagination and Other Stories* (London: Jonathan Cape, 1934), 'The Bath' and 'The Palace', *Country Tales* (London: Reader's Union, 1938); and John Lindsey's *Vicarage Party* (London: Chapman and Hall, 1933).

5   'Ex Cathedra'. *The London Aphrodite*. no. 2 (October 1928), 160.

Powys, H.E. Bates, Nina Hamnett, and many others. In addition to many other limited edition books and booklets, he also published The Blue Moon Booklets between 1930 and 1937, which featured many of the same writers and often dealt with working-class, revolutionary, or anti-establishment themes.[6] Lahr drew into his influence such writers as Hugh MacDiarmid, John Gawsworth, Rupert Croft-Cooke, Olive Moore, Nancy Cunard, Rhys Davies, Anna Wickham, James Hanley, Count Potocki of Montalk, Malachi Whitacher, Oswell Blakeston, Ronald Duncan, Julian Symons, Walter Allen, A.J.A. Symons, Leslie Halward, C.H. Norman, Philip Lindsay, Gay Taylor, Gerald Kersh, Hamish MacLaren, E.W. Martin, A.S.J. Tessimond, L.A. Pavey, Charles Duff, and many others, several of whose careers he facilitated and promoted.[7]

While Lahr was very closely involved in the literary market, he did so in a very informal way, and he situated himself in opposition to the kinds of commercial mechanisms upon which his patrons depended for their literary success. The space of his shop replicated this effect and provided the physical node for the networks that circulated around Lahr. In the process of creating the space and culture of his shop, Lahr engaged with print culture in ways that suggest an anti-marketing strategy that approached print culture with a great deal of irony. Much of Lahr's influence can be mapped in his publishing activities, as is illustrated in his publication of James Hanley's limited edition short story *The German Prisoner* from within the overlapping spheres of influence and related publishing activities emanating from the shop. This chapter discusses this publication at some length, describing the ways in which it situates Lahr and his shop within the complex and competing interests of the market, and when viewed from this perspective, *The German Prisoner* becomes a destabilising print object that mirrors the shop from which it emerged.

Charles and Esther Lahr: The Progressive (and Unprogressive) Bookshop

Charles Lahr was born Karl Lahr in 1885 in Bad Nauheim in the German Rhineland, the eldest of fifteen children in a peasant family.[8] As a young man in pre-war Germany, he became active in politics and committed himself to anarchism, a commitment he kept for the rest of his life. In 1905, he fled Germany to evade conscription into the Kaiser's army. He arrived in London in October and lived there until his death in 1971. He gave up his German citizenship and never became a British citizen, so he was legally stateless, and for this reason was fond of claiming that nobody owned him. Just before the First World War, he owned

---

    6   For a complete bibliography of Lahr's publications, see Goodway.

    7   Many writers describing their time in shop provide lists of names like this one. See, for example, Kenneth Hopkins, *Corruption of a Poet*, 112; and Rhys Davies, *Print of a Hare's Foot: An Autobiographical Beginning*, 111.

    8   Biographical information on Lahr comes from Goodway and from Sheila Lahr's autobiography, *Yealm*, http://www.militantesthetix.co.uk/yealm/CONTENTS.htm.

a small bookshop in Hammersmith, but this venture was interrupted by his first internment. For several years before and after the war, he also found work cycling between London barbershops collecting and returning razors. This work afforded him the opportunity of visiting bookshops and collecting and selling books. One of the shops he visited starting in 1919 was Harold Edwards's Progressive Bookshop at 68 Red Lion Street in Holborn.[9] Fortunately for Lahr, at this time he also met his wife, Esther Archer,[10] a Jewish factory worker from East London, who bought the Progressive Bookshop from Edwards for £25 in three instalments.[11] Due to Charles' poor or nonexistent bookkeeping, and to his generosity to struggling writers, the shop was always on the verge of bankruptcy; as Edwards recalls, what money he made was 'lost in his publications', for 'money was the last thing that had any interest for Charlie … What he enjoyed was the constant stream of writers and artists going in and out of the shop'.[12] He rarely made money from the sale of books either, for 'the kind of book that interested Charlie was always that of some obscure modern writer whom he thought to be good'.[13] Many of these writers were those who, with Lahr's help, went on to long and successful careers.

The progressive bookshop was not only a literary institution but also a clubhouse for intellectuals, politicians, and activists on the left, the shop being a port of call for such figures as R.M. Fox, F.A. Ridley, George Padmore, C.L.R. James, and many others. In an unpublished typescript written for David Goodway and titled 'Rogues, Scoundrels, and Liars', C.L.R. James writes that it is impossible for him to think about his 'intellectual formation in the 1930s without thinking of Lahr'. He explains that his

> introduction to Marxism and pretty rapidly [his] conviction that Stalin and the Stalinists were the greatest historical liars and political scoundrels whom [he] had ever read or heard of are entirely associated as far as an individual is concerned with Charlie, his bookshop, his pamphlets and his concern to get for [James] what he thought would be of use to [him].[14]

Lahr himself was well acquainted with the power and physical restrictions of the state. Aside from his first internment, he spent six months in prison for selling stolen books, and during the Second World War he was interned again. These last two imprisonments, Lahr thought, were motivated not simply by his criminal

---

[9]   Harold Edwards, 'Harold Edwards – A Revolutionary Youth', unpublished typescript, private papers of David Goodway, 6.

[10]   Archer was an Anglicisation of her maiden surname Argeband. According to David Goodway, Lahr claimed that they deliberately used the name Archer rather than Lahr because of anti-German sentiment in the aftermath of the Second World War. Later they used the name "E. Lahr' for the shop and some of its publications.

[11]   Edwards, 7.

[12]   Ibid. 8.

[13]   Ibid.

[14]   C.L.R. James, 'Rogues, Scoundrels, and Liars', an unpublished typescript written for David Goodway.

activities and German background but also by his anarchist beliefs.[15] Taken together, his anarchist, German, anti-establishment, and criminal identifications placed him on the economic and political margins of British life, and this seems to have been a position from which he was happy to operate. According to C.L.R. James, although Lahr did not belong to any political party, he 'was one of the most genuine political revolutionaries [he] ever knew'.[16] Lahr 'was not a distinct personality. He was just a well-built, good-looking man, always physically fit who knew what he wanted in life (egalitarian socialism if I may phrase it for him), a born fighter but one who accepted without moaning or regret the circumstances in which the modern world had put him'.[17] He 'did not carry himself well. He just carried himself, looking at you straight in the eyes, concerned about politics and yet, as much as any man I have known politically, with a never failing background of goodwill, good nature and an interest in your personal welfare'.[18]

While the spirit of the shop is largely associated with Lahr, it was originally the product of Esther Lahr's ambitions, and her removal puts into sharp contrast the experiences of other prominent women bookstore owners who helped produce and define modern literature. If Lahr's role in the history of book culture has been almost forgotten, then this is even more the case for Esther, who was removed from her place in literary history. When The Progressive Bookshop opened in 1921, it was, as mentioned above, purchased and operated by Esther, whose name, 'E. Archer', appeared on the letterhead and as publisher of many of the shop's books. Although Esther provided the original ambition and investment for the shop, she receded from its daily operations from 1927 onwards when she gave birth to the first of two daughters and moved into suburban exile in Muswell Hill. The shop's fate might have been different had it remained in the business-savvy and politically active hands of Esther. Before meeting Charles, she was a well-known open-air speaker, and she turned her ideals to practice when she organised

---

[15]   H.E. Bates's fictionalisation of Lahr's trial in the story 'No Country' depicts Lahr (renamed Oscar) claiming that he was set up in order to deport him because he was an alien and a known communist. The story highlights Lahr's statelessness, his certainty of political persecution, the narrator's dismissal by the judge as a 'literary man', and the court's ultimate indifference to communism, fascism, or any other political motive. Oscar is simply a man of no country falling into indifferent legal mechanisms. In a letter to Geoffrey West, however, Bates confides that he thinks that the affair was a 'frame-up ... with political reasons behind it and Charles was definitely afraid they would deport him'. H.E. Bates to G.H. West, 25 January 1931, G.H. West Papers, HRC. According to Lahr's daughter, Sheila Lahr, however, other booksellers had learned that Lahr was selling under the Net Book Agreement prices, and when Foyles discovered that their books were being stolen and sold by Lahr, they notified the authorities. Sheila Lahr, *Yealm*, http://www.militantesthetix. co.uk/yealm/ yealm7.htm.

[16]   C.L.R. James, 'Rogues, Scoundrels, and Liars', an unpublished typescript written for David Goodway.

[17]   Ibid.

[18]   Ibid.

the largely female workers of her workplace, the East End Rothman's cigarette factory, for the IWW.[19] Her movement into bookselling was another extension of her political commitments, as an early letter from the Irish nationalist and communist writer Liam O'Flaherty suggests:

Dear Comrade:

You didn't do too bad at all with the magazine [*The New Coterie*] and I should think if you keep up the standard you will make good ...

I am eagerly looking forward to my visit to London. I have a short play[20] which I will bring to show you. You might like to use it for the next number of *Coterie* and then issue it as a booklet. It would go very well. It's the best thing I've done. I like your idea immensely of getting things out in this manner. It's the only way to escape the public and make the bourgeoisie *pay*.[21]

In these early years of the shop, Esther was, at least as much as Charles, the 'middleman' publisher of *The New Coterie*.[22] The magazine cover, with its William Roberts image of jubilant mechanised workers, was also an announcement of *her* political and aesthetic commitments. Further, O'Flaherty's satisfaction in 'publishing in this manner' in order to 'escape the public and make the bourgeoisie *pay*' is an ambiguous statement that suggests slyly exploiting the bourgeois market for left and highbrow literature, which would set the tone for the kind of subversive and self-conscious publishing activities that increasingly characterised the shop's output. However we read this letter, it is clear that Esther was closely engaged in the alternative publishing activities of the shop, and she participated in its counter-cultural literary production. Her influence in the shop's operations is evident in much of the early archival material, which on the whole offers a much more professional air, with attractive advertisements and letterhead. Even in the later days of the shop's life, all instances of organisation, cataloguing, and financing were handled by Esther, if only in the less programmatic way that her reduced role allowed. Had she remained at the reins, she might have become a more prominent figure than Charles, perhaps taking her place alongside some of the great women making modernism of her time. Such a role seems to have been her ambition. An early letter (written on Progressive Bookshop letterhead) from Esther to Sylvia Beach demonstrates the kinds of connections and role to which Esther aspired:

---

19   Ken Weller, *'Don't be a Soldier!' The Radical Anti-War Movement in North London 1914–1918* (London: Journeyman, 1985), 67.

20   The play, 'Darkness, A Play in Three Acts', appeared in *The New Coterie* 3 (Summer 1926), 42–68.

21   Liam O'Flaherty to Esther Lahr, 2 February 1926, Liam O'Flaherty Papers, HRC.

22   The periodical was a revival of *The Coterie* and was edited by Paul Selver, T.W. Earp, and Russell Green.

Dear Miss Beach:

I have just received the copy of *Le Navire D'Argent* which you sent to the Editor of *The New Coterie*, which I am publishing. Could you send me 12 copies of the journal and I will send cash by return. Our first number is coming out early in November. I will send you some prospectuses as soon as they come from the printers, also a show-card, and a dozen copies of No 1 ... I called at your shop last year in August and I suppose you will remember me,

Yours sincerely,

(Miss) E. Archer[23]

At this stage of the shop's development, more than a year before her marriage and the birth of her first child, *Miss* Archer independently began to establish herself within the world of publishing and bookselling. Looking at the strangely bracketed title, (Miss), it is tempting to imagine that after writing the gender neutral 'E. Archer' she self-consciously revised her signature to announce herself to the publisher of *Ulysses* as a fellow bookwoman.

Unfortunately, Esther did not take her place in book history; instead, she ended up stifled in the Lahrs' Muswell Hill home. As her eldest daughter recalls in her autobiography, Esther's frustrated entrepreneurial and literary ambitions left her ill suited for domestic family life:

[I]n later years, when she no longer worked in the bookshop which was hers but which had become my father's, [she lamented] her isolation in this dull, conventional suburb. By then she was marooned, largely by poverty, at the edge of which we coped for the next few years because by the end of 1929 ... the book trade slumped. Later, it might have recovered, but in my father's unbusinesslike hands this became more and more unlikely.

When my mother was overcome by the pain of living, she screamed against the four walls between which she was trapped and her voice bounded off each wall and hit us, her children, buffeting us into corners, driving us from room to room. My father is never there to be caught in the desperate anger for he is a man who comes home for an evening meal only and to sleep.

Sometimes my mother ... blindfolds herself with a dark band as the only way to escape ... I sit on the edge of a chair, watching and listening to her, the tears running down my face, for I am convinced that this temporary blindness is permanent and that her maiming is mine also.[24]

---

23   Esther Archer to Sylvia Beach 12 October 1925, Maurice Saillet Collection of Sylvia Beach and Shakespeare and Company, Series II, Box 263.8, HRC.
24   Sheila Lahr, *Yealm*, http://www.militantesthetix.co.uk/yealm/CONTENTS.htm. This deeply affecting vision of Esther's frustrations is prefigured in William Roberts' portrait of her. William Roberts and Jacob Kramer were regular visitors to the Lahr home,

Despite this suffocating depiction of Esther's house-bound existence, it would be inaccurate to recall Esther solely as a defeated professional and political woman, for there is evidence of the high regard in which she was held, particularly when Lahr's six-month incarceration freed her back into the shop's daily affairs. Nevertheless, the sad irony is that Esther's experience was captured by the artists to whom her shop catered so well; while she sat at home minding children far from the traffic of Red Lion Street, Anna Wickham, for example, strode into the cramped space of the shop to talk literature and politics, the same Anna Wickham who had written in 1915 in a chapbook published by Harold Monro's Poetry Bookshop,

> Alas! for all the pretty women who marry dull men,
> Go into suburbs and never come out again,
> Who lose their pretty faces, and dim their pretty eyes,
> Because no one has courage or skill to organize.[25]

This promising labour organiser and businesswoman was removed from the bookshop that she began and that might never have had the influence that it did if not for her vision and her capital. This is a sobering reminder of the challenges faced and overcome by other women booksellers.

A Literary Rowton House

Launched by Esther's vision and carried by Charles's inspiring character and energy, the shop drew a wide array of agents in the field of literary production.[26] It was frequented daily by the sorts of people a young and struggling writer needed to meet, including editors, anthologists, reviewers, publishers, booksellers, collectors, publisher's readers, BBC writers, and literary scholars, and Lahr actively influenced the networks within this field. For instance, Lahr served as a patron to many writers, supporting them financially or supplying them income

---

and Roberts knew the Lahrs intimately. Roberts' treatment of Esther echoes her conflicted lives. The contrasting halves of her face show a dark and frustrated glare on the left side and a bright and open vision on the right. Kramer's head study sketch of Esther in *The New Coterie* 2 is also striking for its forceful features and closed eyes.

[25]   Anna Wickham. 'Meditation at Kew', *Contemplative Quarry* (London: The Poetry Bookshop, 1915), 14.

[26]   In this way, Lahr operates in terms of Pierre Bourdieu's conception of art as a manifestation a dynamic field of producers, which not only includes 'the direct producers of the work in its materiality (artist, writer, etc.) but also the producers of the meaning and value of the work – critics, publishers, gallery directors and the whole set of agents whose combined efforts produce consumers capable of knowing and recognizing the work of art as such … In short, it is a question of understanding works of art as a manifestation of the field as a whole, in which all the powers of the field, and all the determinisms inherent in its structure and functioning, are concentrated'. Pierre Bourdieu, *The Field of Cultural Production* (New York, Columbia University Press, 1993), 37.

through publishing their work or selling their manuscripts to collectors, most notably to the collector and millionaire head of Electric and Musical Industries (EMI), Sir Louis Sterling. The following letter is representative of many early letters from H.E. Bates before fame and success freed him from his dependency on Lahr:

> I detest writing you again, but could you forward a note on the MSS again? Things have been damned hard this summer, what with the stories not selling well and my having to work on the new novel to the exclusion of everything else. I promise to become famous one day and so repay you (if you still live!). Could you send something for the weekend? Cape owes me money, but he's tight-fisted.[27]

Here we see Lahr interacting within the intersecting interests of publishers dealing with authors, authors building their reputations and careers, and collectors speculating in those reputations, all navigating across a literary market determined by the relative values of short stories and novels in sales seasons. While in the simplest terms this letter shows Lahr providing financial assistance, he was engaged in a much wider field of influence and was able to exploit many connections with reviewers and other prominent figures in the publishing industry, as a letter from Rupert Croft-Cooke further illustrates:

> my new novel comes from Jarrolds on Friday. Will you, for the love of God, do all you can for it? I'm so terrified that it will be lost in the Autumn floods. I know that if you can find time to see and write to a few people you can make all the difference. You will, won't you? And make a bit of a show of it?[28]

Lahr also operated as a kind of informal agent or go-between for writers' business affairs, as he did when Gollancz was considering *Lady Chatterley's Lover*[29] or when Reginald Moore wrote to ask whether Lahr thought Modern Reading should publish a collection of Rhys Davies's stories.[30] Basically, Lahr was well positioned to materially affect the careers of writers and to contribute to the production, dissemination, and reception of literature.

And these more clearly 'institutional' roles associated with the physical production and dissemination of printed materials need to be further qualified by a much less tangible but arguably more pervasive and subtle influence. Davies's obituary suggests that Lahr's role depended just as much upon the bicycle as it did upon bookshop, upon a kind of mobility belied by the geographical fixity of the shop. As Kenneth Hopkins explains in his autobiography, *The Corruption of a Poet* (1954), '[n]ot only did Charles know everybody, but everybody knew

27   H.E. Bates to Charles Lahr, undated, Sterling Library, V36 i.
28   Rupert Croft-Cooke to Charles Lahr, undated, Sterling Library, MS985/1/6.
29   Russell Green to Charles Lahr, November 12 1928, Sterling Library, MS985/1/11.
30   Reginald Moore to Charles Lahr, undated, Sterling Library, MS895/1/18.

Charles, which is quite another thing'.[31] Hopkins suggests that even when Lahr was not directly involved in aiding specific individuals, he acted as a catalyst for the interactions of writers, publishers, critics, and booksellers; he was a principal agent through whom connections were made and careers were influenced. David Goodway reports Hugh MacDiarmid's assessment of Lahr's role in these same terms: 'Charlie had an infectious love of life, an irrepressible gaiety, and a deep rooting in a sardonic contempt for all conventional values, all "received" opinions; and he was therefore a splendid catalyst of all sorts and all conditions of men and women'. As a result, he could 'rescue them from stodgy influences elsewhere'. He kept 'abreast of things', possessing 'the capacity to take a lively interest in all that was going on', and hence was able to draw a wide range of people together who, in turn, interacted creatively with one another'.[32]

All of the recorded memories of the shop describe the shop's nodal institutional role in similar terms. R.M. Fox remembers it as a 'rendezvous for rebels and world shakers with an interest in books and ideas'.[33] Rupert Croft-Cooke describes it as a 'literary Rowton House' to which 'most writers of the years between the wars, owe ... a great debt'.[34] Walter Allen, author and friend of the Auden group, describes the shop as 'a resort for rebels and eccentrics' and recalls that it seemed to have 'existed as a place for the exchange of literary news and gossip of a not quite orthodox kind'.[35] John Taylor Caldwell, assistant and secretary to Guy Aldred, claims that the shop was 'visited at some time or other by all radical visitors to London'.[36] As these reports make clear, until it was bombed out of existence in the Blitz, The Progressive Bookshop was a prominent left literary salon in London between the wars.

Counter Space in The Progressive Bookshop

Under Lahr's influence, the shop developed a distinct character, and much of the material effects of his work depended upon the production of a space that facilitated this informal literary institution and that drew an eclectic crowd. In the photographic images of Lahr that survive, we can see him standing in front of his shops, or bending over the bargain bins on the streets in front of other bookshops. This record preserves his role as one that partly operates in the space where the shop spills out upon and merges with the public thoroughfare. We can

---

[31]   Kenneth Hopkins, *The Corruption of a Poet* (London: James Barrie, 1954), 112.

[32]   Goodway, 51.

[33]   R.M. Fox, *Smokey Crusade* (London: Hogarth Press, 1938), 180.

[34]   Rupert Croft-Cooke, *The Numbers Came* (London: Putnam, 1963), 131.

[35]   Walter Allen, *As I Walked Down New Grub Street* (London: Heinemann, 1981), 105–06.

[36]   John Taylor Caldwell, *Come Dungeons Dark: The Life and Times of Guy Aldred* (Glasgow: Anarchist, Luath Press, Barr, 1988), 62.

think of bookshops as 'interstitial spaces' or 'third spaces',[37] as Ray Oldenberg defines them. These spaces straddle the worlds of public and private, creating spaces of sociability that can potentially transform public transactions. In this way, they echo Walter Benjamin's reflection that he made his 'most memorable book purchases on trips, as a transient', and that 'cities revealed themselves to [him] in the marches [he] undertook in the pursuit of books!'[38] His library and his collection of printed memories merge with the streets and blur the public and private realms in the moving life of the city. Bookshops fuse the private act of reading with the public act of consumption and sociability where the public commercial display and imaginative and intellectual activities merge. Part of their potency is in their openness and the consequent inclusiveness that brings diverse people together in new and unexpected ways. As mentioned, Lahr's institutional role was an informal one, and many of the connections between his patrons were of the most casual kind. This reminds us that we are not always or necessarily dealing with the systematic or organised creation of a coherent literary coterie or body of literature but with the often incidental friendships and associations that make up a literary culture.

When we think of the bookshop as a social and lived space, we acknowledge that these spatial interactions take shape within the often competing claims of culture, politics, and the market. Henri Lefebvre identifies one of the principle forms of space in which we live as the 'dominant form of space, that of the centres of wealth and power, [which] endeavours to mould the spaces that it dominates'.[39] It is a space, for instance, that normalises capitalist exchange, division of labour, bureaucratic impenetrability, patriarchal power, the primacy of the nuclear family, and so forth. However, this dominant space always houses counter-spaces and contradictory spaces, spaces that highjack dominant spaces and repurpose them into leisure or liberating ones. In doing so, they question or change the nature of that dominant space. As Laura Miller has argued, bookshops often operate in this way. As merchants of culture, as economic agents who transform an economic exchange into an intellectual or political activity in excess of the immediate act of commercial exchange, booksellers fashion spaces that

---

[37]   Ray Oldenburg, *The Great Good Place* (New York: Paragon House: 1991); the connection between third spaces and bookshops is discussed in Audrey Lang and Jo Royle, 'Bookselling Culture and Consumer Behaviour', *The Future of the Book in the Digital Age*, ed. Bill Cope and Angus Phillips (Oxford: Chandos Publishing, 2006), 115–34; see also Laura Miller, 'Shopping for Community: The Transformation of the Bookstore into a Vital Community Institution', *Media, Culture & Society* (May 1999), 21 (3), 385–407, for a discussion of the bookstore as a space of community within a commercial context.

[38]   Walter Benjamin, 'Unpacking My Library', *Illuminations*, ed. Hannah Arendt (New York: Schocken Books, 1968), 63.

[39]   Henri Lefebvre, *The Production of Space*, trans. Donald Nicholson-Smith (Malden, MA: Blackwell, 1991), 49.

implicitly revise dominant commercial activity.[40] As a social space and a lived space, The Progressive Bookshop revises the dominant commercial space of the city, offering an alternative literary community and shadow economy for aspiring and professionalising authors. In this way, the shop is a counter-space, revising the imperatives of commercial exchange supposedly defining the bookshop.

Bookshops can be excessive, impractical, and distinctive in ways that few other commercial spaces can. Kenneth Hopkins, who lived in Lahr's spare room above the shop between May 1938 and July 1939,[41] provides one representative description of The Progressive Bookshop that captures this particularly eclectic commercial space:

> The shop was about ten feet by twelve, and the front wall was all window. The door was at the side opening not into the street but into the passage. As the window was lined floor to ceiling with books, and had also a screen at the back, practically no light penetrated into the shop. The walls were lined with books, and in the middle was a gas radiator over which a rickety arrangement of shelves supported, precariously, great piles of periodicals, books, pamphlets, a typewriter, string, about two-thirds of a loaf, several pipes and various oddments of indiarubber, cheese, carbon paper, matches and pipe dottles. These last were close to the radiator, drying for future consumption.
>
> With one thing or another occupying the floor space, little remained save a rectangular area with a slight depression at the back in which [Lahr's] chair was established. The clear space was a bit larger than the top of a dining table, and provided standing space for about four people at a time.[42]

The shop was dirty, dusty, eclectic, and, above all, small. The cramped nature of the space is the common detail remembered by those who visited The Progressive Bookshop, and this feature, more than any other, enabled the intense interaction for which it has become known. Lahr's shop had none of the 'large, comfortable paneled rooms'[43] that Osbert Sitwell remembers above The Poetry Bookshop, nor was there room for the Serbian rugs and antique furniture of Shakespeare and Company.[44] Here people from all spheres of the literary world were literally forced

---

[40]   Laura Miller, *Reluctant Capitalists: Bookselling and the Culture of Consumption* (Chicago: University of Chicago Press, 2006), 214–20.

[41]   His letters to John Cowper Powys in the Harry Ransom Center bear Lahr's address during this period. The first one in part reads, 'I love Lahr; he's a fine chap. My room – a room of my own! – over his shop – is lined with books; it has a bed, a table, a chair or two, gas fire and a light, all for 5/- a week; and no extras, and no questions if a bring a friend in!!' Kenneth Hopkins to John Cowper Powys, undated, Kenneth Hopkins Papers, Box 51, HRC.

[42]   Hopkins, 99–100.

[43]   Joy Grant, *Harold Monro and the Poetry Bookshop* (Berkeley: University of California Press, 1967), 3.

[44]   Noel Riley Fitch, *Sylvia Beach and the Lost Generation: A History of Literary Paris in the Twenties and Thirties* (New York: Norton, 1985), 42.

into interaction with one another. H.E. Bates recalls the shop as 'little more than a cubicle, about 12 feet by 8 feet, its walls lined with books, paintings and drawings from ceiling to floor'.[45] Although 'never capable seemingly of holding more than six people, [the shop] always seemed to be populated by a couple of dozen, with more chatting and lounging away in the passage outside'.[46] The social world that Bates recalls emerges as a casual, eclectic, informal, and levelling interstitial space. There

> were men and women from all walks of life: poets, novelists, artists, solicitors, schoolmasters, businessmen, book collectors in search of first editions or autographed copies, journalists and editors. It would take far too long to name even a fraction of the persons of small or considerable eminence who foregathered there; but among artists was Pearl Binder ... and William Roberts; and among writers Rhys Davies, O'Flaherty, T.F. Powys, Nancy Cunard, Rupert Croft Cooke, Malachi Whitaker and a host of others.[47]

These descriptions are confirmed by the report of Lahr's younger daughter, Oonagh, who recalls that the shop held four people with 'two more in the passageway between it and the next shop, and three or so lurking and chatting on the pavement where the books in the front window and stacked in front did not impede conversation'.[48] The shop was cramped, yet uncontained, paradoxically confining and liberating at the same time: physically confining yet socially liberating. It was just as much (or more) a lived social space as it was a commercial one where, as Walter Allen recalls, 'Books were bought and sold', but 'in an as it were absent-minded way',[49] for, as Hopkins tells us, the 'habitués of Lahr's shop were called customers only as a courtesy, for it really functioned more as a club'.[50]

So, by all accounts, the shop was never primarily a commercial space but a communal and even anti-commercial one set against the mouthpieces and authorities of official literature. As such, it catered to a bohemian crowd of artists whose virtue was the neglect they suffered. The Progressive Bookshop crowd, Rupert Croft-Cooke writes,

> never expected, as writers or artists, to be anything but poor unless they hit the jackpot in their own profession. They were threadbare, ill-shod and unshaven, not in the abominably affected manner of today [1960s] but because they had not the money to buy clothes and shoes, or, very often, razor blades. Naturally enough, success was unforgivable even to contributors of the *New Coterie* so

---

[45]   H.E. Bates, *The Blossoming World: An Autobiography*, vol. 2. (London: Michael Joseph, 1971), 52.

[46]   Ibid., 53.

[47]   Ibid.

[48]   Oonagh Lahr, personal correspondence with the author, January 2006.

[49]   Allen, 106.

[50]   Hopkins, 108.

that H.E. Bates was already looked upon with suspicion. Established writers were unmentionable except with contempt.[51]

The shop was a tiny but vibrant space. It was eclectic, levelling, and bohemian, operating in a strained relationship to a market that many of its literary professional patrons depended upon, resented, and worshipped.

Anti-Marketing in The Progressive Bookshop

Lahr consciously cultivated the culture and community of his shop through various anti-marketing activities that playfully manipulated print culture in and around the shop. For George Woodcock, the anti-establishment benevolent misrule of The Progressive Bookshop was publically announced in Lahr's penchant for creating mock news stories on street placards from pasting headlines into odd arrangements, such as 'Professor Joad's Daughter Elopes with Pope',[52] 'Hitler punches the Pope', 'Mussolini 100 not out', 'Mr. Chamberlain on "The Hollywood I Love"', and 'Stalin Kisses Trotsky'.[53] According to Woodcock, these posters were not merely 'jests for [Lahr's] own delight, [… for] his celebrated posters also served to attract the customers he preferred, the kind who made his bookshop one of the recognized gathering places of writers during the years between the Great Wars'.[54] With these headlines, Lahr manipulated print media to announce the sort of community he sought and cultivated the intellectual space of The Progressive Bookshop.

The potential disruptiveness of Lahr's anti-marketing is represented in John Lindsey's fictional account of Lahr in his novel *Vicarage Party* (1933), which replicates the many biographical accounts of Lahr and the shop and which portrays Lahr's antibourgeois, anti-establishment, and anti-capitalist methods. In the novel, the store is approached by a Vicar looking for the kind of book that Orwell, echoing sexist dismissals of mass culture, describes in 'Bookshop Memories' as 'the average novel – the ordinary, good-bad, Galsworthy-and-water stuff which is the norm of the English novel [and which] seems to exist only for women'.[55] In the shop window, the Vicar perceives that the shop 'was most untidy. The books were arranged anyhow'.[56] As for the clientele, 'Everyone in or near the shop was talking. People kept appearing and taking a book away'.[57] When the Vicar tries to intercept the proprietor, a 'man with a beard [who] kept rushing in and out of the

---

[51]   Croft-Cooke, 156–57.

[52]   George Woodcock, *Letter to the Past* (London: Fitzhenry & Whiteside, 1982), 176.

[53]   Hopkins, 100.

[54]   Woodcock, 176–77.

[55]   George Orwell, 'Bookshop Memories', *Facing Unpleasant Facts* (New York: Mariner Books, 2009), 40.

[56]   John Lindsey, *Vicarage Party* (London: Chapman and Hall, 1933), 214.

[57]   Ibid., 214.

shop carrying piles of books', the proprietor mutters, 'For Christ's sake, get out of the way!'[58] The Vicar reassures himself:

> He'd come to buy Galsworthy and that was more than most of these people seemed to be doing, standing about with their hands in their pockets, gossiping, slandering people and suddenly running over the road to the public house opposite.
> He'd come to buy Galsworthy. He was a customer. They'd treat him with respect when they knew that: the same respect they did at Bumpus', where he had an account.[59]

The Vicar's faith in the respectability ensured by a mutual worship of commercial exchange is, of course, not shared by the proprietor of the shop. The key moment of shock and displacement occurs while the Vicar waits for the proprietor to return and examines a book whose jacket displays a review by the Bishop of Brighton: 'Just the book Christian men and women have been waiting for, for so long'.[60] On opening the covers, however, he discovers a book on birth control titled 'What Every Wife Should Know'. The dust-jacket has been switched, but the Vicar does not get the joke, and he wonders if there is some mistake; he even experiences a small religious crisis: 'The Bishop of Brighton did not believe in Birth Control, did he?'[61] This fictional subversion of the book's paratextual elements upsets expectations concerning the coherence and consistency of book production and unsettles the Vicar's pious confidence in Bishops and Bumpuses. It is similar in nature to Lahr's subversion of newspaper headlines and is generally illustrative of Lahr's anarchist attack on conventional pieties and the forms of print that sustain them.

These subversive printing practices are most evident in Lahr's Christmas cards. Designed and printed by Herbert Jones, they contained irreverent seasonal poems written by the Progressive Bookshop coterie. Christmas was and still is an important time for bookshop sales, and Christmas cards were staples of the trade.[62] Orwell's recollection of Christmas marketing in the bookstores is indicative of the commercial culture that Lahr's cards parodied:

> At Christmas time we spent a feverish ten days struggling with Christmas cards and calendars, which are tiresome things to sell but good business while the season lasts. It used to interest me to see the brutal cynicism with which Christian sentiment is exploited. The touts from the Christmas card firms used

---

[58]   Ibid.

[59]   Ibid.

[60]   Ibid., 215.

[61]   Ibid., 216.

[62]   For example, Charles B. Anderson and G. Roysce Smith, eds, *The American Bookseller's Association's Manual on Bookselling: How to Open and Run Your Own Bookstore* (New York: Harmony Books, 1974) includes chapters on 'Greeting Cards' and 'Personalized Christmas Cards'.

to come round with their catalogues as early as June. A phrase from one of their invoices sticks in my memory. It was: '2 doz. Infant Jesus with rabbits'.[63]

Lahr's Christmas cards exploit this spirit of 'brutal cynicism'. For example, in 'A Christmas Sermon', Arnold Wareham's speaker listens to a sermon on 'Humility' and sits 'ashamed [he] could not hurl him down / And whip him naked through the town'. He ends proclaiming,

> Oh! much too cheaply sold
> Was Judas' merchandise. For now "tis gold
> That mass-betrayal earns the unctuous knaves
> Who preach submissiveness to slaves!

John Brophy's 'Epitaph, On Two Parents of the Old School' describes two parents who 'brought up their children wisely and well / In the fear of their parents, the Empire, and hell'. In patriotic spirit, they sent their sons to die in the Great War, and then 'happy in War Loan and comfort and pride, / Albert and Martha slept, ate, and died'. The whole set of cards announced Lahr's refusal to profit from one of the book trade's seasonal staples and expose the hypocrisy of commercial culture.[64] One can almost imagine Lindsey's Vicar picking up one of Lahr's cards and purchasing it in his devotion to the sanctity of commerce.

Lahr's mock headlines, his resistance to mainstream marketing, and his various printed materials intervene in the print culture of advertisement and mass-circulation publication to market his shop as a kind of (anti)establishment for writers on the fringes of the literary marketplace and whose work sought to unsettle what they regarded as a bourgeois complacency. This resistance, however, was not as simple as it might have appeared on the surface. As a closer look at the some of the publishing activities of the Progressive Bookshop community demonstrates, Lahr was engaged in a complex manipulation of book production as a manifestation of competing interests across questions of class, readerships, literary markets, and obscenity.

Publishing *The German Prisoner*: Materialising Networks

In March 1930, Eric Partridge wrote to Lahr to introduce him to James Hanley, the working-class author who would soon become the subject of controversy for his sexualised novel of working-class alienation, *Boy*. The letter provides another illustration of Lahr's influence, and it marked the beginning of a relationship that led to Lahr's publication of Hanley's short story *The German Prisoner*, a

---

[63]   Orwell, 40.

[64]   Regardless, the cards did apparently sell well, as a letter from Eimar O'Duffy indicates. Eimar O'Duffy to Charles Lahr, undated but written on O'Duffy's 1931 Blue Moon Christmas Card, uncatalogued Charles Lahr Material, HRC.

limited edition book that materialises the literary and political networks of The Progressive Bookshop:

> James Hanley, the author of *Drift* (first edition exhausted on publication; I want you to read this book), has come to London looking for a job, either with a publisher as reader or anywhere as a general office help or even as a manual worker. If you know of anything at Chatto and Windus or elsewhere for him, I'd be grateful.
>
> I do suggest, also, that you ask him to submit to you three or four stories with a view to inclusion in 'The Blue Moon Booklets'; he is thoroughly worthwhile. I hope to publish one of his stories in *The Window* in July, but you might be able to do something with some story of his before that date. Drop me a line to tell me if I may say to him: 'Send some stories along to Lahr', or 'Go and meet Lahr'.[65]

Not only did Hanley meet Lahr but also he lived in Lahr's home for several months where he wrote *The German Prisoner*, which was published not as a Blue Moon Booklet but as a limited edition from Lahr's Muswell Hill address. In this story, two animalised working-class soldiers from Manchester and Dublin get lost in the fog of a First World War wasteland. The surreal dehumanising dislocation of their experience is interrupted when a beautiful young German soldier stumbles across them. This aestheticised figure becomes the focus of their confusion, rage, and victimisation, leading them to beat, sodomize, and kill him. They subsequently beat each other to near death before a stray shell finishes them off. In Lahr, Hanley found one of the few publishers willing to take on such sexually violent and controversial material, and the story of its publication places Lahr in the matrices of obscenity, art, censorship, and the market.

In keeping with Lahr's anti-bourgeois counter-space, much of his publishing activities engaged with the censorship of literature and sometimes involved publishing potentially 'obscene' literature, as was the case with Hanley's *The German Prisoner*. In the late 1920s and early 1930s, Lahr published a number of works that drew the attention of the censors or that that flirted with or challenged the definitions of obscenity. In 1928, for example, during Home Secretary Joynson-Hicks's anti-Lawrence campaign, Lahr corresponded with Lawrence and began a relationship that included distributing 112 copies of the second edition of *Lady Chatterley's Lover*, publishing an unexpurgated authorised limited edition of *Pansies*, and negotiating and eventually publishing, covertly, a posthumous third edition of *Lady Chatterley's Lover* in London.[66] Two of Lahr's Blue Moon Booklets

---

[65]   Eric Partridge to Charles Lahr, 25 March 1930, James Hanley Papers, Box 3.7, HRC.

[66]   Craig Monro, 'Lady Chatterley in London: The Secret Third Edition', *D.H. Lawrence's 'Lady': A New Look at Lady Chatterley's Lover*, ed. Michael Squires and Dennis Jackson (Athens: University of Georgia Press, 1986), 222–35; Christopher Pollnitz, 'The Censorship and Transmission of D.H. Lawrence's Pansies: The Home Office and the 'Foul-Mouthed Fellow', *Journal of Modern Literature* 28.3 (2005), 44–71.

also addressed this repressive literary context. Richard Aldington's *Balls and Another Book for Suppression* (1930) parodies the moral invective of the literary police: 'Once more I raise my voice in protest, with the belief that the immense public which applauds all my utterances will eventually force the authorities to take action and suppress all books not approved by me and my family'.[67] The book that offends him in this essay is a recent publication of Shakespeare's *Songs*. Similarly, John Arrow's *J.C. Squire v. D.H. Lawrence* (1930) offers a direct reply to Squire's article in *The Observer* of 9 March 1930. In this essay, Arrow claims that Squire's success and the 'honorable niche he now occupies' has turned him into a missionary who, unlike Lawrence, obscenely capitulates to the market in his call for the censorship of Lawrence's paintings.[68] By the time Lahr published Hanley's *The German Prisoner*, therefore, he was intimately engaged in publishing, printing, and bookselling practices that directly thwarted the suppression of literature. The homoerotic violence of this story clearly engages the limits of the obscene in ways that Lahr could not help but be aware of.

Not surprisingly, much of Lahr's publishing took the form of limited and special editions written by the shop's regulars. This is particularly significant for a story like *The German Prisoner*, which pushes the limits of the obscene and, therefore, engages the limited and special edition's ambiguous relationship to the both the artisanal literary market, on the one hand, and the sale of salacious material, on the other. Lahr's engagement with potentially obscene materials made him well versed in such matters, and he was no doubt conscious of the inextricable commercial, moral, and aesthetic implications of limited edition publication. His experiences publishing Lawrence is evidence enough, but he was still at it in the late 1930s. When Kenneth Hopkins was living at the shop, Lahr persuaded Hopkins to offer his *Progress of Love*, a 'naughty work',[69] to one of the most prestigious limited edition presses, the Golden Cockerel Press, which had published several writers of the Progressive Bookshop crowd.[70] However, as Hopkins put it, the press 'expressed ... their fear and terror of the law whose wrath not to incur they have declined'.[71] Lahr encouraged Hopkins to take advantage of the limited edition market in the knowledge of the limited special edition as potential outlet for sexually explicit material.

As is well established, the principal reason that the special edition was exploited as a means of evading the attention of the censors is because it ostensibly markets

---

[67] Richard Aldington, *Balls and Another Book for Suppression* (London: E. Lahr, 1931), 9.

[68] John Arrow, *J.C. Squire v. D.H. Lawrence: A reply to Mr Squire's article in 'The Observer' of March 9th, 1930* (London: E. Lahr, 1930), 10.

[69] Kenneth Hopkins to T.F. Powys, 28 April 1938, Kenneth Hopkins Papers, Box 51.38, HRC.

[70] Gay Taylor, one of the original founders of The Golden Cockerel Press, was a Progressive Bookshop regular.

[71] Kenneth Hopkins to J.C. Powys, 14 May, 1938, Kenneth Hopkins Papers, Box 51.38, HRC.

itself to an elite audience. By virtue of their cost and high quality, such books, it was argued, were not intended to corrupt those regarded as most susceptible to their salacious influences (women and the working classes). The Golden Cockerel Press, for example, defined itself in precisely these anti-commercial terms. It was established, as they claim in their first prospectus, in the belief of 'the inadequacy of the commercial system of publishing ... as the vehicle of the intelligent and artistic expression of the time'.[72] They eliminate 'the profit-making middlemen and directorate which in the commercial system come between author and working printer, the inventor of the book and its maker'.[73] As such, the Golden Cockerel Press believes that a good piece of work has its 'natural public'.[74] It is a more pure form of publication, disassociated from the corrupting influence of the market, unprostituted and, therefore, incapable of offering sex for sale.

This commercial purity, further, ostensibly proved the artistic legitimacy of the authors against a more generally corrupting literary mass market, a notion that many of the Progressive Bookshop crowd exploited. In an undated[75] manuscript of an article on book collecting entitled 'The Nose', Rhys Davies (who published seven special editions with Lahr and others) speaks of special editions in very high terms: 'In a world where the cinema, the two-penny lending library, tinned music and hysterical newspapers are becoming ever more popular, it is a relief to come across a leisurely designed book produced in the tradition, more or less, in the illuminated missals of old'.[76] Davies here regards the special edition as an escape from the degradations of a mass market. However, even here, the professional author slips through when Davies acknowledges that the collection of limited editions is 'entirely a business proposition' in as far as we 'all live by profit', and he praises book collectors for they each do as much for the author as 100 lending-library borrowers.[77] For the most part, however, Davies conceives of the special edition as functioning in a realm beyond the taste of the popular consumption of newspapers, popular music, lending libraries, and the cinema, conferring upon their authors their proper dues as artists.

---

[72]   Desmond Chute, 'The Golden Cockerel Press', First Prospectus. in *Cock-a-Hoop: A Bibliography of The Golden Cockerel Press. January 1950–1961 December with a list of the prospectuses 1921–1962. Compiled by Christopher Sandford and David Chambers* (Middlesex: Golden Cockerel Press, 1963), 57.

[73]   Ibid., 58.

[74]   Ibid., 58.

[75]   This article was probably written in 1935 for Gilbert Fabes, the Rare Book Manager of Foyles Bookshop and a regular of the Progressive Bookshop who wrote one of Lahr's Christmas cards. In 1935, Davies wrote to Fabes agreeing to contribute to Fabes's 'Symposium': 'Shall be glad to make a contribution to the Symposium. Hope to be able to cast some light on book-collecting'. Rhys Davies to Gilbert Fabes, 21 October 1935, Rhys Davies Papers, Box 8.8, HRC.

[76]   Rhys Davies, 'The Nose', Rhys Davies Papers, Box 5.5, HRC.

[77]   Ibid.

Of course, Davies was not unequivocal about the special edition. The context in which he wrote an essay on book collecting, was not the context in which he wrote to a *TLS* reviewer. When writing to G.H. West of his Golden Cockerel Press special edition, Davies is dismissive: 'I've just had a book of four stories taken by the Golden Cockerel Press: a limited edition at 21s. I become more expensive every year! A pity my own financial state doesn't increase accordingly'.[78] Similarly, when he wrote West to 'tout' for a review of his special edition *The Skull* (1936), he admitted to the pomp of such ventures: 'He's [Vincent Stuart] made rather a handsome job of the book, though of course from our "literary" point of view a short-story all decked up and costing 25/- seems unnecessary, [though] I suppose something can be said for the labour of a genuine craftsman, as this young man seems to be'.[79] Suddenly, when talking to West from this purely 'literary' point of view – from the discourse of criticism rather than of collecting – the elaborate production of a limited edition is an unnecessary intervention between the writer's work and its consumption.

These contradictory perceptions of limited editions derive from the fact that these books offered a form of publication for writers who, like many assisted by Lahr, had not yet broken into the mainstream metropolitan publishing industry. The limited edition established writers' artistic credentials and marketed their value to the very mainstream publishing industry that had so far rejected them. It is a literary commodity that secures its place in the market by denying the market, defining, as Lawrence Rainey argues, 'a kind of productive space insulated from the harsh exigencies of the larger marketplace'.[80] By bypassing 'a broad public receptive to standardized products (such as the six-shilling novel) and suspicious of novelty', it addressed a minority readership looking for the distinction of products that signalled 'an essentially precapitalist economic structure, an artisanal economy producing luxury goods in limited quantities for aristocratic consumption'.[81] By the time Lahr was publishing limited editions, they were well established as a normative mechanism in establishing a writer's artistic credentials in mainstream publishing.[82] Lahr, therefore, worked within the common Modernist paradox that John Fordham applies to Lahr's community in his study of James Hanley. The shop 'embraced milieux as diverse as the metropolitan artistic avant-garde, the privileged circles of metropolitan publishing and bookselling, and the extensive network of political comradeship'.[83] It published radical pamphlets, little magazines, and expensive special editions, and Lahr's 'alternative publishing strategies placed him at the metaphorical centre of the continuing modernist

---

[78]   Rhys Davies to G.H. West, 9 May 1932, Rhys Davies Papers, Box 1.4, HRC.

[79]   Rhys Davies to G.H. West, 13 July 1936, Rhys Davies Papers, Box 1.4, HRC.

[80]   Lawrence Rainey. *Institutions of Modernism: Literary Elites and Public Culture* (New Haven: Yale University Press, 1998), 100.

[81]   Ibid., 101.

[82]   Ibid.

[83]   John Fordham, *James Hanley: Modernism and the Working Class* (Cardiff: University of Wales Press, 2002), 93.

dilemma, since he aided and encouraged those writers who displayed [an] ... anti-bourgeois outspokenness and integrity ... , yet employed those very means which guaranteed the institutional status quo – the fetishisation of the work of art as commodity'.[84] This conflict is played out in Lahr's publishing activities, which materialise the aesthetic, political, and commercial matrices negotiated within the shop's community.

In producing *The German Prisoner* as a limited edition, Lahr could be said to be operating in an anarchist opposition to consumer culture, but one could also argue that he was marketing very carefully within that consumer culture. We might further argue that by dealing in potentially obscene material in the form of a special edition, he both crassly flaunted obscenity and sought to evade the attention of the censors.[85] In Lahr's publication of *The German Prisoner*, we have a working-class story marketed in the non-commercial distinction of the luxury book where art and pornography and the class associations of each overlap. It is a complex and unsettling book, which seems quite at home alongside Lahr's other disruptive printing activities.

A sense of the marketing and reception of *The German Prisoner* is gleaned from the marketing and reception of the Furnival Books, a series that was not only published at the same time, but which shared an almost identical bibliographic resemblance to *The German Prisoner* and which was also entirely a Progressive Bookshop community affair. The publisher, Alan Steele,[86] was a regular at the shop, the series editor was H.E. Bates, and the contributors are a collection of Progressive Bookshop patrons and correspondents, including Rhys Davies, Liam O'Flaherty, T.F Powys, and Hanley. Hanley was informed of the Furnival series by Lahr,[87] and his contribution, *The Last Voyage*, is not only dedicated to Lahr's daughter, Oonagh, but, like *The German Prisoner*, is introduced by Richard Aldington. One can almost imagine the series' birth during a chat in Lahr's shop, and one can regard *The German Prisoner*'s publication as replicating this simultaneous publishing endeavour. Indeed, Bates' letters to Steele during the

---

[84]   Ibid., 94.

[85]   Two articles offer useful insights in reading the book along these lines: Margaret Stetz 'Sex, Lies, and Printed Cloth: Bookselling at the Bodley Head in the Eighteen-Nineties', *Victorian Studies: A Journal of the Humanities, Arts and Sciences* 35.1 (1991), 71–86; and Rachel Potter, 'Obscene Modernism and the Sale in Salacious Books', *Modernism/Modernity* 16.1 (2009), 87–104.

[86]   Alan Steele began his career with W.H. Smith and ran the Macfarlane & Steele chain of bookshops in Sussex. He joined Frederick C. Joiner as co-director of wholesalers William Jackson (Books) Ltd in 1927. Joiner and Steele dabbled in pornography and traded and transported such banned books as D.H. Lawrence's *Lady Chatterley's Lover* and *Pansies*, and James Joyce's *Ulysses*. Steele was largely in charge of their publishing imprint, Joiner & Steele. F.A. Mumby and Ian Norris, *Publishing and Bookselling*, revised edition (London: Jonathan Cape, 1974), 370–71.

[87]   Letter from James Hanley to Alan Steele, 25 May 1930, Cambridge University Archives, Add. 8698/H50.

publication of the series are peppered with references to Lahr, and Lahr brokered the inclusion of T.F. Powys's story in the series,[88] all while Hanley was living in Lahr's Muswell Hill home and writing *The German Prisoner*.[89]

Joiner & Steele advertised the Furnival Books with the claim that 'they will enable the man with a slender purse to possess a set of books that will include work by some of the best short-story writers and artists of the day and, at the same time, be finely printed and bound'.[90] They claimed, therefore, that they wished to bring the more specialised book to a wider reading public: to bridge the gap between the special edition market and the mass market, yet they maximised on the associations of rarity with quality by limiting the edition to 550 copies, fifty of which were not for sale. The price, each book sold for 10s 6d, was certainly at the low end of a special edition, which generally went as high as 25s, or up to 40s for *Pansies* and 4£ for the special edition of *Lady Chatterley's Lover*;[91] however, low as the price is, it still suggests greater respectability in being half a guinea: an affordable prestige. The form, price, and advertising of the Furnival books marketed highbrow authenticity to middlebrow pocketbooks, blurring the line between aesthetic distinction and commercial exploitation.

The correspondence between Bates and A.E. Coppard highlights the Progressive Bookshop community's awareness of this conflict.[92] In response to Coppard's resistance to being published in a series that favoured collectors in search of a commodity over readers in search of literature, Bates agrees that there is 'something like a vicious principle behind it all, and the thought of one's labours reposing on collector's shelves like mere stocks and bonds awaiting a rise in the market is utterly damnable'.[93] He goes on to agree with Coppard's preference for

---

[88]   Letter from T.F. Powys to Charles Lahr, 22 April 1929, Box 18 HRC; Letter from T.F. Powys to Charles Lahr, 22 April 1931, T.F. Powys Papers, Box 18, HRC.

[89]   The printer of *The German Prisoner* is not identified, but based on the similarities; it is tempting to assume that Lahr used the same printers used for the Furnival series, which was the Chiswick Press.

[90]   Qtd in 'Furnival Books', Review of *Key of the Field* by T.F. Powys, *The Hessian Prisoner* by H.E. Bates, *The Man From Kilsheelan* by Liam O'Flaherty, and *The Stars, The World and the Women* by Rhys Davies, *Times Literary Supplement*, 27 March 1930, 268.

[91]   John Worthen, *D.H. Lawrence: The Life of an Outsider* (London: Allen Lane, 2005), 119.

[92]   Another excellent illustration of the Progressive Bookshop community's obsessive sensitivity to the complexities, opportunities, and hypocrisies of the various literary markets of the time is illustrated by Herbert E. Palmer's Blue Moon Booklet *What the Public Wants* (1931), a short story about a writer, Jabez Williams, who desperately adopts different styles and genres in various publishing media, vainly trying to establish a literary career. At one point, the imagist allusions of his name (Ezra Pound and William Carlos Williams) become clear as he composes a 'loose kind of rhymeless poem in praise of China and Japan', which 'Lord Beaverbrook's most enthusiastic readers' condemn as 'an attack on Empire Free Trade'. At another point, Jabez proposes *A Magazine for Authors, Critics and Reviewers*, the aim of which 'would exist mainly in the interest of the reviewer'.

[93]   H.E. Bates to A.E. Coppard, 19 June 1929, A.E. Coppard Papers, Box 32.5, HRC.

'readers rather than investors' but assures him that the retention of copyright for future publication in magazine and book form 'opens up the probability of not fewer readers for you but a great many more'.[94] A few days later, Coppard's more commercial concerns become clear in Bates' continued solicitation:

> Even if you refuse, however, I think you might like to know something of what Jackson's [who are also wholesalers] have been doing for you during a good many years. No one has – in the bookselling world, at any rate – more faith in your work than they have had: what's more, they've expressed this in a practical way by taking more of your work than any other firm in London. For *Silver Circus* alone they subscribed some hundreds before publication. You can't sniff at that – and they also have asked me to point out to you the double benefit which is bound to come from this new series of theirs, for they mean to place orders at once for the previous works of all who are contributing'.[95]

The Furnival series appears here as a wholesaler-cum-publisher's advertising campaign to sell larger quantities of mainstream publication books. Coppard agreed to contribute to the series.

Similarly, Liam O'Flaherty's introduction to Rhys Davies's contribution to the Furnival series, *The Stars, The World, and The Women*, is the perfect articulation of that Progressive Bookshop conflict between bohemian indifference and professional aspiration. In 1930, both O'Flaherty and Davies were aware that Davies had not yet established himself in the commercial market, and the foreword to the story reads like a neurotic attempt to both justify Davies's right to commercial success and celebrate his more artistically legitimate removal from it in the form of the limited edition book. O'Flaherty describes the literary world as a fortress:

> Established writers are within, comfortable, with money in their pockets, good wine in their bellies, and with their minds dulled with success. Young writers are roaming about outside in the slums that surround the fortress, consorting with the ruffians and tuffs of the alleyways. They jeer at those within, hurl stones at them and lampoon them. Those within keep out those without, by every foul means.[96]

The established writer is only half envied for the comfort and success he has gained. O'Flaherty's foreword, and by extension the Furnival series as a whole, seeks to 'escape the domination of the fortress' by demonstrating how 'cultured book-lovers should draw the attention of the public to good writers. If the public responds by buying good books, instead of the books recommended by the critics in the great literary journals, then good writers can buy their own weekly wine

---

94 Ibid.
95 H.E. Bates to A.E. Coppard, 23 June 1929, A.E. Coppard Papers, Box 32.5, HRC.
96 Liam O'Flaherty, 'Foreword'. *The Stars, The World, and The Women* (London: Jackson, 1930), 7.

and turkey'.[97] O'Flaherty imagines a noble group of artists who, with sympathetic publishers like Alan Steele and Charles Lahr at their backs, may bypass the cultural hegemony of the established literary authorities and liberate the public from the tastes of mainstream cultural producers. Furthermore, the positional work of the foreword and limited edition format are reinforced by the subject of Davies's story, which features a poetic working-class intellectual driven to madness and death by the middle-class aspirations of his consumerist wife, themes replicated in *The New Coterie* stories that first attracted Lahr to Davies's writing.

The German Prisoner, which shared an almost identical bibliographic form with the Furnival books and which was published at the same time and sold at the same price for the same limited numbers, fifty of which were also not for sale, and which included another foreword by Aldington, replicates this ambiguous place in the literary market. Lahr, as the reluctant capitalist running a business frequented by professional writers intimately engaged in the commercial and cultural subtleties of limited edition publication, was well aware of these tensions. Indeed, when reading the bibliographic and linguistic codes of the book in relation to one another, *The German Prisoner* manifests this ambiguity.

If the form of the book sought a certain kind of reader, Aldington's introduction sought to shape that reader into one capable of appreciating this story. Of course, Aldington's credentials are part of the book's commodification. He is not only a recognisable representative of avant-garde poetics but also a war veteran who had recently published a best-selling novel on the war, *Death of A Hero* (1929). His name alone carried weight, but his introduction goes even further in seeking to invent the kind of audience required for this book's positive reception. He attacks the reading public in terms that justify Hanley as an authentic working-class writer and constructs the audience that the book requires. Mainstream literature in England, he claims, serves a 'bourgeois senility', and he rails against the majority of contemporary novelists: 'I am sick of them, you are sick of them, we are sick of them'.[98] He implicates the readership in Hanley's story, creating a community through performative speech and naming readers into complicity. Hanley, he tells us, has an authenticity that supersedes the typical institutions that uphold the literary elite: 'Most modern authors are lamentable deficient in experiencing and feeling. From Prep School to Public School to University to literary salons – what do they know of life? How much do we care how beautifully they say nothing? Bur Mr Hanley has the great essential of a writer – he has lived, and he has something to say'.[99] All of this is a careful positioning of an eccentric working-class writer within terms that might carry him into the public sphere, communicated safely in this nebula cultural authority. Indeed, Aldington's introduction announces that this book is not only about the war but also about the literary mechanisms that transmit

---

[97]   Ibid.

[98]   Richard Aldington. 'Introductory Note', *The German Prisoner* (London: Charles Lahr, 1930), 3.

[99]   Ibid., 4.

this story. It is a book that stands against a 'senile censorship' and 'professional novelists who thrust themselves on the public by every device available to pushing tradesmen'.[100] And even the reading public that he briefly called into complicity is also the public that feels that it cannot sympathise with men who talk like Elston and O'Garra: 'Gentlemen! Here are your defenders; ladies! Here are the results of your charming white feathers. If you were not ashamed to send them into war, why should you blush to read what they said in it?'[101] The professionals, the tradesmen, and the censoring reading public are denounced, until one wonders how this book is expected to circulate at all.

Appropriately, like the limited edition medium itself, Aldington seeks to bypass the mechanisms of literary production, rhetorically eliding his own function as a cultural mediator: 'Mr James Hanley needs no introduction from me. The quality of his work is such that it is bound to obtain a public for him, though it will also create opposition'.[102] Echoing the 'natural public'[103] of the Golden Cockerel Press prospectus, Aldington claims Hanley needs no 'introduction', for his 'public' somehow already exists; however, this rhetorical gesture only heightens our awareness of the mechanisms it seeks to dismiss, as does Aldington's emphatic and paradoxical iteration of a full name, 'Mr James Hanley', who needs no introduction. Aldington negotiates Hanley's name within a literary market that has not yet admitted him to a secure position of worth. He dismisses the institutions that confer publicity and yet represents them himself; indeed, the dismissal of the market *depends* upon the market and is in fact just another way of positioning oneself *within* the market.[104]

All of the paratextual elements of the book echo the culture and community of The Progressive Bookshop in terms of both its left political leanings and its self-conscious literary commercial conflicts and obsessions. They also situate Hanley within an avant-garde literary market; and, so placed, the book, both its bibliographic form and textual content (its bibliographic and linguistic codes) are implicitly engaged in relationships between class, consumption, readership, and aesthetics. These questions revolve around the production of a book by a working-class writer writing about working-class characters but dressed in leisure-class (and salacious) clothes and sold at a middle-class cost.

---

[100] Aldington, 4.

[101] Ibid., 6.

[102] Ibid.

[103] Chute, 58.

[104] The same may be said of William Robert's frontispiece. Roberts' Vorticist credentials are as sound as Aldington's Imagist ones, and Roberts, like Hanley and Aldington, was a veteran of the First World War. His art, both in the frontispiece specifically and in his work more generally, stands as a visual analogue to Hanley's abstract depiction of trench warfare, and he provides the pre-approved rubric through which Hanley may be understood and praised, and his visual representation of Hanley's story argues for the value of the narrative every bit as actively as Aldington's introduction.

The story itself is deeply engaged in class anxieties that draw attention to the class implications of special edition publication and readerships. The two main characters, Elston and O'Garra, are emphatically working class. O'Garra comes from 'Tara Street, known as the filthiest street in all Dublin' and Elston comes from the 'filth and rottenness', and the 'smoke and fog and grease of Manchester'.[105] These descriptions of their urban origins closely mirror the descriptions of trench warfare, which emphasises that, for them, the experience of war is only an extension of a pre-existing condition of industrial victimisation. They do not share the bucolic pre-war adolescence of their middle-class contemporaries. The lost innocence that features so prominently in the war literature of the officer classes is for them the lie that elides their more general condition of abasement.[106] The story, therefore, confronts the class associations of the aesthetic treatments of the war, as will be particularly evident in the formal aestheticisation of the German prisoner himself.

Further, this urban and working-class depravity is also the fear of mass consumption. The most vividly described of the two animalised working-class soldiers, O'Garra, is described within the context of decayed and rotting mouths, which symbolically places him in the context of the corrupted forms of consumption. O'Garra 'discovered it was his mouth that used to frighten the women. It was his most outstanding characteristic. It made him something more than a man. A Threat. The children of Tara Street used to call him "Owld click", because he made a peculiar clicking sound with his false teeth'.[107] This working-class man is associated with the threat of a rotten and artificial consumption that was typically associated with mass-produced goods – books included – and their consumers. There is an immediate and tangible difference between this figure of urban degradation and corrupted consumption and the finely made book associated with artisanal and pre-capitalist production. When read in the context of the standardised products of the modern mass market, the surreal description of the warscape has a similar effect:

> One saw nothing. Nothing. There was something infinite about the action of feeling. One was just conscious that the night was deluged by phantom-like movements. That was all. Far ahead the sky was lighted up by a series of periodic flashes. Then a vast concourse of sound, then silence. The roads were impassable. The men were separated, relying on an occasional whisper, an occasional feel of hand or bayonet, to establish contact with one another. Crawling beneath wagons and guns, now held up by mud.[108]

---

[105]   James Hanley, *The German Prisoner* (London, 1930), 8–9.
[106]   Anne Rice, '"A Peculiar Power about Rottenness": Annihilating Desire in James Hanley's "The German Prisoner"', *Modernism/Modernity* 9.1 (2002), 77–78.
[107]   Hanley, 8.
[108]   Ibid., 11–12.

The texture of the finely made book invites one to read such passages in the context of the sensuous experience of reading a crafted object, and in this context, the warscape echoes descriptions of the market as a function of mass culture. The entire passage moves us away from genuine, tangible, human experience. It is communicated in the incompletion of sentence fragments. The impersonal pronoun, 'one', obtrudes insistently on the first half of the story, muffling one's identification with anything more than the most general experience. 'Feeling', sensation, has grown infinite, unable to terminate in the touch of a known object, a recognisable sound. What does appeal to sensation, flashing lights, and a concourse of sound, does not form into meaning. Human contact is only occasional, the feel of a disembodied hand devolving into the violent impersonality of the bayonet. This whole world is base, and uncertain materiality: being 'held up by mud' is not only to be obstructed by clinging earth but also to be supported by an uncertain foundation. The amorphous, oozing, liquid atmosphere of the story as a whole accords well with the fear of a mechanised literature and of a consumer society that creates a nebulous mass of unfeeling and undiscerning consumers: A world in which meaningful contact with other human beings is becoming more and more difficult to achieve, the kind of world that the special edition ostensibly stands against. Indeed, O'Garra's hideous and rotten mouth figuratively opens up to include the entire warscape: 'the earth in convulsion seemed a kind of yawning mouth, swallowing noise'.[109]

In contrast to this oozing, liquid, and uncertain world, the German prisoner stands as a formally aesthetic figure from a different tradition. He seems to step into the surreal and uncertain wasteland from another reality:

> He was a youth, about eighteen years of age, tall, with a form as graceful as a young sapling, in spite of the ill-fitting uniform and unkempt appearance. His hair, which stuck out in great tufts from beneath his forage cap, was as fair as ripe corn. He had blue eyes and finely moulded features.[110]

He is an anachronism, as out of place in this landscape as his uniform is ill-fitting. His youth is figurative as well as literal, recalling that lost innocence that O'Garra and Elston cannot share. He is also rural and natural, 'graceful as a sapling' and 'fair as ripe corn', where O'Garra and Elston are urban and corrupt. Most importantly, however, he is an aesthetic object; with his 'finely molded features', he stands out as a vivid idealisation in a story that is otherwise surreal and basely realistic. Aware of the German soldier's distance from themselves, O'Garra and Elston refer to him in earthy, scatological, and homophobic language in order to reduce him to their level of experience: They refer to him as a 'sod', a 'bugger', and curse him, saying 'Shit on you'.[111]

Inevitably, the soldiers must destroy him:

---

[109]   Ibid., 18.
[110]   Ibid., 24.
[111]   Ibid., 25.

The two men now fell upon the prisoner, and with peculiar movements of the hands began to mangle the body. They worried it like mad dogs. The fog had brought about a nearness that was now driving them to distraction. Elston, on making contact with the youth's soft skin, became almost demented. The velvety touch of the flesh infuriated him. Perhaps it was because nature had hewn him differently. Had denied him the young German's grace of body, the fair hair, the fine clear eyes that seemed to reflect all the beauty and rhythm and music of the Rhine. Maddened him. O'Garra shouted out:

'PULL his bloody trousers down'.[112]

At this point, they stick a bayonet up the German boy's anus, O'Garra wants to 'back-scuttle the bastard', and Elston sticks a horse-hair up his penis.[113] This natural and beautiful boy is out of place in this story, appearing once again as an aesthetic object, not only with 'finely moulded features', but now reflecting all the 'beauty and rhythm and music' of the Rhine. He is a refugee from a different aesthetic tradition being torn apart in this piece of sadomasochistic Modernist working-class fiction.

On the level of the text, one can read this violent feminisation of the aestheticised body as a revolt against the aesthetic ideals inspiring so much war literature – one thinks of Wilfred Owen's Keatsean poetics and beautiful corpses. However, when one steps back to consider the scene in the context of the reading experience, the production of the book, and the book's place in the market, this working-class resistance to leisure-class aesthetics is repeated in the tension of the special edition in the mass market, which seeks to elide its own commercial function through an appeal to the art-value of the book. In a tangible and physical way, the finely made aesthetic object of the book *is* the German Prisoner; it even bears this name on its cover. The sensuousness of the reading experience and the class associations of this reading act are violently and disturbingly undermined by the homoerotic rape of the principle object of sensuous pleasure and aesthetic form within the story. When one further reflects that the book was bound in buckram and fifty were printed on vellum, the fleshly quality of this book is even greater. This opens a new reading of that moment when the two men make 'contact with the youth's soft skin' and become infuriated by the 'velvety touch of the flesh', one that alludes directly to one's hands on the book.

While I do not claim that all of these interpretations were the conscious work of any one contributor to the production of this book, it is not a coincidence that a book such as *The German Prisoner* arose from within the field of cultural production that circulated around and through Lahr's anarchist interstitial or counter-space. It is a book that engages and revises the full range of the limited edition's fetishisation in commodity culture, whether it is that of the artistic distinction, readerly privilege, or erotic pleasure. If, like the Furnival books with which it shares such a close bibliographic and institutional relationship, it sells

---

[112]   Ibid., 32.
[113]   Ibid., 33.

a certain consumer identity, then one might argue that it implicitly attacks that identity at the same time it exploits it. To be playful with some of the popular perceptions of anarchism, one might regard *The German Prisoner* as the book as briefcase bomb – the seemingly harmless object that insinuates itself into a place of comfort, ease, and pleasure, then suddenly and violently explodes, destroying its privilege as art-object and the distinction of a reading act through a working-class narrative that brings us the front lines of class conflict.

It is difficult to say what audience this book was aimed at or how it was received, especially when Aldington appeals to a reader that is both allied with and opposed to the subject matter and when the luxury edition published in a small print run provides non-mainstream publication but also appeals to the kind of privilege the story attacks. However, this confusion replicates the confusion of the narrative: the victimised working-class protagonists are also oppressive monsters; the sexually explicit homoeroticism is also a grotesque homophobic self-loathing; the innocent victim of horrible violence is also the representative of divergent class experiences or even the fetish figure of 1930s fascism. It is an uneasy tale that leaves everything it touches unsteady, including the material conditions of the publication and the mechanisms that transmit an author into the literary marketplace.

The German Prisoner is important not simply as a story by a writer drawn into a particular community but also as a physical artefact that emerged from within the networks of a particular site of cultural and commercial exchange, beginning with a letter written to the community's central bookseller. In this case, the catalytic node of Charles Lahr and his shop was essential. And, despite the special edition's cache as anti-commercial, and despite Aldington's rhetorical dismissal of the 'public', *The German Prisoner* may be read as an unsettling though deeply implicated positioning of Hanley within the competing claims of various literary markets that circulated around a bookseller who made it his business to produce and disseminate literature in various forms to receptive and sometimes unsuspecting readers.

As a bookshop owner, Lahr was widely engaged in the literary market and the entire field of literary production. The shop itself served as a catalytic space that facilitated the meaningful interaction between the various players within this field. Lahr's role, however, is not unambiguous, for the shop was a counter-space, one that was necessarily embedded in the dominant space that it defies or revises. The point is not whether or not, or to what extent, Lahr and his shop offered resistance to the dominant capitalist space and dominant publishing industry. Such an argument separates what is in fact inseparable and obscures the more complex operations of literary commercial culture. The point is that the commitments and actions of the man, the commercial activities of the shop, the networks of the community, and the publishing activities emerging from within these networks were all part of the internal differences within commercial, aesthetic, or political activities. The Progressive Bookshop did not undermine commercial culture; it re-imagined it through exploiting its materials within literary institutions, commercial activities, and book production.

Postscript

The Progressive Bookshop is long gone. Bombed in the Blitz, it has been physically erased from the urban streetscape. Lahr kept shops afterwards, one in Woburn Walk, one in Little Newport Street, and his last was in the basement of the Independent Labour Party headquarters. Nevertheless, The Progressive Bookshop lives on not only in the printed materials produced by Lahr but also in the archival record and in the vivid written memories of those who visited the shop. George Woodcock recalls visiting Red Lion Street in 1941 after it had been bombed:

> Red Lion Street had been changed utterly by the war since the days when I first went there to visit Charlie Lahr. Houses had been knocked out by bombs, and those that stood between the gaps, like teeth left in an old man's mouth, were shored up with the timbers that were already blackened by the weather and beginning to decay. Some of the spaces had been made into fire-fighting reservoirs which on a clear day brightly reflected the sky and the clouds; others had been left for the fire weed to fill all summer with its magenta flowering. Destruction had brought its own beauty.[114]

Woodcock's description of bombed-out London is couched in the absence of a figure who was central to his own political and literary development, and the destruction and decay cannot quite overcome a defiant vitality associated with the man and his shop. As Rhys Davies wrote in a letter to Bates regarding Lahr's opening of his next shop in Little Newport Street, 'Battered, bombed and bloody, he still rises, in his sandals and his beard'.[115]

---

[114] Woodcock, 269.
[115] Rhys Davies to Geoffrey Harry West, 16 September 1941 HRC.

Chapter 7
The Grolier Poetry Book Shop:
From Couch to Cultural Icon

David Eberly

Established in 1927 by Adrian Gambet and Gordon Cairnie, the Grolier Poetry Book Shop describes itself as the 'oldest continuous bookshop' devoted to the sale of poetry.[1] The plate glass window of the store's single 404 square foot room fronts Plympton Street, which runs between Adams House and Harvard Yard in Cambridge, Massachusetts. The Academy of American Poets recognised the Grolier's iconic status when it designated the store as a 'National Poetry Landmark' in 2004. One of thirty-one sites honoured, it takes its place alongside City Lights, the only other book store cited; the Woodberry Poetry Room, located a block away in Harvard's Lamont Library; and McLean Hospital, a nearby mental institution which provided care to a number of the store's more famous customers.

'No one who loves poetry, and Cambridge', Donald Hall has written, 'fails to praise the Grolier Book Shop'.[2] Generations of American poets have entered the Grolier to talk and shop and, later, to celebrate it. Boston poet William Corbett offered a representative list of customers in his guidebook *Literary New England*: 'Robert Lowell, Charles Olson, Elizabeth Bishop, Richard Eberhart, Donald Hall, Helen Vendler, Robert Creeley, Jim Harrison, Paul Hannigan, Gail Mazur, and the photographer Elsa Dorfman'.[3] (Many of their photographs, often taken by Dorfman, have hung 'on the little wall space not taken up by bookshelves'.[4])

---

[1] The designation of the Grolier Poetry Book Shop homepage as '.org' and not '.com' illustrates the tension between the commercial and cultural aspects of the Grolier, which continues to operate as a store even as it labels itself as a non-profit cultural institution. As indeterminate as its for-profit status, the store's name itself shifts from 'Book Shop' to 'Bookshop', depending on the source, as if to separate or combine its elements. 'Book Shop' will be used throughout this essay, unless quoted.

[2] Donald Hall, *Unpacking the Boxes* (Boston: Houghton Mifflin Harcourt, 2008), 86.

[3] William Corbett, 'Cambridge', *Harvard Review* 5 (Fall 1993), 104.

[4] Corbett, 104; the list of American poets who have gathered to praise the Grolier through the decades is formidable. A 1971 issue of *The Antioch Review* published thirty-six poems for Gordon Carnie on his birthday and included Conrad Aiken, Robert Bly, Fanny Howe, Denise Levertov, Guiseppe Ungaretti, and Richard Wilbur in addition to many of the poets listed by Corbett. Thirty-five years later, Doug Holder would gather a newer generation of poets to recognise Louisa Solano, among whom were John Hildebidle, Richard Kostelanetz, Ruth Lepson, and Kathleen Spivak, less known, but no less passionate about the store.

In October 2002, more than 800 people jammed Harvard's Sander's Theater to recognise the Grolier's seventy-fifth anniversary at an event sponsored by the Poetry Society of America and hear an equally stellar group of poets, including Frank Bidart, Eamon Grennan, and Philip Levine, celebrate the store's history, so interwoven with their own achievements. Standing before the auditorium of poetry lovers, Hall recalled his first visit to the store as a Harvard freshman in the 1940s when he bought a new volume of poems by Richard Wilbur and showed the crowd 'the now worn and well-read book'.[5]

The Grolier has had only three owners since its establishment in 1927. Each one brought a distinct character to the store. Gordon Cairnie, who founded and owned the Grolier until his death in 1973, financed it with his wife's wealth, treating the shop as an illustrious poetic 'boy's club'. Lacking his means, Louisa Solano borrowed $15,000 and bought the store after Cairnie's death, transforming it into a business which supported her, however marginally, and served an international community of poets and their readers for thirty years. Ifeanyi Menkiti, the bookshop's current owner, earned his salary as a philosophy professor at Wellesley University until his retirement in 2014. Confronted by the dramatic shifts in the book-reading and book-buying habits of the public in the last two decades, Menkiti has sought to preserve the Grolier as an cultural entity, separated from the selling, if not the marketing, of books. Distinctly different in personality, each owner has bought, sold, and protected the volumes of poetry contained on the shelves lining the walls of the small room which is the Grolier, and each has fostered a unique relationship with the public that sustains it. Together, they represent the modes of commerce which constitute the history of the independent American bookstore across almost a century of bookselling.

'Atchison, Topeka, and Santa Fe'

A Canadian and 'stern contrarian', Gordon Cairnie started the Grolier Book Shop with his friend Adrian Gambet, who soon lost interest in their joint enterprise. Cairnie remained the store's owner until his death almost fifty years later. Like many other stores of the era – Sylvia Beach's Shakespeare & Company in Paris and Frances Steloff's Gotham Book Mart in New York, for example – the history of the Grolier reflects the spirit and idiosyncrasies of its sole proprietor. A graduate of Ontario Agricultural College and 'erstwhile potato inspector', Cairnie ran his store in 'unforgettable style', warning away hapless shoppers with 'a hand-lettered sign on the door warning "No Textbooks, No Science Books ... Just Literature", and refusing to sell books to those he didn't think would give them a good home'.[6] The store's books were arranged in no discernible order, and its centre table was

---

[5]   Amanda Paulson, '400 square feet of poetic punch', *Christian Science Monitor*, 17 October 2002, 11.

[6]   Corbett, 104.

piled with the little magazines and broadsides that characterised the ferment of American poetry at the time.

If Cairnie could discourage the curious with a shouted 'Shut the Goddam Door', he also warmly welcomed the poets who entered the small, smoke-filled room. Cairnie, Corbett writes with astonishment, 'actually loved poets, famous or forever unknown, for themselves'.[7] Those so favoured found a home. 'Gordon's generosity is huge', Donald Hall wrote when introducing a selection of poems in honour of Cairnie's birthday. 'So is his reputation for grumpiness ... We were all frightened of him at first. He is monosyllabic and abrupt, a shy man ... Eventually I stopped at least once a day, like all the other writers. I sat on a sofa and Gordon introduced me to his old friends – Conrad Aiken, Horace Reynolds, Robert Creeley, Richard Wilbur'.[8] Cineaste Rob Nilsson later saw the 'utter scorn' that Cairnie heaped on him as a test. 'If you could see through it, you'd be the kind of guy Gordon liked', and welcomed to the shop.[9] Steve Glines, founder of the Wilderness House Literary Retreat, has left a similar portrait of Cairnie. An impecunious eighteen year old, Glines caught Cairnie's attention for his habit of buying books of older poets. Cairnie discovered that he 'used to summer about a mile or so from my mother's house in Nova Scotia and he knew all the neighbors and characters of Poplar Hill'. After their long chat, 'Gordon made me feel welcome even if I wasn't a "known poet"',[10] Glines recalled.

'Cambridge is not Paris and the Grolier Bookshop is not the Cafe Floré', Hall judiciously noted. 'But the Grolier provides the best elements of a literary café – a place where writers can hang around, talk or be silent, and remain unharassed'.[11] Perched on the edge of Harvard Yard and visited by a stream of poet-academics and their acolytes, the Grolier under the ownership of Cairnie resembled not so much the Floré as a thirteenth-century Parisian bookshop operating under the system known as *pecia*. Under this system, as Andrew Pettigree describes it in *The Book in the Renaissance*, 'privileged booksellers were permitted to rent out specially made exemplar copies of set texts' to students who had no other access to them and who 'copied them, or had them copied, before returning them'.[12] The arcana of letterpress and pamphlets sold or lent by Cairnie to impoverished Harvard students may remind one of the scarce and ephemeral texts of medieval Paris. Nilsson recalls an incident in which Cairnie sold him a signed first edition of Conrad Aiken's *Blue Voyage* at a price commensurate with 'an embattled student's bank

---

[7]   Ibid.

[8]   'Thirty-Six Birthday Poems for Gordon Carnie with photographs of the poets by Elsa Dorfman', *Antioch Review* 30. 3/4 (Autumn 1970–Winter 1971), 311.

[9]   Rob Nilsson. 'In Praise of Praise'. *cinesource*, 3 May 2012. http://cinesourcemagazine. com/index.php?/site/comments/in_praise_of_praise.

[10]   Steve Glines, 'The Poetic Look', *Boston Area Small Press and Poetic Scene*, 12 November 2005. http://dougholder.blogspot.com/2005_11_13_archive.html.

[11]   Antioch, 312.

[12]   Andrew Pettigree, *The Book in the Renaissance* (New Haven: Yale University Press, 2010), 9.

account', a gesture of Cairnie's 'incorruptibility', one which is not far removed from the cloister.[13]

Yet Carnie's Grolier did have a flavour of the literary café about it. The 'commerce of thinking, of books and bookstores', described by Jean-Luc Nancy in his book of the same title, can be seen as a commingling 'that has something of the mêlée about it': people, books, ideas, flying off the shelves in community, as his translator notes:[14] It is this community that is celebrated by those who knew the Grolier under Cairnie's ownership. 'The Grolier', Hall writes, 'crawls with the ghosts of writers and cronies, dead or moved away, who used to live there. Gordon is the locus of these people, the source of both news and old stories ... Gordon is the link between generations of writers, an institution of continuity in a place of continual change'.[15] Such a place, Nancy writes, 'can be called the bookstore of the soul', recalling the commerce of Pettigree's Scholastic bookshop.[16]

The Grolier's books might have been read, jotted on, borrowed, and passed around, but, all Cairnie's contemporaries agree, they were seldom sold. Cairnie, Hall has written, 'sits on his sofa and writes postcards ... He fills a 1927 Daily Reminder (or something like that) with notes and orders. He sells a few books, stays home when he pleases, and sometimes closes to drink beer and talk'.[17] As Hall succinctly put it in his poem 'Gordon of the Grolier Book Shop', 'He never broke even'.[18] Cairnie's business habits were as irregular as his hours. 'His correspondence', Solano recalled, 'was stuffed under the middle cushion of the couch ... And bills he considered paying were stuffed into the back behind the pillows'.[19] Under Cairnie's proprietorship, the store 'was more a club than a shop'. Because it was partially funded with his wife's investments – the Atchinson, Topeka, and Santa Fe, as Cairnie joked – 'he could afford to give away books and ignore such trivialities as business operations'.[20] Solano remembers that 'you never even saw money'. Cairnie 'kept the change in his pockets. So you were led to believe that yes, books could sustain you physically. Of course ... they can't, however much we'd like them to'. Solano would later qualify this memory. 'The

---

[13]   Nilsson, http://cinesourcemagazine.com/index.php?/site/comments/in_praise_of_praise.

[14]   Jean-Luc Nancy, *On the Commerce of Thinking: Of Books & Bookstores*, translated by David Wills (New York: Fordham University Press, 2009), xvii.

[15]   Antioch, 312.

[16]   Nancy, 42.

[17]   Hall, 86.

[18]   In a conversation with me, Louisa Solano observed that many of the postcards that Cairnie wrote were to customers reminding them of outstanding payments. I am grateful to Louisa for the many discussions about the store that we have shared over the years and for the more formal interview that she gave me on 15 July 2012.

[19]   Lisa Hammel, 'Boston Bookshop's Birthday', *The New York Times*, 28 September 1983, C 13.

[20]   Paulson, 11.

thing is – his account book was meticulously kept'.[21] In other words, as Doug Holder observed, 'Gordon intended to receive money for his transactions, he just never collected'.[22] Writing Cairnie's obituary in *The Harvard Crimson* in 1973, the young poet Michael Ryan concluded, 'Perhaps they can keep the store going, but that's not the point, is it? I must have been there 200 times in my five years, but I only bought a dozen or two books. No one ever went to the Grolier for books'.[23]

If Gordon Cairnie's Grolier housed the 'soul' of book commerce, however penurious, it would have resided in the couch stuffed with correspondence and invoices that dominated the shop. No memoir fails to mention it. As Nilsson noted, if you could see through Cairnie's bluffness, 'you would sometimes be invited to sit on his old leather couch. He sat in only one place, and that part of the couch was worn down to the springs'.[24] Sitting there, the young, male would-be poet could imagine himself joining the lineage of the poetic greats who had sat in the same spot next to Cairnie.

Not all, however, shared this view. Poet Laureate Robert Pinsky countered those memories of Grolier's halcyon days with a more trenchant one delivered at the store's seventy-fifth anniversary celebration. Looking back from the vantage point of 2002, he praises the less cliquish proprietorship of Louisa Solano:

> Cairnie scared me when I was a shy, covertly arrogant young schmo slinking into the Grolier to buy poetry books … I would try to get in and out as quickly as possible, an outsider at what felt like a private club, On Gordon's couch sat geeky, sneery Harvard students in cowboy hats, eating Big Macs and talking about Charles Olson.

> When Louisa took on the store she got rid of the couch … Along with the couch went the poetry geeks. I remember how cheerful, welcoming, freshly dusted the place felt and how happy I was that this curly-headed young woman had made the place seem lighter, brighter, more open.[25]

---

21 Solano, interview with the author.

22 Amy E. Brais, 'Louisa Solano to be Honoured at the Somerville News Writers Festival', *Boston Area Small Press and Poetry Scene*, http://dougholder.blogspot. com/2005/10/louisa-solano-to-be-honored-at.html.

23 Michael Ryan, 'Gordon Carnie–1895–1973'. *The Harvard Crimson*, 24 July 1973.

24 Nilsson, http://cinesourcemagazine.com/index.php?/site/comments/in_praise_of_ praise; Cairnie's couch seems to attract as many descriptions as it does depicters. Donald Hall remembers Nilsson's 'old leather couch' as 'a lumpy green sofa' on which Cairnie smoked his pipe; Rosemary Herbert reports it to have been 'insect-infested'.

25 Rosemary Herbert, 'Books: A Haven for the Well-versed', *The Boston Herald*, 20 September 2002, 7.

'Flying in the face of business reality ... '

The daughter of an emeritus professor of Romance languages at Harvard University, Louisa Solano discovered the Grolier Book Shop when she was fifteen years old and working at the Cambridge Public Library. 'I worked at the library the public library until 5 o'clock. Then I'd tear over there ... I dusted the bookshelves and swept the floor and ran errands ... I tore down Saturday mornings with a cup of tea for Gordon and sat on the steps of the book store waiting for him. I often drank the tea myself because his hours were very irregular'.[26] At the time, Solano was 'chronically, acutely shy. I hardly ever opened my mouth. I was the youngest person there usually'.[27] And yet she would declare, 'I knew then that I would own it someday. And I have never been so sure of anything in my life'.[28] At the age of twenty-six, with the help of one of Cairnie's executors, Solano found fifteen friends who each guaranteed $1,000 so the she could purchase the store, when many thought it should be closed down in Gordon's memory.

Solano quickly changed the shop. She threw out the iconic couch and took down the forbidding signs. A feminist, she added books written by women to the store's original stock, making sure, as she told a later interviewer, that there was an 'equal ratio' of poetry by men and women, 'even in the face of criticism by customers who asked for "real poetry" when handed books by female poets'.[29] In doing so, Solano 'democratized it out of the white male poet syndrome and moved the store to more involvement with the community'.[30] The large plate glass window became a place on which could be found the flyers for local poetry readings and workshops, as well as provocative exhibits of broadsides and books focused of political topics of the day: nuclear disarmament, feminism, and AIDS prevention among the many progressive causes that she supported. While these changes demonstrated Solano's desire to end the male 'club' atmosphere that enveloped the store, they also reflected broader societal changes in the academic and creative worlds it served. Harvard and Radcliffe, for example, began jointly admitting male and female students to their classes in 1975, in much the same *zeitgeist* as Solano 'admitted' male and female poets to her shelves. Two additional bookstores catering to feminist and gay and lesbian readers opened nearby: New Words in Cambridge in 1974, and Glad Day in downtown Boston in 1979. All three were profitably sustained by their diverse audiences.

At the same time that she shifted the Grolier culturally, Solano also altered it commercially, changing its focus to an all-poetry bookstore. The Grolier had begun as a fine press bookstore, filled with limited first edition books by writers of the period like Edna St Vincent Millay and John Galsworthy. Gradually, Cairnie

---

[26]   Hammel, C13.
[27]   Doug Holder, ed., *Louisa Solano: The Grolier Poetry Bookshop*, second edition (Somerville, MA: Ibbetson Street Press), 4.
[28]   Herbert, 4.
[29]   Ibid.
[30]   Holder, 4.

shifted the store to a more literary one, and he became one of the leading poetry booksellers on the East Coast. At the start, Solano attempted to run the Grolier as a general bookstore. She soon realised, however,

> that if I were to survive, I'd have to decide what this bookstore represents. After a month of sleepless nights, I decided to make it a poetry bookstore ... My decision to make it a poetry bookstore was because how undervalued poetry was. In this country, the only way anything gets respected is by money ... If I could create a poetry bookstore that actually existed on commercial terms, people would say: 'Look it's got some worth'. And it worked.[31]

It continued to work until the commercial environment that supported the store for decades vanished. As Solano later said when interviewed, 'Flying in the face of business reality may not make good business sense, but it can make a business'.[32]

'An all poetry book store can survive',[33] Solano added. The history of the bookstore in America suggests a different outcome, however. As John Hrushka observes in *How Books Came to America*:

> In the colonies, and later in the republic, the notion of sustaining a bookstore by selling nothing but books, or even books and stationery, was ridiculous ... Signs in the window of Sparrow Horton's Woburn Book Store in Woburn Massachusetts, advertised newspapers and periodicals, pictures frames, wallpaper, window shades, toys, insurance, steamship tickets, but no books ... Even in the largest markets – Philadelphia, New York, and Boston – booksellers needed to supplement their stock of books with a wide variety of wares simply to survive'.[34]

Hrushka's description does not differ much from the business model of Walmart, which delivers its books like cartons of paper goods, or its rival of Barnes & Noble, which has decreased its floor space for books and filled it with cards, games, Ugli dolls, and coffee cups to survive. (Barnes & Noble further reduced its floor space for books in order to market the Nook, in a failed attempt to compete with Amazon's Kindle.) Nor have independent bookstores proved immune to the pressure to decrease their square footage for books and replace it with similar, if more tasteful, merchandise. The entrance to the Brookline Booksmith, an exemplary survivor, is piled with ceramic plates and bowls and other knick-knacks, and its display tables of books is pushed away from the door. Indeed, the

---

[31]   Doug Holder, 'Interview with Louisa Solano', *Wilderness House Events*, 24 July 2006, http://wildernesshouse.blogspot.ca/2006/07/interview-with-louisa-solano-guest-aug.html.

[32]   Louisa Solano, interview with the author, 'Write that down', Louisa said to me during our interview, repeating it word for word.

[33]   Ibid.

[34]   John Hrushka, *How Books came to America: The Rise and Fall of the American Book Trade* (University Park: Penn State University Press, 2011), 100.

marketing strategies of the American supermarket, developed after World War II, mimicked those of expanding bookstores of the post-war era, which, for example, introduced shelves placed in front of counters to encourage browsing, and box-cutting to sell text books in bulk. The marketing of food and books both fell prey 'to the crass trifecta of volume, efficiency, and commercialism'.[35] The Grolier remained stubbornly antithetical to all three values.

Implementing her business model to sell only poetry books, Solano expanded the Grolier's stock from the 400 titles sold by Carnie to 9000 titles by 1983; it later rose to 19,000 before decreasing in the store's final years.[36] At the same time, she constructed the floor-to-ceiling bookshelves that have characterised the shop's small space since then, placing its overstock well over the heads of its customers. These high bookshelves came to define and enclose the confined space of the store. The invention of bookshelves, Andrew Piper has argued, created an 'infrastructure' of books, insuring their stability. 'Like medieval readers who were taught to put ideas in certain places in their minds, when I browse I am locating ideas in a physical space, to be returned to later'.[37] This physical space, embodied for decades in the Grolier's single room, is now threatened by online browsing. 'When we browse online', Piper writes, 'there are no corporeal connections being made between what we have seen and where we have seen it ... Without books and their shelves, we lose a fundamental component of what it means to browse, to glance at books'.[38] At its peak, the Grolier 'always held booklovers in its thrall', a Boston paper reported. 'It is an eminently browsable place'.[39]

Solano arranged the content of her store's shelves according to principles which have remained in effect since. Poets were shelved alphabetically from A-Z. This alphabetical display was punctuated by titles grouped by nationality, ethnicity, and interest: African American, British, Gay and Lesbian, and Haiku among others. (Language poets would be added later.) Irish poetry took pride of place by the door, perhaps reflecting Solano's friendship with Seamus Heaney, as well as with other local Irish poets like Desmond O'Grady. Together with these titles, Solano kept an unrivalled array of the broadsides, little magazines, and chapbooks that

---

[35] Ted Stirphas, *The Late Age of Print: Everyday Book Culture from Consumerism to Control* (New York: Columbia University Press, 2009), 58.

[36] The inventory of the Grolier has been well documented throughout its existence, since each book had to be inventoried and valued annually for tax purposes. Solano publicised the extent of her stock to market the store. See Lawrence Biemiller, 'Stories from the Chronicle: A Bookstore for Poets and Lovers of Verse', http://www.iceandcoal.org/nfa/grolier.html; Hammel; and David Mehegan, 'Independent Thinking', *The Boston Globe*, 19 November 2003, C1.

[37] Andrew Piper, *Book Was There: Reading in Electronic Times* (Chicago: University of Chicago Press, 2012), 120.

[38] Ibid., 121.

[39] Herbert, 4.

poured from the ephemeral presses of the era.[40] In making her alterations, Solano simultaneously fashioned a space that facilitated access to her expanded inventory while encouraging the increasingly diverse customer base of poetry readers upon which she would build her early commercial success.

In doing so, Solano exemplified Julie Rak's observation that 'The physical organization of the store also reflects its mandate and principles' and may operate as 'social action'.[41] As she noted in her study of Canadian book stores,

> Unlike other culture industries, book selling attracts customers who often do *not* endorse big-box retailing and who actively oppose the forces of globalization, even as they participate in everyday capitalism. In some localities at least genre [like poetry] as social practice is used to bring books to readers, readers to books, and – these entrepreneurs hope – new and useful ideas to the people who need them.[42]

Solano not only brought books to readers and readers to books but also created a space that brought authors to readers, further breaking down the barriers of the book industry. Under Solano's ownership, the Grolier became a place of readings and author signings, where customers not only browsed the books displayed on its shelves but met their authors as well. Long lines formed for book signings by established writers like May Sarton, while small clusters of friends and supporters greeted poets publishing their first volumes. Solano also established a poetry reading series which took place in the common room of Harvard's Adams House a short half-block from the store. While the series featured well-known poets like Seamus Heaney and Donald Hall, who were champions of the shop, it was best known for introducing poets drawn from the same diverse community which supported the Grolier during its early years. As a result, Solano's reading series quickly distinguished itself from readings hosted by the neighbouring Blacksmith House and the local universities surrounding it, which increasingly attracted poets published by established commercial and academic publishers.

Perhaps the most important innovation made by Solano, together with the Cambridge poet Gail Mazur, was the establishment of the Grolier Poetry Prize. Such prizes were rare before they became the financial mainstay of literary magazines, small presses, and writing programs. Like the far more prestigious Yale Series of Younger Poets, the Grolier Prize sought to recognise new poets at the start of

---

[40] 'I happen to love small press', Solano has said. 'To me the small press is the supporter of poetry ... When I first came to the Grolier there were all these small pamphlets in the store. I was the first to carry *Language Magazine*; I was the first seller to carry many of the small press literary magazines'. Holder, *Louisa Solano: The Grolier Poetry Bookshop*, 7.

[41] Julie Rak, 'Genre in the Marketplace: The Scene of Bookselling in Canada', *From Codex to Hypertext: Reading at the Turn of the Twenty-First Century*, ed. Anouk Land (Amherst: University of Massachusetts Press, 2012), 167.

[42] Ibid., 171.

their careers. After several years, Jeanne Henle, an Eastern Michigan University Librarian, established the Ellen LaForge Memorial Poetry Foundation under the auspices of the Grolier to honour her sister who wrote poetry throughout her life, and yet remained unpublished.[43] The Grolier Prize rules were strengthened to reflect Henle's desire to support the discovery and encouragement of unpublished poets and excluded previously published poems or poems that had been submitted elsewhere for publication, thus reinforcing Solano's own commitment to diversity, unorthodoxy, and youth. The Prize proved to be a respected and visible start for many young poets. Scattered among its winners are familiar poets like Debra Gregor, Lucie Brock-Broido, Timothy Liu, Susan Wheeler, and the Pulitzer Prize winning and Poet Laureate Natasha Tretheway.[44]

Despite these innovations, the Grolier continued to resemble other small, independent bookstores of the era, reliant on its proprietor for its survival. Solano laboured many hours in the store, assisted by a continually changing cohort of young assistants – students, acquaintances, relatives, and friends. The store's profitability remained inextricably linked to the health and hard work of its owner. In that, Louisa Solano joined a long lineage of sole proprietors of whom Shakespeare and Company's Sylvia Beach and Gotham Book Mart's Frances Steloff were two of its most prominent women. Her similarities to Beach are significant. Beach's struggles to keep Shakespeare and Company profitable despite its renown presage Solano's own. In a 1929 letter to Ernest Hemingway, Beach apologised for not running the author's errands: 'Hemingway dear please forgive me for not doing any of the things that you asked me to do'.[45] Beach then followed with a litany of tragicomedic events: her facial neuralgia 'that doesn't sound bad but hurts awfully'; Adrienne Monnier's grippe with two relapses amid her struggle to proof the French translation of *Ulysses*; and the illnesses of her assistant Myrsine and her little girl, which forced Beach 'to do everything alone at the busiest time of the year'.[46] Her letter paints a daunting portrait of the travails of bookstore ownership.

Like the Grolier four decades later, Shakespeare and Company depended on the opportune support of others to survive; gifts from her friend and heiress Bryher, and later from her life-long friend Marion Peter, whose 1936 check proved 'most

---

[43]   Solano resigned as President of the Ellen LaForge Foundation in 2007 after the sale of her store. The Foundation is now affiliated with the William T. Joiner Center for the Study of War and Social Consequences at the University of Massachusetts, Boston, which also sponsors the Grace Paley Award for community activism. University of Massachusetts, Boston, was the academic home of many of the poets and writers who long supported the Grolier.

[44]   A member of the Dark Room Collective of African American poets formed in Boston twenty-five years ago, Tretheway won the Grolier Prize before her first book, *Domestic Work*, was published in 2000. Tretheway is emblematic of the poet whom the Grolier Book Shop welcomed and the Grolier Prize sought to encourage.

[45]   Keri Walsh, *The Letters of Sylvia Beach* (New York: Columbia University Press, 2010), 124.

[46]   Ibid., 125.

opportune at this moment when my business has reached a new low'.[47] Far worse than the financial insecurity that Beach endured was the physical toll inflicted by her effort to keep her store open. As Beach wrote to Paul Leon, 'I have sacrificed my health to such an extent that my headaches, which the doctors agree are due to fatigue and mental strain, have not yet yielded to any treatment'.[48]

Louisa Solano also suffered from a life-long illness which severely impacted her ability to manage the Grolier and eventually contributed to its demise. Solano was diagnosed in her forties with temporal lobe epilepsy. In addition to triggering debilitating seizures, temporal lobe epilepsy can also affect the personality of its sufferer. For many years after her diagnosis, Solano shared her diagnosis with only her closest friends. Later, she became more public about her illness and spoke openly about its effect on her customers. As she told Doug Holder in a 2005 interview,

> I know people have accused me of looking through them or being a snob. Actually when I am doing this it may be in the midst of a Petit Mal. People say that I sometimes yell at them or say some really horrible things, but quite frankly I have no memory of it most of the time … To apologize is to say that I am responsible, but I am really not. People don't comprehend how this disease controls one's personality.[49]

Solano struggled with her epilepsy for many years as her customer base shrank and her business eroded, often as impacted by the side effects of her medication as her illness. The decline of her store was paralleled by the decline of her health. In 2006, she sold the store after sustaining a community of poets and poetry readers across thirty years in the book industry and against the ever-growing trends that threaten all bookstores, let alone the all poetry bookstore.

'A marvelous, cluttered anachronism … '

Writing about the Grolier in the *Chronicle of Higher Education* in 1996, Lawrence Biemiller described a bookstore that was essentially unchanged since Solano took it over and which would remain so until its sale. 'As bookstores go', he stated, 'the 404-square-foot Grolier is a marvelous cluttered anachronism'.[50] Its books remained alphabetised, although an overflow of F's now blocked access to the E's, and the store's computer and telephone crowded 'into a paper-strewn niche … complicating access to everyone from R through Z'.[51] Solano continued to run the shop by herself, working from noon to six-thirty and serving from twenty-

---

[47]   Ibid., 176.

[48]   Ibid., 142.

[49]   Brais,   http://dougholder.blogspot.com/2005/10/louisa-solano-to-be-honored-at. html.

[50]   Biemiller, http://www.iceandcoal.org/nfa/grolier.html.

[51]   Ibid.

five to 100 customers on a busy day.[52] 'Everyone thought I would be gone in a day', Solano told Biemiller.[53] It took much longer than that, but less than a decade after Biemiller's article appeared, foot traffic had vanished, and only a handful of customers wandered in, as Solano, relying on day-by-day sales, sought a buyer.

The same economic conditions that forced Solano to sell the Grolier led to the bankruptcy of the much larger Wordsworth Books located a few blocks away. At its zenith from 1982 to 1992, Wordsworth 'sold more books published by Harvard University Press than did all the bookstores in Europe', according to its owner, Hillel Starvis.[54] Starvis blamed the deep bulk discounting of books by Barnes & Noble and other chains, changes in Harvard Square which saw the closure of locally owned enterprises and the rise of national chains like Gap and Abercrombie & Fitch, and, most importantly, the rise of Internet commerce.[55] Having opened the store with what was a record loan for a bookstore of $56,000 from the Small Business Administration, Wordsworth closed with an inventory of $1,000,000 and debts totalling $1,500,000.[56] When it closed, Wordsworth Books joined a dismaying list of defunct bookstores that, small and large, once characterised Harvard Square: Reading International, Cambridge Booksmith, Pangloss Bookshop, McIntyre & Moore Booksellers, Starr Book Shop, The Book Case, and others, including the Harvard University Press Display Room.[57] As Solano said in an interview given at the time of her competitor's closing, 'the "imaginative atmosphere" of the old Harvard Square has been pushed out by the chain stores'.[58]

While a special arrangement with Harvard University, which leased the store's space for a miniscule $200 a month, preserved the Grolier from the rapidly rising rents of the Square, the store suffered like Wordsworth from the deep discounting introduced by Barnes & Noble, which had become the manager of the Harvard

---

[52]   Ibid.

[53]   Ibid.

[54]   Jack Thomas, 'Closing Store has Them at a Loss for Words', *The Boston Globe*, 1 December 2004. http://www.boston.com/ae/books/articles/2004/12/01/closing_store_has_them_at_loss_for_words/.

[55]   Publicly and privately, Solano would add a fourth economic reason for her store's financial demise: shoplifting. As she noted in a *New York Times* article on the subject, she was not protected from theft by size or specialisation. In fact, as sole proprietor, she made an easier mark. Thieves, she noted, worked in pairs. Despite the magnetic security system she had invested in, Solano estimated she had lost $29,000 in 2003. See Judith Rosen, 'Literary Thugs and Book Thieves', *New York Times*, 17 May 2004, 19.

[56]   Judith Rosen, 'Grolier Poetry Bookshop Goes Nonprofit Route', *Publishers Weekly*, 22 June 2012, http://www.publishersweekly.com/pw/by-topic/industry-news/bookselling/article/52661-grolier-poetry-book-shop-goes-nonprofit-route.html.

[57]   When it closed, the president of the Harvard Square Business Association predicted 'that the space will lease out'. Almost a decade later, only half of the space was let; the store's large lower level, whose windows front Brattle Street, remained empty, eventually to be replaced by a bank.

[58]   Claire Provost, 'Grolier Book Shop to Close', *The Harvard Crimson*, 18 March 2004. http://www.thecrimson.com/article/2004/3/16/grolier-book-shop-to-close-the/.

Coop, the area's dominant bookstore (Coop 'members' also receive annual rebates on their purchases). 'Often located in prime city locations', John Thompson has written, 'book superstores were designed as attractive retail spaces that drew customers in and encouraged them to browse',[59] offering them coffee shops and sofas, an ironic recap of Cairnie's well-worn couch. The deep discounts of 30–40 percent on best sellers and 10–20 percent on other titles made by the chains could not be matched by independent bookstores. The Grolier was particularly vulnerable to these discounts; the bread-and-butter volumes of established poets published by Knopf, Norton, and Farrar Straus Giroux, together with related trade biographies and other titles, were now available for much less at the Harvard Coop and the other bookstores surrounding it, including the independent Harvard Bookstore, located – literally – next door. Solano herself was near bankruptcy as early as 1997, and was facing a reported debt of $50,000, when a group of local poets staged a fundraising drive and rescued the store.[60] Throughout the country in the years following, 'More and more independents closed down', Thompson states, 'forced out of business by the two-pronged pressure of rising overheads (especially the rising costs of real estate) and declining revenues'.[61] By 2006, when Solano sold the store, independent bookstores accounted for only 13 percent of all book revenue, and membership in the American Booksellers Association had been decimated.

'What was the straw that broke the camel's back that made you feel that you might need to put the business up for sale?', Solano was asked in a 2005 interview. Admitting that she had been supporting the store on her charge card for the past two or three years, 'it came to the point when I had to pay and I couldn't'.[62] The Grolier, she observed, 'actually existed on mail-order business for many years. In 1998, the Internet started coming up, and gradually ate my business'.[63] Or, as she stated more bluntly in a later conversation, 'Amazon'.

Amazon's rise as an Internet retailer and its impact on the book trade industry has been well documented. According to Thompson, 'In just ten years, Amazon had risen from nothing to become one of the most important retail outlets for publishers'.[64] But, argues Ted Stirphas, 'Rather than referring to amazon.com as an online or Internet bookseller, perhaps it would be more apt to call it a large-scale, direct-to-customer warehouse bookseller whose interface would be the World Wide Web'.[65] Understood from this perspective, Amazon can be seen as a continuation of the carton-cutting, shopping cart strategy of the Barnes &

---

[59] John B. Thompson, *Merchants of Culture: The Publishing Business in the Twenty-First Century* (Malden, MA: Polity Press, 2010), 28.

[60] Michael Kenney, 'Poetry Bash makes a Splash', *The Boston Globe*, 18 August 1997, C6.

[61] Thompson, 31.

[62] Brais, http://dougholder.blogspot.com/2005/10/louisa-solano-to-be-honored-at.html.

[63] Ibid.

[64] Thompson, 42–43.

[65] Stirphas, 101.

Noble Annex, which viewed books as 'fully fungible or interchangeable staples meant to be purchased in bulk, much like flour, salt, cooking oil, or even toilet paper'.[66] In fact, before settling on books as Amazon's first product, Jeff Bezos, the company's founder, considered some twenty other commodities. Later, Amazon added to books an array of products ranging from toys and electronics to clothing and household appliances, becoming a twenty-first-century version of Sparrow Horton's Woburn Book Store.

While Amazon's underlying business model may seem less innovative than at first glance, it nevertheless introduced significant changes that altered the profitability of the book trade for brick-and-mortar stores. First, Amazon offered an astounding range of titles – claiming access to over a million books when it started business,[67] suddenly rendering Grolier's carefully built-up stock of 15,000 titles miniscule in comparison. Second, Amazon's database offered search capabilities and access to sources previously available to librarians and book sellers, but not the book-buying public. As a result, Amazon eliminated the need for customer service and interaction that had been the mainstay of specialised bookstores like Shakespeare and Company and the Grolier for decades. The availability of e-books themselves, however, did not affect Solano's decision to sell the Grolier. Four years after its sale, John Thompson noted that e-book sales still represented only a small portion of sales for trade publishers; reported revenue was very modest. 'The early proponents of the e-book were right', he argued in 2010, 'when they said the future was digital; they were just wrong about the timescale'.[68]

At the same time that Amazon began its extraordinary growth, changes in the university library business, driven by economic factors, decreased Grolier's sales. For many years Solano had cultivated not only poets and writers but also acquisition librarians who 'special ordered' poetry books from the store. Pressured by increasing costs driven by scientific periodical subscription prices that rose an astronomical 320 percent in two decades, and squeezed by shrinking university budgetary support, libraries curtailed their purchases of books. As Harvard University Librarian Robert Darnton noted as early as 1999, 'Until recently, monographs used to account for at least half their acquisition budgets. Now it amounts to 2.5 percent'.[69] Moreover, as library acquisition budgets shrank, librarian supporters of the Grolier could no longer justify their purchases from the store when the same title was available at a significantly lower price from Amazon or other distributors. The cumulative effect of electronic marketing, discounting, and cost cutting proved insurmountable.

---

[66]   Ibid., 67.
[67]   Thompson, 41.
[68]   Thompson, 314.
[69]   Robert Darnton, *The Case for Books: Past, Present, and Future* (New York: Public Affairs, 2009), 71.

The most dismaying effect of e-trade was the inexorable disappearance of the store's unique and supporting customer base. Ten years before the sale of her store, Solano fondly described two ideal customers:

> There was an engineer from NASA who walked into the store after reading about it. He said, 'Teach me something about poetry'. Now he has one of the largest collections in the country. Another customer sent $600 every other month and told me to send small-press books to various schools where his children had gone. I met him only once, at the very beginning, but he helped keep the store alive for years, and helped pay the small-press bills.[70]

In the end, there was one thing Solano offered 'that none of her competitors could: intimate knowledge of and opinions about poetry'.[71] This knowledge, it seemed, ceased to matter. The Grolier's customers had vanished, and with it the book sales that had kept the store marginally profitable for years. Near the end of her career, Solano learned a lesson that she had not anticipated thirty years before, that 'good poetry does not always make good business'.[72]

Ultimately, Solano's proprietorship succumbed not only to the changing business climate of the book business but also to the conditions that have defeated many sole small business owners – poverty, illness, and age. Having supported herself on revolving credit for the final few years of her ownership, Solano found that she could not afford even the Harvard Real Estate company's subsidy of the store's rent. Facing an option to renew, Solano took the company's advice and offered to sell the lease with the contents of the store, bringing to a close a two-year long search for a buyer. Even then, Solano might not have chosen to so do had it not been for her declining health. As she wrote in a letter announcing the store's sale, 'The decision to sell is not one I would have chosen except for the fact that for the four months in the last twelve, I had enforced absences because of my health. This is no way to run a store: it creates the idea that the business is closed or that the owner has small interest in the customer'.[73] After fifty-one years of involvement, and thirty-one of ownership, Solano relinquished the store to its new owner, Ifeanyi Menkiti.

Two years later, on 21 June 2008, a small group of friends and supporters gathered to unveil a Cambridge city plaque in Louisa Solano's honour.[74]

---

[70]   Biemiller, http://www.iceandcoal.org/nfa/grolier.html.

[71]   Paulson, 11.

[72]   Provost, http://www.thecrimson.com/article/2004/3/16/grolier-book-shop-to-close-the/.

[73]   Margery Snyder, 'Solano Bids Farewell to the Grolier Poetry Shop', *About.com*, 28 March 2006. http://poetry.about.com/b/2006/03/28/louisa-solano-bids-farewell-to-the-grolier-poetry-book-shop/html.

[74]   In her interview with Claire Provost, Solano had expressed the desire for a 'blue marker' from the Cambridge Historical Society to designate the site as a historical landmark – for which no need exists as long as the store sign hangs above the door – and, jokingly, that a street be named after her. She came close to getting her wish fulfilled.

Recognising the Grolier Book Shop's renown as 'a wellspring for new and well-known poets'; acknowledging Solano's 'critical knowledge and deep appreciation of poetry; and citing her many accomplishments and awards, including the Women's National Book Association Award, the Cambridge Peace and Justice Award, and a special Excellence in Business Award among others, the Cambridge City Council dedicated the intersection of Bow Street and Plympton Street as 'Louisa Solano Square'. As Solano said, 'When you consider that almost five decades of my life have been spent in and around that corner, I can't think of a better location'.[75]

'This is not a business – it is a cultural institution'

Like many others before him, Ifeanyi Menkiti discovered the Grolier Book Shop as a graduate student at Harvard University, where he was studying philosophy in 1969 with John Rawls. Menkiti's long involvement with the store from youthful customer to mature board member of the LaForge Foundation gave him a unique perspective about the bookstore he attempted to preserve when buying it. Having known the two owners who preceded him, Menkiti sought 'to maintain the organization Solano brought to the store, and perhaps bring back some of the lingering Cairnie encouraged'.[76] Where Solano threw out Cairnie's couch to announce a dramatic change in ownership and attitude, Menkiti disabled the alarm system and cameras installed by Solano 'in order to create a friendlier atmosphere'.[77] Born in Nigeria, Menkiti has published four volumes with well-known small presses like Third World Press and Pomegranate Press. Perhaps because he is a poet, Menkiti expressed the wish that he would like 'to bring back some of the old conversation, to have people come and enjoy the place'.[78]

Menkiti's position as a philosophy professor at Wellesley College has also meant that, like Cairnie, he did not have to depend on the Grolier for his livelihood. In a 2006 interview given when he bought the Grolier, Menkiti stated that while he had no deadline for success, he knew that he could not run the store at a loss indefinitely. 'My hope', he said then, 'is that the store can sustain itself'.[79] Six years later, he told *Publisher's Weekly*, 'I [still] don't understand retail; I

---

[75]   Doug Holder, 'Louisa Solano Corner in Cambridge, Mass', *Boston Area and Small Press Scene*, 7 May 2008, http://dougholder.blogspot.ca/2008/05/louisa-solano-corner-in-cambridge-mass.html.

[76]   Janice O'Leary, 'Poet Takes to Business with a Passion', *The Boston Globe*, 30 April 2006, 11.

[77]   Daniela Caride, 'Nigerian Poet Pens New Verse in Book Shop's Tale', *Bay State Banner*, 17 May 2007, 16.

[78]   David Mehegan, 'He Keeps a Haven of Poetry Alive', *The Boston Globe*, 3 June 2006, D2.

[79]   Ibid.

don't understand business'.[80] His initial plan to sell books and organise events to 'catapult Grolier into the black'[81] proved unsuccessful; the Grolier could not sustain itself as a traditional bookstore in the face of increasing online sales and the deepest recession since the 1930s. In the intervening years, Menkiti dipped into his own funds to replenish the store's inventory; reduced the store's staff; launched the Grolier Discovery Award, a successor to the Ellen LaForge Memorial Poetry Prize, to attract the interest and support of the poetry community; and founded a new Grolier imprint to publish the work of contestants and other poets.

Surprisingly, Menkiti also established a new 'poetry room' above the Bloc 11 Café in Union Square Somerville, where many of the area's students and artists had relocated to escape the high cost of Cambridge housing. 'Madness', its inaugural fundraising event, celebrated the link between the Grolier and many of its more famous patrons, whose psychologically tormented lives had taken them to neighbouring McLean's Hospital. In creating a poetry room, and moving it away from the university that had so long sustained the store, Menkiti demonstrated the accuracy of Andrew Piper's observation that

> The bookstore, long thought dead, is being reimagined as a space of temporary respite, but also material encounter. In place of the timelessness of the independent bookstore, like Shakespeare & Company, or the sheer inertia of the big box store like Barnes & Noble … in these newly reimagined spaces we are getting in touch with the stuff of reading – not just books but the numerous objects to which they are related. The bookstore is being reconceived as a space of transitory materialization.[82]

If Menkiti re-imagined the Grolier as 'a space of transitory materialization', he also drastically altered the underlying premise of it as a book *store*. In 2012, Menkiti created the non-profit Grolier Poetry Foundation to provide support for poets and to publish their work while maintaining the physical space of the store, which will no longer be dependent on the all-but-nonexistent sales of its physical stock. In making his decision, Menkiti explicitly acknowledged that the Grolier 'is not a business, it is a cultural institution'.[83] Menkiti sees his work as ensuring that the Grolier endures as 'more of an educational institution and cultural institution than as an engine of commerce'.[84] If its reconfiguration as a non-profit has potentially freed the Grolier from the tyranny of books sales, the strategy is not without risk. Peter Frumpkin, in *On Being Nonprofit*, argues 'nonprofit and voluntary action is

---

[80]   Rosen, http://www.publishersweekly.com/pw/by-topic/industry-news/bookselling/article/52661-grolier-poetry-book-shop-goes-nonprofit-route.html.

[81]   Caride, 16.

[82]   Piper, 127–28.

[83]   Kaivan Mangouri, 'Bookstores Forced to Turn a Page', *Boston.com*, 25 June 2011. http://www.boston.com/ae/books/articles/2011/06/25/bookstores_forced_to_turn_a_page/.

[84]   Jan Gardner, 'Grolier Poetry Book Shop Plans Fund-raisers', *The Boston Globe*, 12 May 2012, http://www.bostonglobe.com/2012/05/12/word/WWCHuBIDa19ICWZz8QHSdM/story.html.

an important *instrument* for the accomplishment of tasks that the community sees valuable'.[85] Perhaps more importantly for the Grolier, which is reshaping itself as an organisation while maintaining a physical location as a store, the non-profit sector 'can be seen as valuable because it allows individuals to express their values and commitment through work, volunteer activities, and donations'.[86]

Securing the future of the non-profit Grolier Foundation may prove as difficult as sustaining the for-profit store. The leadership and professional expertise required for success is no less demanding for a non-profit venture than for a commercial one. A clear definition of mission and a committed board capable of making significant contributions to sustain the organisation and to guarantee its financial security and insure that it is not dependent on the vicissitudes of small donations and fundraising events will be required if the newly established Grolier Poetry Foundation is not to become one of the 'hundreds of thousands of nonprofits ... apparently inactive despite remaining on the IRS rolls'.[87]

In creating the Grolier Poetry Foundation, Menkiti has answered Jean-Luc Nancy's call to launch books into what he described as 'the bookstore of the soul, the free space of devouring of and by the pure Idea, the labyrinth of books that are read, jotted on, forgotten, and dust covered',[88] as much a concept as a commercial space. Will the Grolier Book Shop survive? In his retirement from his Wellesley professorship, Menkiti plans to stay engaged with the Grolier, whose purpose he sees in the eyes of an impoverished high school student who spent three hours reading in the Grolier. 'How do you quantify this joy and service', he asked?[89]

---

[85]   Peter Frumpkin, *On Being Nonprofit: A Conceptual and Policy Primer* (Cambridge, MA: Harvard University Press, 2002), 22.

[86]   Ibid., 23.

[87]   Ibid., 175; as a nonprofit professional and with Ifeanyi Menkiti a former director of the Ellen La Forge Foundation, I can anticipate the hard work necessary to establish the new Foundation.

[88]   Nancy, 42.

[89]   Rosen, http://www.publishersweekly.com/pw/by-topic/industry-news/bookselling/article/52661-grolier-poetry-book-shop-goes-nonprofit-route.html.

Chapter 8
Sylvia & Company

Katy Masuga

On the southern quay of the Seine, the *Rive gauche*, directly opposite Notre Dame Cathedral, in a very early seventeenth-century former monastery, sits the English-language bookshop Shakespeare and Company, run by Sylvia Beach Whitman. She began learning the ropes as early as 2003 at age twenty-one, eventually taking over the shop in 2006 from her father, George Whitman, who founded the shop in 1951 and passed away at age ninety-eight in December 2011. The *rue de la Bûcherie* is one of the oldest streets on the Left Bank, serving in the Middle Ages as the location for the distribution of old, boiled meats to feed the poor. Despite the orthographical similarity to the French term *boucherie* for 'butcher', the small alley is actually named after its more ancient use as a port for setting logs in the River Seine (from *bûche* meaning 'log'). According to Sylvia Whitman, the building that houses Shakespeare and Company was constructed around the time of Shakespeare's *Tempest* (roughly 1610). This past serves as a metaphor not only for the longstanding reputation of the shop itself but also of its many transformations: it is an island refuge withstanding storms of commercial and cultural change.

Shakespeare and Company's transition from book publisher, lending library, and literary focal point during the first part of the twentieth century to its current status as an important tourist attraction and historical-interest site that still promotes and sustains its business as a bookshop and space for literary culture has been made not without difficulty, but it certainly continues to remain successful. Due to the disappearing market for small, privately owned and operated bookstores, literary businesses like Shakespeare and Company have been threatened with extinction and have creatively developed new approaches to survive the corporate and Internet-based book market. With its capacity to transform itself while also remaining true to its original philosophy as a sanctuary for writers, artists, and booklovers, Shakespeare and Company continues to occupy a vital position, both physically and psychologically, for understanding the development and impact of small bookshops on modern literature and literary culture over the course of the twentieth century and into the twenty-first.

This continuity derives from Shakespeare and Company's capacity to reinvent itself while remaining faithful to Sylvia Beach, George Whitman, and Sylvia Whitman's visions. Currently, this persistence and longevity into the twenty-first century is taking the form of very concrete efforts to keep a certain fire alight that continues to attract 200 to 400 visitors to the bookshop a day. Recent endeavours include the bi-annual literary festival, a revitalisation of George Whitman's *Paris Magazine* from the 1960s, and a writing prize for new writers. These key elements are provisional in the sense that for bookstores like Shakespeare and Company to survive the reinvention of book culture through advances in technology, drastic and deliberate measures must be taken. As Laura J. Miller affirms in *Reluctant Capitalists* (2006), independent booksellers must become more astutely business-minded like their mass market, corporate rivals.

Perhaps even more important in the twenty-first century, independent booksellers must undertake a task that appears counterintuitive to the impending and continuing rise in an Internet-based, electronic book market: they must *remain* integral and active in tangible events and interests. In other words, independent bookshops must not lose their foothold in the real world of old books and even older histories. At the same time, there is something fundamentally different about Shakespeare and Company that sets it apart not only from other independent booksellers but also from its local competitors in Paris. Before investigating what makes Shakespeare and Company thrive even more now than in the past, attention must first be turned toward its history and what makes it a unique bookshop in the first place.

'Opening bookshop in Paris. Please send money': Financing Joyce

The history of Shakespeare and Company in Paris goes back to Sylvia Beach's original bookstore at 8 *rue Dupuytren*, established in 1919 in a former laundry shop near the regal, early seventeenth-century Luxembourg Palace and Gardens. Born in 1887 in Baltimore, Maryland to a Princeton minister, Beach went to Paris during her studies and remained there for the rest of her life, becoming lifelong partners with Adrienne Monnier, who had already founded the first lending library in France, known as *La maison des amis des livres* (The House of the Friends of Books).[1] Already aware from the start that her undertaking was a risky endeavour, particularly in a foreign and non-English based environment, Beach wired her mother for the initial support: "Opening bookshop in Paris. Please send money.'[2] Indeed, Shakespeare and Company's many successes and near failures have necessarily been made possible through the fundamental components of private generosity, non-judgemental hospitality, and bi-directional communality. Its longevity and success is, of course, also based on this very spirit of risk founded on very personal and literary passions.

Despite its unassuming appearance, Beach's Shakespeare and Company quickly became widely popular, attracting not only Anglophone expatriates but also international tourists and French Parisians alike. Its rapid growth as the only English-language bookshop in Paris at the time led to its 1921 relocation to a larger space around the corner at 12 rue de l'Odéon, coincidentally and conveniently directly across the street from Monnier's shop. Beach's bookshop itself remained

---

[1]   Shari Benstock, *Women of the Left Bank: Paris 1900–1940* (Austin: University of Texas Press, 1987), 196.

[2]   Sylvia Beach, *Shakespeare and Company* (Omaha: University of Nebraska Press, 1991), 17.

in the Odeon location until its permanent closure more than twenty years later in 1941 with the occupation of France during World War II.

With amateur interest in French literature but no formal education and no experience as a bookseller or publisher, Beach and her bookshop nevertheless gained immediate and lasting recognition for her daring publication of James Joyce's controversial *Ulysses* in 1922. In her memoir *Shakespeare and Company* (1959), Beach recalls asking Joyce: 'Would you let Shakespeare and Company have the honor of bringing out your *Ulysses*?'[3] She foresaw her own illustrious reputation, writing to her sister in 1921, 'Holly I am about to publish *Ulysses* of James Joyce ... *Ulysses* is going to make my place famous. Already the publicity is beginning and swarms of people visit the shop on hearing the news'.[4] Indeed, after the publication of *Ulysses*, Shakespeare and Company had its reputation well established, not only as the pre-eminent English-language bookshop in Paris up through the war years but also as a reputable avant-garde publisher of one of the most important works of the twentieth century, cementing a legacy and significance that continues to the present.

At the same time, the struggle to publish *Ulysses* did not guarantee financial success – far from it. The publication took its toll on Beach and her bookshop, nearly causing her bankruptcy, as she financially helped support Joyce and his family from her modest earnings. Thus, the romantic image of Shakespeare and Company as an ideal independent bookstore, in terms of a business model, could not be further from the truth. In order to finance the publication of *Ulysses* in the first place, Beach arranged subscribers to pay in advance for their copies. However, the cost of publication far exceeded the subscriptions, despite the anticipated popularity of the book. This discrepancy had in part to do with Beach's indiscriminate flexibility with Joyce, based on what she saw as her interminable admiration of his genius. Yet, it was also simply a reflection of the precarious business of independent bookselling and publishing. Itself financed by independently wealthy patrons, Beach's shop in turn provided Joyce and his family with extensive personal loans for the next twelve years, including the unforeseen labour of the preparation and publication (and promotion) of *Ulysses*. In her memoir, Beach discreetly writes that Joyce 'enjoyed spending the way some people enjoy hoarding' and recalls how a patron once noted that Joyce 'spends money like a drunken sailor'.[5] Despite supporting his spending habits out of her self-appointed necessity as a publisher to underwrite her author, Beach disdained them, and her business suffered the consequences.

Ultimately, after *Ulysses* became recognised as the momentous work of the twentieth century that it is today, Beach relinquished her rights to its further publication after ten years, at Joyce's request. Shortly after Beach gave up her rights, *Ulysses* was bought out by Random House in America. This deal effectively disintegrated any recovery of lost funds due to Beach. In her collected

---

[3] Ibid., 47.
[4] Ibid., 85.
[5] Ibid., 196–97.

correspondence is a letter Beach wrote to Joyce, finally expressing her controlled and polite anger: 'I already have many expenses for you that you do not dream of, and everything I have I give you freely. Sometimes I think you don't realize it … The truth is that as my affection and admiration for you are unlimited, so is the work you pile on my shoulders'.[6] Beach, however, never posted the letter.

As a poignantly noteworthy example of the independent bookshop publishing the great work of genius, Shakespeare and Company historically and presently continues to provide numerous examples of the state of the industry in terms of what to do and what not to do, what is manageable, and what are the right decisions both for the market and for 'culture', which often appear, as experienced today in new ways, to be mutually exclusive or at least in conflict. The intricate financial relationship between Joyce and Beach serves as a synecdoche of the greater quandaries independent booksellers and publishers face today. Having devoted her entire labours, personal, physical and financial, to the publication, reprinting and management of *Ulysses* over the entire course of the 1920s, Beach found herself unable to publish anything else, aside from several small publications of parts of Joyce's work in literary journals.[7] She rejected, for example, D.H. Lawrence's *Lady Chatterley's Lover*, even after Aldous Huxley and Lawrence himself pleaded with her to bring it out. Though it is clear she was actually not fond of Lawrence's book, Beach also simply could not take on any other projects.

Adrienne Monnier benefited financially from the publication of *Ulysses* to an extent, as it prompted renewed excitement in the French-speaking literary community. In *Paris Was our Mistress* (1947), Samuel Putnam recalls, 'And *Ulysses* in French garb was soon to be on the bookstalls'.[8] In 1925, Monnier began a literary review at *La Maison des amis des livres* called *Le Navire d'Argent*, which published, among other significant cultural works, parts of *Ulysses* in French as it was being written in 1920. *Le Navire d'Argent* was well known and respected, also bringing out, for example, a translation of T.S. Eliot's 'The Lovesong of J. Alfred Prufrock' translated by both Monnier and Beach. Monnier's connections to intellectuals and the avant-garde in Paris allowed her to reap the benefits of Joyce's work in ways that Sylvia, as his publisher in the trenches, could not. Thus, far from being a straightforward enterprise, the business of publishing books, even in what appears to be the best of cases – or, at least, the mythological tale of Joyce's *Ulysses* that everyone knows today – reveals instead the likely and persistent hardships faced by those still working at it in the present.

As with many business undertakings in the late 1920s, however, Monnier's *Le Navire d'Argent* went bankrupt with the American stock market crash and

   [6]   Keri Walsh, ed., *The Letters of Sylvia Beach* (New York: Columbia University Press, 2010), 319.

   [7]   See Noel Riley Fitch, *Sylvia Beach and the Lost Generation* (New York and London: W.W. Norton & Co Inc, 1983).

   [8]   Samuel Putnam, *Paris Was Our Mistress: Memoirs of a Lost and Found Generation* (London: Plantin Publishers, 1947), 235.

subsequently ceased printing after 1929. It was in this same year that Monnier brought out the complete French translation of Joyce's *Ulysses*. After numerous translators' quarrels and the usual financial troubles (also faced with a widespread pirated circulation of the original English *Ulysses* in America), Monnier successfully published its French translation, *Ulysse*, in February 1929, seven years after its first complete appearance in English. At the same time, this French publication signalled the end of Monnier's professional relationship with Joyce, which was followed two years later with the end of their personal relationship. This inevitable break came in the wake of the fallout from the strained financial difficulties between Joyce and Beach concerning *Ulysses*'s copyrights.[9] Though a far cry from their original camaraderie, Beach and Joyce did remain cordial to one another until Joyce's death in 1941.

In *Women of the Left Bank* (1986) Shari Benstock notes how the story of the relationship between Joyce and Beach is often reported in unclear or misguided terms. Benstock writes that such accounts suggest that Beach reaped untold financial rewards from the publication of *Ulysses* (a belief Joyce is thought to have held) or that she was not entitled to any royalties or benefits from its publication anyway and was causing undue animosity between the two. Although these claims are false, it is interesting to note the very complex and abstruse circumstances that led to them and the impact they have on contemporary ideas about Shakespeare and Company or, in general, on the nature of the role and purpose of independent bookshops that publish. Pointing out the deep inaccuracies in the stories of the history of Joyce and Beach, Benstock points to Fitch's biography *Sylvia Beach and the Lost Generation* (1983), which reveals the precise financial history of both Joyce and Beach, noting the former's extravagant expenses and indebtedness to Beach and the latter's silent resentment and acceptance and subsequent destitution and personal sense of betrayal.

Once Beach was able to right her accounting books nearly a year after the break with Joyce, it became painfully evident that she not only had not made any profit whatsoever from *Ulysses* but had incurred great losses. Luckily, but also necessarily, both Beach and Monnier's bookshops were underwritten to a large extent by their close friend Bryher, who, herself an artist and writer, was also the daughter to the ship-owner and financier John Ellerman, the wealthiest man ever in England during his lifetime and up to his death in 1933.

These financial and personal struggles between Beach and Joyce, in light of the publication of *Ulysses*, remain tremendously relevant today. Considering the difficult balance between personal and business relationships, but also – very significantly – the important developments and demands in the ever-changing market of literature publishing, the legacy of Beach and Joyce's partnership serves as a monument to the future of small presses and independent bookshops. Their example raises, first and foremost, the question of the possible survival of such unique and personal enterprises at all in the new age.

---

[9]   Benstock, 227.

In *Paris Was Our Mistress* (1947), Samuel Putnam writes: 'For the place de l'Odéon was a time-honored center of intellectual life',[10] but once World War II took over, that 'center of intellectual life' was altered forever. Beach's shop was forcefully and permanently closed in 1941 when she refused a high-ranking German officer her last copy of *Finnegans Wake*. Threatened with his imminent return to confiscate her books, Beach immediately hid her collection, with the help of nimble friends, in the building's attic apartment and removed all traces of her shop within two hours. The officer never found her collection, but Beach herself was arrested and spent six months in an internment camp. Upon her release, Beach returned to her apartment above the vacant bookshop, where she quietly lived among her hidden book collection until the liberation of Paris in 1944. It is said that Hemingway personally liberated Shakespeare and Company, with Beach writing in her memoir: 'I flew downstairs; we met with a crash; he picked me up and swung me around and kissed me while people on the street and in the windows cheered'.[11] Through all of her hardships – her unwavering commitment to Joyce, her belief in the success of her bookshop, her stance against the Nazis – Beach once said: '*Jusqu'à tous la terre*' ('A fight until the end').[12]

Les Amis de Shakespeare and Company: A Nexus for the Arts

Before the Second World War and the end of Beach's Shakespeare and Company, not only did the shop serve as the publisher of one of the most important works of the twentieth century but it also was a bookstore, of course, as well as a lending library and a reading room with lectures and events, serving as the nexus for the literary and arts scene in Paris for nearly a third of the entire twentieth century. The sense of community was evidently strong and impacting and has affected the shop and its contemporary namesake successor – the Shakespeare and Company of George Whitman. Basing his own principles on those set down by Beach, Whitman has been able to carry on the legacy of Shakespeare and Company through his almost nonchalant and casual approach, catering above all to camaraderie, open-handed munificence, and a fundamental love of books and reading, while somehow letting the business fall in step behind.

In a particular instance, this vein of camaraderie reaches back to Beach in the 1930s, when it was feared Beach might go bankrupt, friends set up a subscription group known as Les Amis de Shakespeare and Company.[13] Taking after Monnier's example, this group arranged for readings to be held in Beach's shop, inviting T.S. Eliot, Bryher, Dorothy Richardson, Ezra Pound, Robert McAlmon, and many

---

[10]   Putnam, 97.

[11]   Beach, *Shakespeare and Company*, 220.

[12]   Qtd in Adrienne Monnier, *Les Dernières Gazettes* (Paris: Mercure de France, 1961), 81.

[13]   Adrienne Monnier, *Les Gazettes d'Adrienne Monnier: 1925–1945* (J. Julliard: Paris, 1953), 122.

others, also including French writers such as André Gide, Paul Valéry, André Breton, Guillaume Apollinaire, and Tristan Tzara to participate. During this time, not only was Beach a good friend to Eliot, Stein, Hemingway, and Joyce but also, of course, to many more writers, including Fitzgerald, Sherwood Anderson, Nancy Cunard, and, naturally, a major part of the Anglo, expatriate population in Paris in general. In a letter written in protest of the pirating of *Ulysses* in America, Beach collected more than 150 signatures from her friends, faithful customers, and supporters, including those named above as well as Richard Aldington, H.D., Albert Einstein, Havelock Ellis, E.M. Forester, Knut Hamsun, Hugo von Hofmannstahl, D.H. Lawrence, Mina Loy, Maurice Maeterlinck, Thomas Mann, W. Somerset Maugham, J. Middleton Murray, Gabriel Miro, Jose Ortega y Gasset, Luigi Pirandello, Jean Prévost, Bertrand Russell, Miguel de Unamuno, H.G. Wells, and Virginia Woolf. Regardless of the forms in which success may come, indeed, community has always been at the heart of Shakespeare and Company.

The celebrity list of "les amis" of Shakespeare and Company is long, and the shop has been immortalised in many of their novels as well. In *A Moveable Feast*, Hemingway writes of the shop: 'On a cold windswept street, this was a warm, cheerful place with a big stove in winter, tables and shelves of books, new books in the window, and photographs on the wall of famous writers both dead and living'.[14] Hemingway refers to numerous writer-friends in the memoir-novel, explaining the origin of 'the Lost Generation' moniker: a reproach overheard by Gertrude Stein from the patron of her auto garage toward his young, inept employee. She quickly adopted the derogatory phrase to refer to the new wave of what she perceived to be disillusioned and misguided youth searching for meaning through writing and a bohemian lifestyle in Paris during the interwar years. In her authoritative and self-assured manner, Stein declared (according to Hemingway): 'You are all a *génération perdue* ... That's what you are ... You are a lost generation'.[15] If this moniker still to reverberates among the stalls at the current Shakespeare and Company, it comes in the form of the patrons who seek out the essence of Stein's phrase by partaking in the capitalist enterprise that has made Hemingway's *A Moveable Feast* one of the three bestsellers of the bookshop, the other two being Saint-Exupéry's *The Little Prince* (*Le petit prince*, 1943) and Hugo's *The Hunchback of Notre-Dame* (*Notre-Dame de Paris*, 1831).

Nevertheless, beyond the mythical and magical elegance that contemporary Paris lovers look for from the little bookshop on the bank of the Seine, what really makes Hemingway's text timeless is his Whitmanesque expression of the individual's collective experience in the world. He writes, 'There is never any ending to Paris and the memory of each person who has lived in it differs from that of any other'.[16] Such claims as this encourage independent booksellers in general to struggle for the preservation of the singularity of the human experience in an

---

[14] Ernest Hemingway, *A Moveable Feast* (London: Arrow Books, 2004), 20.
[15] Ibid., 18.
[16] Ibid., 126.

industry that appears to be overwhelmed by the mindless grind of the corporate machine. If Hemingway's words continuously remind the sentimental reader that Paris is a moveable feast through the very fibres of the text, then it is indeed possible to sustain the belief in the business of bookmaking and selling itself.

What we learn from this period is not that 'it was better in the good old days' but that our own struggles and efforts within a common literary body retain the quality and spirit of the struggle of wanting to balance a hopefully lucrative business with a meaningful expression of culture, in whatever forms that struggle manifests itself. For Beach, this balance was supported by uncompromising principles, regardless of the market, of war, and of literary trends. In her own words, Beach declares: '*Nous ne sommes pas à vendre*' ('We are not for sale').[17] As simultaneously stoic and naïve as this claim may be, as a business model it still manages to support the survival and success of the current Shakespeare and Company. And even if Beach suffered under the weight of her own principles, it is still a testament to the influential and monumental effect her bookshop continues to have on independent booksellers worldwide.

Socialist Utopia as Bookstore: George Whitman

After World War II, the future of Shakespeare and Company took a vastly new direction. George Whitman, a friend of Beach's of a later generation, sailed to Paris in 1946 with the Merchant Marines, leaving his native Massachusetts for good. He befriended the young Lawrence Ferlinghetti two years later in Paris, who was doing his doctorate in poetry at the Sorbonne. The two became lifelong friends, and Ferlinghetti finally left Paris for San Francisco where he established his bookshop City Lights in 1953. Just prior, in 1951, Whitman opened his English-language bookshop *le Mistral* across from Notre Dame, having begun collecting books while himself a student of literature at the Sorbonne. In her diaries, Anaïs Nin wrote, 'There was George Whitman, undernourished, bearded, a saint among his books, lending them, housing penniless friends upstairs, not eager to sell, in the back of the store, in a small overcrowded room, with a desk, a small stove'.[18] As his small student room had served as a literary point of contact for friends and fellow students including Ferlinghetti, so too did *le Mistral* become a lending library and a place for Anglophones in Paris to discuss literature and the arts.

After Beach's death in 1962, Whitman renamed his bookshop Shakespeare and Company in her honour. In light of such an homage, biographer and critic Keri Walsh calls Beach 'the patron saint of independent bookshops',[19] and Benstock calls her 'the patron saint of literary experimentalism'.[20] Beach's effect on the

---

[17] Monnier, *Les Gazettes*, 78.

[18] Anaïs Nin, *The Diary of Anaïs Nin: 1947–1955*, vol. 5, ed. Gunther Stuhlmann (San Diego, New York, London: Swallow Press, Harcourt Brace Jovanovich, 1974), 202.

[19] Walsh, xxv.

[20] Benstock, 206.

literary-minded in Paris was significant enough for Whitman to understand the profundity, both culturally and economically, that naming his shop after hers would have. Although Beach's Shakespeare and Company had already been permanently closed since 1941, Whitman's shop did not open until 1951 – after the war and after his studies. Whitman never formally asked Beach for permission to change the name of *le Mistral* to Shakespeare and Company, recalling with a childlike grin across his near century-old face: 'I was afraid she'd say "no" ... even though I knew she wouldn't'.[21] Choosing instead to honour her after her death, Whitman himself received the honour of inheriting many of Beach's books to his new Shakespeare and Company, such as her personal Simone de Beauvoir collection.[22]

Not only did Whitman adopt Beach's style, building uneven, towering bookcases to cover every inch of the old shop with a quiet reading room upstairs (also opening a separate antiquarian next door), but he also took Beach's sense of generosity several steps further by making his the only completely free lending library in Paris and also by allowing those travelling through Paris to stay in the shop free of charge. The only responsibility of these 'tumbleweeds' has been to work in the shop a handful of hours a day and to write a personal statement about themselves, including thoughts on their writerly aspirations. A selection of the tumbleweeds' personal statements from the 1960s and 1970s was published in the 2010 issue of *The Paris Magazine*, which itself is Sylvia Whitman's relaunch of George Whitman's original magazine from the 1960s.

The tumbleweeds' accommodations are modest, sleeping on old mattresses, pulled out onto the floor of the reading room and an adjoining room after the shop closes. Without much in the way of facilities, the tumbleweeds maintain fidelity to the early twentieth-century origins of Beach's shop – only the old fireplace that Hemingway so admired is lacking. Eating modest meals and often using the city's public baths, "the tumbleweeds are warmed by books!" jokes the young Sylvia Whitman.[23] Beside the fact that the shop does, of course, have standard hot water radiators, Whitman has also suggested she would actually one day like to restore the old fireplaces.

The notion of the 'tumbleweed' comes from Beach's Shakespeare and Company. In *Exile's Return* (1934) Malcolm Cowley remarks: 'We were like so many tumbleweeds sprouting in the rich summer soil ... rolling and drifting over the wide land'.[24] Although the reference is to himself and the figures he knew in Paris during the 1920s, like Hemingway, Fitzgerald, E.E. Cummings, Pound, and others, it of course also applies – almost literally – to all the young artists and writers who continue to roll into the warm embrace of Shakespeare and Company and eagerly take up their duties as bookshelvers and booksellers

---

[21] George Whitman, interviewed by Katy Masuga, 20 June 2010.

[22] Sylvia Beach Whitman, interviewed by Katy Masuga, 8 July 2010.

[23] Ibid.

[24] Malcolm Cowley, *Exile's Return: A Literary Odyssey of the 1920s* (New York: Penguin Books, 1994), 36.

under the guidance of Sylvia Whitman. In his autobiographical experiences as a Shakespeare and Company tumbleweed in the late 1990s, Jeremy Mercer recalls George Whitman as saying, 'I like to tell people I run a socialist utopia that masquerades as a bookstore, but sometimes I don't know'.[25] Despite changes over the years, Whitman's credo still holds true.

Thanks to his generosity, the door to Shakespeare and Company remains open to the tumbleweeds in need of a creative community and a mattress to sleep on. Whitman adopted this open policy for his shop by drawing from his experiences travelling in South America as a young man in the 1930s, where, thanks to the locals, he was never in want of a bed or a plate of food. Amazed by their hospitality, Whitman's desire was to adapt it to the urban environment, where such openness is generally less common and accepted. As unconventional as it was and still is, the tumbleweed community at Shakespeare and Company is a reminder of the tremendous and lasting effect that simplicity of community can have both on change and peace and in bringing people together toward compassion and human understanding.

This concept of the tumbleweed also applies, of course, to the group of writerly bohemians who bridge that gap between Stein's *lost generation* and the contemporary generation of vagabond-volunteers currently in residence at the bookshop, namely, the 'Beat Generation'. Their primary residence in Paris, the so-called 'Beat Hotel', was situated at 9 *Rue Gît-le-Cœur*, coincidentally equidistant from Beach's old Shakespeare and Company and Whitman's new Shakespeare and Company. In the 1950s until its closure in 1963, the poets and writers self-dubbed 'the Beats' occupied rooms in this squalid hotel, including William S. Burroughs, Allen Ginsberg, Peter Orlovsky, and Gregory Corso. The Beat Hotel offered the bare minimum (hot water three days a week, clean linens once a month), but its proprietor was sympathetic to artists and writers, having worked in her younger days at an inn visited by artists including Monet and Pissarro. Thus, the unofficially named Beat Hotel became a base for the Beat writers. It was here that Burroughs finished *Naked Lunch* (1959) after returning from Morocco, where Ginsberg began his poem *Kaddish* (1959) after extensive travel with Orlovsky, and Corso composed *Bomb and Marriage* (1958) after bumming around Europe.

Through Whitman's friendship with Ferlinghetti, the Beats knew Whitman's Shakespeare and Company (then *le Mistral*) and were regulars, particularly in light of its best attractions being free: book-borrowing, poetry readings, home-cooked meals, and, of course, a place to sleep as needed. Reflecting on the Beats' poor cooking facilities and humble lodging, Whitman explained, 'They were in and out of here nearly every day!'[26] As some of the first to come to, as well as participate in, Whitman's poetry readings, the Beats also attended the Sunday tea parties, which were held right up until George Whitman's death in December

    [25]   Jeremy Mercer, *Time Was Soft There: A Paris Sojourn at Shakespeare and Company* (New York City: St. Martin's Press, 2005), 40.

    [26]   Alix Sharkey, 'The Beats Go On', *The Observer*, 3 March 2002, http://www. theguardian.com/books/2002/mar/03/classics.features.

2011 in his small, irregular flat upstairs, covered with books and old portraits of everyone from Colette to Joyce to Henry Miller to Lawrence Durrell to Ted Joans.

Although it is this living history of Shakespeare and Company itself that in many ways enables the bookstore's success, there are specific measures that the Whitmans have undertaken to prolong that success in the face of a changing market. Technically, Shakespeare and Company competes for its English-reading clientele with a handful of other English-language bookshops in Paris, which have included The Village Voice, The Red Wheelbarrow Bookstore, San Francisco Book Company, The Abbey Bookshop, Berkeley Books, Galignani, the oldest English-language bookshop on the Continent, and a handful of others. Despite the image of a 'free love' community within the English-language bookselling business in Paris, full of like-minded booklovers, welcome and willing to share ideas, books, speakers and even readers, it still remains a cut-throat business, as demonstrated in the unfortunate recent closure of several of the oldest and most beloved English-language bookshops in the city including The Village Voice in 2012. Shakespeare and Company itself is able to sustain itself within this image of the free love approach through some very specific undertakings.

Essential to its survival are the activities previously mentioned, including the festival, literary prize, magazine, history book, and cafe but, above all, tourism, standing out as a must-stop cultural and historical destination for travelling English-speakers worldwide. Another very significant element that also plays a major role in Shakespeare and Company's continued success is the Whitmans' proprietorship of the portion of the building in which the shop is housed and until recently, the tumbleweeds volunteer-style employment. In terms of the latter, the functioning of the shop is no longer dependent upon the tumbleweeds service, however. Their responsibilities have been reduced to opening and closing the shop and some book shelving, as the recent success of the shop has permitted the expansion of regular, full-time paid staff from seven in 2011 to over twenty-five in 2015.

In terms of the former element that lowers the shop's overhead, ownership of the property, of course, does not indicate luxury under the rooftop of Shakespeare and Company. On the contrary, George Whitman occupied the same, incredibly modest apartment at the top of the building until his death, leading the same bohemian lifestyle since his first arrival in the 1940s. Shakespeare and Company occupies one-third of the old seventeenth-century building, fitting in six small rooms that roughly cover a modest 140 square meters on two floors. The shop accommodates 200–400 visitors a day – sometimes with a queue at the door – who are mostly Parisians in winter and tourists in summer, and who are not necessarily native Anglophones.

In 2006, George Whitman was awarded the '*Officier des Arts et Lettres*' ('Officer of Arts and Letters') in France for his lifetime contribution to the arts. Ferlinghetti wrote of him, 'He's certainly carried forth the glorious tradition, because he's a real bibliophile – and that's a dying breed these days'.[27] Ever supportive of the down-and-out, George's tradition of opening his shop and home

---

[27] Sharkey, http://www.theguardian.com/books/2002/mar/03/classics.features.

to impoverished travellers has been carried on by his daughter Sylvia, who now restricts the shop's transitory inhabitants to writers and artists in order to manage the increasing influx of the curious vagabonds.

'Get yourself in print': The Literary Prize, Festival, Magazine, History Book, and Café

These tumbleweeds are not only encouraged to write but are required to do so as part of their free lodging at Shakespeare and Company. Those of them who eventually find themselves in print might also thank Monnier, in addition to Beach and the Whitmans, for her equally determined legacy of helping struggling writers. Apart from being a publisher and bookseller, Monnier too was a writer. In one of her essays, she writes to a fictional poet about the difficulties in getting recognition for one's literary efforts: 'Some mornings you write. You no longer have any desire to send your poems to the reviews, your attempts discourage you; but even so you suffer from not seeing yourself *in print*, should that be only for yourself alone. Well then, get yourself in *print*'.[28] Echoing a currently very relevant topic, Monnier's recommendation is to self-publish:

> Go to any printer at all ... When the book is finished, and after you have corrected by hand the three or four magnificent misprints that will not fail to embellish it, send it to all the poets, writers or artists whom you admire, to your friends and acquaintances, to some critics, to the Bibliothèque Nationale and to the municipal library of your town – give it to your mother even ... [29]

Monnier explains the difficulty of getting one's work out to the world and yet also of the importance of working at it despite all obstacles, because seeing oneself in print 'is no small pleasure', and, indeed, in fifty or 100 years 'you will be discovered and put in a place of honor'.[30]

Monnier's work was published in the journals *Mesures*, which she worked on, and *Gazette des Amis des Livres*, her own enterprise, along with her *Navire d'Argent*. She also published her short story collection *Fableaux* in 1932, inspired by her mother's commune in Savoy, written in a style that includes 'the direct, robust speech of the country people',[31] reflecting on the very quality of humility and community that has always permeated the core of Shakespeare and Company. Of course, neither Sylvia nor Monnier (nor any of their writer friends) had to wait fifty or 100 years for their names to be honoured in their craft. Yet it is 100 years later that that honour is still acknowledged and has served as the backbone for the

---

[28] Adrienne Monnier, *The Very Rich Hours of Adrienne Monnier*, trans. Richard McDougall (Lincoln, Nebraska: First Bison Books, 1996), 190.

[29] Ibid., 191.

[30] Ibid.

[31] Ibid., 54.

success of Whitman's Shakespeare and Company, and all of its hopeful publishers and writers, to continue to the present day.

With support from The de Groot Foundation, Shakespeare and Company launched 'The Paris Literary Prize' in 2010 for the best novella by an unpublished writer. An effort to aid in the literary endeavours of aspiring writers, Shakespeare and Company has always opened its doors to new voices. One of the most encouraging aspects of its seemingly indestructible longevity has been Shakespeare and Company's ability to transform itself by retaining a sense of tradition and 'old-fashioned' communality in its business dealings.

In 2003, the young Sylvia Whitman not only began taking over her father's shop but also simultaneously started Festival and Company, run out of Shakespeare and Company. After its initial success, the festival was subsequently designated an independent cultural enterprise and established to take place every few years, featuring a variety of events across the arts, including soirées with performances in historic buildings, such as the *Hôtel de Ville* (the city hall, built 1533, completed 1628), a fourteenth-century converted convent, and the *Square René-Viviani*, the park of the *Église Saint-Julien-le-pauvre* (Church of St Julien the Poor) directly next to the shop, which itself is still served by its nineteenth-century 'Wallace fountain' out front.

Despite its high profile drawing power and its glamorous evening affairs, the festival is not-for-profit and is free and open to the public. It centres upon a calendar of literary events: readings, lectures, and roundtable discussions, presented by invited, well-known writers and based upon a central theme. The first festival in 2003 was entitled 'Lost, Beat and New: Three Generations of Writers in Paris' and included such writers as Jim Haynes, Carolyn Cassidy, and Alan Sillitoe. The 2006 festival featured events on travel and writing, with participants including Geoff Dyer, Noel Riley Fitch, and William Dalrymple. In 2008 it focused on memoir and biography and included Paul Auster, Siri Hustvedt, Alain de Botton, and Charlotte Rampling. In 2010, the festival brought together the topics of storytelling and politics and included André Schiffrin, Phillip Pullman, Ian Jack, and Will Self. Of course, with its cult of personality, its readings, regulars, workshops, tumbleweeds, and free wine and cheese after each weekly reading or event, 'Shakespeare and Company', as Erica Wagner declared in her editorial on the 2010 Festival and Company website, 'is *always* a festival'.[32]

In addition to the festival and the Paris Literary Prize, the transformative efforts of the young Whitman have also brought a revival of the elder Whitman's sporadic literary publication *Paris Magazine*. First printed in 1967 and not again until the 1980s for only two runs, Sylvia's first issue of *Paris Magazine* (2010) features old and new writers, including Saadat Hassan Manto, Irène Némirovsky, Alexander Kluge, Michel Houellebecq, Jeanette Winterson, Marie NDiaye, Jesse Ball, and Rivka Galchen. In her introduction, Sylvia Whitman writes, 'It's the spaces books

---

[32]   Erica Wagner, 'Editorial', *The Shakespeare and Company Literary Festival 2010: Storytelling and Politics*. http://www.festivalandco.com/index.php?page=517.

inhabit, the people they attract and the character they exude'.[33] Readers can peruse those spaces, people and character in the recent and more extensive *Shakespeare and Company, Paris: The Rag & Bone Shop of the Heart* (2015), a salient and meticulous in-house publication on the intricate and meandering history of the shop. Echoing her father's claim in 1967 that the writer requires 'a world that is sufficiently disorganized to allow [her or] him to subvert it', the young Whitman notes, 'We are still sufficiently disorganized and hope the writer and reader might find the right kind of electricity'.[34]

Benefiting from another expansion venture, literary patrons can now find their own daily dose of the Shakespeare and Company electricity at the new, adjacent café, between the original shop and the neighbouring park of the *Église Saint-Julien-le-pauvre* on the *Square René-Viviani*. Partnering with experts in the field, Sylvia joins a relatively recent, predominantly Anglo-based trend in Paris of delivering well-crafted, artisan brew set in an atmosphere less traditionally Parisian with a more informal, social layout. Quite obviously an historic and expert investment, the café is also testament to the everlasting community-minded core of both Sylvias' 'rag & bone shop of the heart'.

Metropolitan Traditions: Ferlinghetti, Calder, Haynes

Sylvia Whitman's Shakespeare and Company, like the original, is a centre for community, and, also like the original, its influence extends beyond itself into wide networks of bookselling and publishing. Founding his own bookshop two years after Whitman, Ferlinghetti also used Shakespeare and Company as his model. The sentiment is reflected in his doctoral dissertation at the Sorbonne: 'The City as Symbol in Modern Poetry: In Search of a Metropolitan Tradition' (1951). Here he examines the presence of 'the city' in the work of Walt Whitman, T.S. Eliot, Djuna Barnes, Hart Crane, André Breton, Vladimir Mayakovsky, Federico García Lorca, and Francis Thompson.[35] Ferlinghetti chose to set up City Lights in San Francisco in 1953 as a sister bookshop to Whitman's Shakespeare and Company in Paris, founding it with Peter D. Martin who returned to New York two years later to open the New Yorker Bookstore. Their idea to create the first all-paperback bookshop in America was widely successful, though first met with scepticism. City Lights Publishers then brought out Ginsberg's *Howl and Other Poems* in 1956, joining Beach as a controversial publisher of potentially obscene material.

Ferlinghetti was charged with disseminating obscene literature but, in 1957, ultimately acquitted, effectively paving the way for a reconceptualisation of the

---

[33]   Sylvia Whitman, 'Shakespeare and Company and The Paris Magazine'. *The Paris Magazine* 4, ed. Fatema Ahmed, 4 (June 2010), 1.

[34]   Ibid., 2.

[35]   Alistair Wisker, 'An Anarchist among the Floorwalkers: The Poetry of Lawrence Ferlinghetti', *The Beat Generation Writers*. Ed. A. Robert Lee (London: Pluto Press, 1996), 79.

'redeeming social importance' of certain controversial works of literature, in the words of the trial's presiding Judge Horn. The trial also firmly established City Lights' reputation as a bookshop and publisher of radical, counterculture literature, which it still maintains today. For its 'significant contribution to major developments in post-World War II literature', City Lights is officially recognised by the San Francisco Board of Supervisors as a historic landmark, as is the building in which it resides.

The tradition of Beach to Whitman to Ferlinghetti and Martin was carried on further by two more Anglo expats in Paris, John Calder and Jim Haynes, both of whom are to this day frequent visitors to Shakespeare and Company and speakers at its events, further expanding the institutional network of independent bookshops and controversial publishing. Friend of Ferlinghetti, Calder is not only one of the foremost scholars and initial publishers of Beckett but also a playwright and poet (publishing his first poem in the local paper at age eight).[36] Calder founded Calder Publications in 1949, which was Beckett's primary publisher in Great Britain beginning in 1955 and continuing through 2007 until rights were transferred to Oneworld Classics and Beckett's non-theatrical works to Faber. Apart from his publication of Beckett, Calder made one of his most notable imprints on literary history by also becoming the first publisher of Henry Miller in Great Britain in 1961, after the Grove Press obscenity trial in 1959 in the United States.

Calder, also a lifelong friend of Beckett, was also the first publisher of Burroughs in Great Britain and known for publishing translations of Tolstoy, Dostoevsky, and Chekhov and also for bringing the writers of the French *nouveau roman* to attention in English translation in the UK. Carrying on a tradition that vividly includes Sylvia Beach as a forerunner, Calder declares in the article 'Publish and Be Damned': 'I only took on things I believed in'.[37] He opened The Calder Bookshop Theatre in 2000, which still exists today, and remains affiliated with Oneworld Classics and Overture Publishing, the latter printing Calder's *Opera Guides* series. In 1962, together with Haynes, Calder organised the Writers' Conference in Edinburgh, which was attended by more than seventy writers, many of whom Calder represented, including Miller, Burroughs, Natalie Sarraute, Alain Robbes-Grillet, and Marguerite Duras.

A radical figure in the literary world from the 1950s through to the present, Calder, like Beach and Ferlinghetti before him, has always been a cutting-edge publisher, taking on projects considered too controversial for the mainstream. Having been introduced to Beckett through Beach upon her visit to New York in 1953,[38] in 1955 Calder met the founder of Grove Press, Barney Rosset, who was

---

[36] John Calder, interviewed by Katy Masuga, 27 July 2010.

[37] Louise Jury, 'Publish and Be Damned: A Defender of Free Speech – A Profile of John Calder', *The Independent* on Sunday, 21 March 2007.

[38] Samuel Beckett was a sometime visitor to Shakespeare and Company in the late 1920s. In 1929, Faber and Faber published Beckett's first work, "Dante ... Bruno. Vico. Joyce.', in a collection of essays with other prominent subscribers of Shakespeare and Company, such as Robert McAlmon, William Carlos Williams, and Eugene Jolas (founder

bringing out Beckett's *Murphy*. Through Rosset, Calder also eventually secured the rights to publish Beckett, taking him off Faber's hands, who considered Beckett obscene and unpublishable. Calder eventually acquired full rights to all of Beckett's work from Olympia Press, run by his friend Maurice Girodias, son of Jack Kahane, notorious publisher of erotica, which was used to finance his publications of other experimental works including Miller's *Tropic of Cancer* in 1934.[39]

Haynes, Calder's colleague, lifelong friend and co-founder in 1966 of the *International Times* in London and in 1967 of *Suck in* Amsterdam, first began his literary legacy in alternative and underground counterculture by opening The Paperback Bookshop in Edinburgh in 1959. Haynes, himself over eighty, recalls the atmosphere, echoing that of the original Shakespeare and Company: 'It was a sort of cultural centre: books and readings, free coffee and tea, a performance space in the front, a gallery in the basement – making it a place that was kind of "jumping"'.[40] With Beach and Monnier as his Parisian independent bookshop guides, Haynes made his shop the first and only in Great Britain to feature all paperback books in its catalogue, also offering free coffee and cookies to its patrons, with an art gallery in the basement and a performance space in the front.

Moving from Edinburgh to London to Amsterdam and finally landing in Paris, Haynes established Handshake Press in 1980, printing some of his own works and some of Ted Joans, Lynne Tillman, and others. Beginning his publishing career at The Paperback Bookshop, Haynes made his debut with Hugh MacDiarmid's *David Hume, Scotland's Greatest Son* in 1962. Also friend to Ferlinghetti, Haynes ran the only bookshop in Britain at the time that sold City Lights' published books.

---

of transition), called *Our Exagmination Round His Factification for Incamination of Work in Progress*, a critical work on Joyce's *Work in Progress*. Beckett was also the first French translator of Joyce's *Work in Progress* despite being a native Anglophone, translating the fragment 'Anna Livia Plurabelle' in 1925, then first published by Monnier in her *Navire d'Argent*.

[39] In the 1920s, Kahane, a friend of Beach's, began taking advantage of the legal systems on both sides of the Channel by publishing banned works in English in France. Kahane first brought out Norah James's *Sleeveless Errand* (1929), leading to him founding the Obelisk Press, which brought out many successful publications including, most famously, Henry Miller's *Tropic of Cancer* (1934) but also a reissued fragment of Joyce's *Work in Progress*, "Pomes Penyeach' (1932), Anaïs Nin's *House of Incest* (1936), a reissue of D.H. Lawrence's *Lady Chatterley's Lover* (1936), Lawrence Durrell's *Black Book* (1938), and four more works by Miller (*Aller Retour New York* [1935], *Black Spring* [1936], *Max and the White Phagocytes* [1938], and *Tropic of Capricorn* [1939]). A writer himself and a deeply reverent admirer of Joyce, Kahane was very impressed with Beach's discovery of *Ulysses* and 'never relinquished the hope of persuading [her] one day to let the Obelisk Press take it over'. Beach, *Shakespeare and Company*, 133. Kahane remained indefatigably desperate to publish Joyce, writing that 'as a budding publisher' his 'dearest ambition was to publish something, anything, by the GREATEST EXPATRIATE'. Jack Kahane, *Memoirs of a Booklegger* (London: Michael Joseph Ltd., 1939), 218.

[40] Jim Haynes, interviewed by Katy Masuga, 7 July 2010.

An immediate success, The Paperback Bookshop was eventually sold by Haynes in 1963 upon his co-founding, with Calder and Richard Demarco, of the Traverse Theatre in Edinburgh, which began its ongoing reputation as the foremost venue in Scotland for new contemporary productions. Haynes also established close connections with the Edinburgh Fringe Festival, founded in 1947 to counterbalance the mainstream Edinburgh International Festival. With its standing as one of the UK's most significant and reputable theatres, the Traverse served as an important reference for validating The Fringe. It was, however, as early as 1960 when Haynes published The Fringe's first catalogue and festival program that it showed the initial signs of serious organisation, drawing up a constitution that promoted free expression and formally disallowed censorship – once again continuing the legacy of the publication of experimental works begun by Beach with Joyce.

Beach's publication of *Ulysses* was an incredibly significant step toward freedom of press, which affected the various endeavours of her Anglo literary inheritors in Paris including Kahane, Whitman, Ferlinghetti, Calder, and Haynes. In the vein of the community of writers and publishers that grew out of the original Shakespeare and Company and continued on with George Whitman's generosity and communal spirit, in the 1970s Haynes created an audio-formatted press called *The Cassette Gazette*, which contained stories and poems read by their authors with the first issue featuring a poem by Ferlinghetti and a story by Bukowski. When Haynes visited Ferlinghetti in San Francisco in 1970s, he gave Ferlinghetti a copy of *The Cassette Gazette*, paving the way for City Lights, and a grateful Ferlinghetti, to become Bukowski's main publisher.

Haynes, Calder, and Ferlinghetti still frequent Whitman's Shakespeare and Company, occasionally as featured guest speakers as part of their events calendar of Monday night readings and lectures but also simply as friends and book patrons of the ongoing literary and cultural community that persists around the shop. Other known and unknown writers and artists are always visiting the shop, either as part of the organised program of events or simply as patrons, including one-time tumbleweeds Ethan Hawke, Jeremy Mercer, and Simon Van Booy.

These literary institutional activities are all central to Shakespeare and Company's survival and are based in the work set down by Beach herself as the proprietor of the original Shakespeare and Company. The endurance of twenty-first-century bookshops might depend in some ways upon learning the lessons of these early twentieth-century bookshops. The remarks from 1924 of the writer Morrill Cody, Beach's friend, still ring true: 'Shakespeare and Company – Paris: Successfully selling English books on a French side street'.[41] An inspiration to a new generation of bibliophile-entrepreneurs, Beach created a legacy that led to the establishment of multiple Shakespeare and Company bookshops around the world. Apart from Whitman's in Paris, there are independent shops in Berkeley,

---

[41]   Morrill Cody, 'Shakespeare and Company—Paris: Successfully Selling English Books on a French Side Street', *The Publishers' Weekly*, 12 (12 April 1924). Appendix I, Walsh, *The Letters of Sylvia Beach*.

Missoula, Prague, Vienna, six in New York, one formerly in Moscow, and two Shakespeare and Sons in Prague and neighbouring Český Krumlov (former home of Egon Schiele).

Although they are officially unaffiliated, they are very much affiliated in spirit and with the new wave of independent bookshops around the world. It might be said that all of these shops share the similar philosophy of providing, in Hemingway's words, a 'clean, well-lighted place' for those who seek out a community among books and booklovers. The Shakespeare and Companies and other shops connect to a heritage that spans backward not only to Beach's shop but also, of course, to Shakespeare himself as the original 'Patron Saint' (*Shakespeare* 102) who inspires readers and writers across the globe literally to participate in the writerly appreciation and subversion.

There does not seem to be any magic formula that has aided such an old-fashioned bookshop as Beach's to make its way through almost the entirety of the twentieth century – with numerous wars and various economic crises – and into the twenty-first century with the dawn and domination of the digital, Internet age. In 1924, Morrill Cody wrote an article for *Publisher's Weekly* writing that Shakespeare and Company is a 'unique bookshop, going contrary to many of the principles laid down for the "successful bookseller,"[42] and that the shop achieves its success in ways far beyond that of just selling books. Because of its interest in supporting not just the book business but also book culture and community at large, Cody has accurately predicted that over time Shakespeare and Company's success would become more evident and in more ways than just the obvious. He writes, 'It will have given aid and encouragement to many writers who might otherwise have been lost in the shuffle, and will have given to many readers a new angle on the personality and intimacy of books and their authors'.[43]

The fact that Shakespeare and Company has survived nearly 100 years through several incarnations is ultimately a testament to the significance of its core values: community, correspondence, and care. Hospitality, the love of literature, and the importance of the book as an object and artefact take precedence over marketing, industry changes, and capitalist enterprise—though of course savvy engagement with the latter allows the former to thrive. This fact is reflected in the shop's motto inscribed across an old beam on the second floor: 'Be not inhospitable to strangers lest they be angels in disguise'. The possibility for angels notwithstanding, the booksellers, tumbleweeds, visitors, and patrons of Shakespeare and Company, old and new, collectively sustain the shop's legacy of peace and love in the joy of books through an understanding deep within, that success is not measured by numbers but by human gestures in the arts.

---

[42]　Ibid., 313.
[43]　Ibid.

Coda

Sylvia Whitman

The independent bookshop is dead. A couple hundred years ago – or so I hear – it was killed by the bicycle. About one hundred years after that, it was the moving picture shows that did the awful deed. If the indie bookshop didn't die when supermarkets began selling books, then it surely met its end when chains moved into its neighbourhood. It was killed once again by online retailers (this time almost fatally so), right before e-readers raised the final dagger.

And yet here we are – some of us, still. There have been serious losses, of course: Gotham Book Mart in New York, The Lion and Unicorn in London and Odile Hellier's wonderful Village Voice Bookshop here in Paris, among many, many other treasured bookstores the world over.

Yet independent bookselling, as a whole, continues – and, recently, it's enjoying something of a renaissance. According to the American Booksellers Association, the number of indie bookstores in the US has grown 19.3 percent in the past few years. At Shakespeare and Company bookshop in Paris, we've only become busier and busier. In the past three years alone, we've grown from a team of seven to twenty-five.

Working in a bookshop is working in a cultural centre, a theatre, a perpetual tea party, a lovers' rendezvous, a place that manifests that delectable Cheever quote: 'I can't write without a reader. It's precisely like a kiss – you can't do it alone'. I feel the same way about selling books and meeting customers.

Readers like bookshops, but – whether occasionally or often – they like the convenience of online shopping, too. As a bookshop owner, I must be mindful that today some desires can be fulfilled at the click of a button.

Amazon founder Jeff Bezos once said: '*Amazon* is not happening to bookselling. The *future* is happening to bookselling'. Of course, the future is ongoing; bookselling is always changing. As small, independent booksellers, we're today able to adapt to the market more quickly than in earlier years: we can ourselves embrace technology and provide efficient online service – all while stocking the most beautiful editions.

I do wonder what the future will bring to these giant global corporations that seem to flourish. The chain bookstores, which once loomed so large, have begun downsizing, some even shuttering all together, dwarfed by Amazon. At the same time, recent events show that publishers and their writers are beginning to balk at the large promotion fees and deep discounts required by Amazon – itself no longer just an e-bookstore, but an 'everything store', a business notably less dependent on profits from book sales.

Being in France provides an interesting perspective. In 1981, the government passed the so-called Lang Law, which limits how much a new book can be discounted to no more than 5% off the cover price. More recently, in 2013, the French senate approved a bill that banned online book retailers from offering free shipping. As a result, Paris has 1025 bookshops.

For readers everywhere, there may never have been a better time to be a customer. Sometimes I see people in the shop's library reading on their iPads, surrounded by the rich tapestry of worn book spines. At first, it was a strange sight, but now I see it simply adds a little extra glow to the scene. Some booksellers, such as Green Apple in San Francisco, have even experimented with selling e-book downloads from inside their shop.

No one can be certain of the future, but I'm confident there will continue to be online companies and electronic books and, yes, even brick-and-mortar bookshops. From our little perch, the last week alone has resounded like fellow bookseller Walt Whitman's barbaric yawp over the Paris rooftops, an exalted joy for what independent bookshops can offer – there was a free event with the brilliant, soulful John Berger, singing children in the upstairs reading room, book-buying from the collection of the late, incomparable Mavis Gallant, the refurbishing of our rare books room, launching our e-commerce site, browsing new titles and gorgeous new editions, chatting with colleagues and welcoming customers.

We're adapting to today's book world, with its new technologies, its new ways to read, whilst steadfastly guarding that kiss, that true kiss one may find only in a bookshop.

References

Aaron, Daniel. 'Disturbers of the Peace: Radicals in Greenwich Village, 1920–1930'. *Greenwich Village: Culture and Counterculture*, ed. Rick Beard and Leslie Cohen Berlowitz, 276–300. New York: Rutgers University Press, 1993.

'After Five Years'. *Publishers' Weekly*, 25 June 1921, 1852–53.

Aldington, Richard. *Balls and Another Book for Suppression*. London: E. Lahr, 1931.

———. 'Introductory Note'. *The German Prisoner*. London, 1930.

Allen, Walter. *As I Walked Down New Grub Street*. London: Heinemann, 1981.

Anderson, Charles B., and G. Roysce Smith, eds. *The American Bookseller's Association's Manual on Bookselling: How to Run and Open Your Own Bookstore*, second edition. New York: Harmony Books, 1974.

'An Hour in the Hampshire Bookshop'. *Daily Hampshire Gazette*, 6 December 1916.

Anonymous. 'Has America A Literary Dictatorship?' *The Bookman* 65.2 (April 1927), 191–99.

Antliff, Alan. *Anarchist Modernism: Art, Politics, and the First American Avant-Garde*. Chicago and London: University of Chicago Press, 2001.

Arrow, John. *J.C. Squire v. D.H. Lawrence: A reply to Mr Squire's article in 'The Observer' of March 9th, 1930*. London: E. Lahr, 1930, 10.

Ashby, Anna Lou. 'Juliette's Door'. *The Library Chronicle of the University of Texas at Austin*. N.S. 5 (1972), 35–37.

Bachelard, Gaston. *The Poetics of Space*. Translated by Maria Jolas. Introduction by John R. Stilgoe. Boston: Beacon Press, 1994.

Baker, Carlos., ed. *Ernest Hemingway: Selected Letters 1917–1961*. New York: Charles Scribner's Sons, 1981.

Barnes, Earl. 'Bookselling: A New Profession for Women'. *Atlantic Monthly,* 116 (August 1915), 225–34.

Bates, H.E. 'The Palace'. *Country Tales*. London: Reader's Union, 1938.

———. 'A German Idyll'. *The Woman Who Had Imagination and Other Stories*. London: Jonathan Cape, 1934.

———. 'No Country'. *Something Short and Sweet*. London: Jonathan Cape, 1937.

———. 'The Bath'. *Country Tales*. London: Reader's Union, 1938.

———. *The Blossoming World: An Autobiography*. Vol. 2. London: Michael Joseph, 1971.

Beach, Sylvia. *Shakespeare and Company*. Omaha: University of Nebraska Press, 1991.

Beard, Rick, and Leslie Cohen Berlowitz, eds. *Greenwich Village: Culture and Counterculture*. New York: Rutgers University Press, 1993.

Benjamin, Walter. 'Unpacking My Library'. *Illuminations*, ed. Hannah Arendt. 59–68. New York: Schocken Books, 1968.

Benstock, Shari. *Women of the Left Bank: Paris 1900–1940*. Austin: University of Texas Press, 1987.

Biemiller, Lawrence. 'Stories from the Chronicle: A Bookstore for Poets and Lovers of Verse'. http:// www.iceandcoal.org/nfa/grolier.html.

Bourdieu, Pierre. *The Field of Cultural Production*. New York: Columbia University Press, 1993.

Bowker, Richard R. 'Bookselling as a Profession – An Address'. *Publishers' Weekly*, 25 May 1918, 1633.

Boyer, Christine. 'Straight Down Christopher Street'. *Greenwich Village: Culture and Counterculture*, ed. Rick Beard and Leslie Cohen Berlowitz. New York: Rutgers University Press, 1993.

Bradley, Sue. *The British Book Trade: An Oral History*. London: The British Library, 2008.

Brais, Amy E. 'Louisa Solano to be Honoured at the Somerville News Writers Festival'. *Boston Area Small Press and Poetry Scene*, http://dougholder. blogspot.com/2005/10/louisa-solano-to-be-honored-at.html.

Brannon, Barbara. 'No Frigate Like a Book: The Hampshire Bookshop of Northampton, 1916–1971.' doctoral dissertation, Columbia, University of South Carolina, 1998.

Brooker Peter, and Andrew Thacker, eds., *Geographies of Modernism: Literatures, Cultures, Spaces*. London: Routledge, 2005.

Browne, Maurice. *Too Late to Lament*. Bloomington: Indiana University Press, 1956.

Butcher, Fanny. 'Ben Hecht's Latest'. *Chicago Tribune*, 18 August 1923, 10.

———. 'Books'. *Chicago Tribune*, 16 August 1930, 4.

———. 'Christmas Books in Review'. *Chicago Tribune*, 15 December 1934, 13.

———. 'Critic Reads Just one Book for Pleasure'. *Chicago Tribune*, 19 April 1932, 19.

———. 'England is Sad, U.S. Gay, British Novelist Finds'. *Chicago Tribune*, 13 October 1919, 13.

———. 'Hemingway Seems Out of Focus in "The Sun Also Rises."' *Chicago Tribune*, 27 November 1926, 13.

———. 'Literary Lions Roar Tribute to English Tongue'. *Chicago Tribune*, 21 February 1919, 5.

———. 'The Literary Spotlight'. *Chicago Tribune*, 16 March 1944, E13.

———. 'Literary Visitors'. *Chicago Tribune*, November 15, 1924, 10.

———. 'New Fitzgerald Book Proves He's Really a Writer'. *Chicago Tribune*, 18 April 1925, 11.

———. *Many Lives – One Love*. New York: Harper & Row, 1972.

———. 'News and Views of Books'. *Chicago Tribune*, 10 September 1922, E24.

———. 'Tabloid Book Review'. *Chicago Tribune*, 8 January 1922, Pt 8, p. 10.

———. 'Tabloid Book Review'. *Chicago Tribune*, 13 June 1920, Pt 1, p. 9.

———. 'Tabloid Book Review'. *Chicago Tribune*, 4 June 1922, Pt 8, p. 14.

———. 'Tabloid Book Review'. *Chicago Tribune*, 7 May 1922, F14.

———. 'Tabloid Book Review'. *Chicago Tribune*, 9 May 1920, Pt 1, p. 9.

———. 'Tabloid Book Review'. *Chicago Tribune*, 19 October 1919, Pt 7, p. 7.

———. 'Tabloid Book Review'. *Chicago Tribune*, 23 October 1921, Pt 8, p. 1.

———. 'Tabloid Book Review'. *Chicago Tribune*, 26 September 1920, Pt 1, p. 9.

———. 'Tabloid Book Review'. *Chicago Tribune*, 4 September 1921, D1.

———. 'You Never Can Sell Poetry'. The *Publishers' Weekly*, 106.13 (27 September 1924), 1154–55.

Caldwell, John Taylor. *Come Dungeons Dark: The Life and Times of Guy Aldred*. Glasgow: Anarchist, Luath Press, Barr, 1988.

Campbell, Lisa. 'Titchner to be First Exhibitor at Foyles Flagship'. *The Bookseller*, 22 May, 2014, http://www.thebookseller.com/news/titchner-be-first-exhibitor-new-foyles-flagship.html.

———. 'Foyles Launches Literary Tours'. *The Bookseller*, 23 May 2014, http://www. thebookseller.com/news/foyles-launches-literary-tours.html.

Canfield, Cass. *Up and Down and Around*. New York: Harper's Magazine Press, 1971.

Caride, Daniela. 'Nigerian Poet Pens New Verse in Book Shop's Tale'. *Bay State Banner*, 17 May 2007, 16.

Churchill, Allen. *The Improper Bohemians*. New York: Dutton, 1959, 63.

Chute, Desmond. 'The Golden Cockerel Press. First Prospectus'. *Cock-a-Hoop: A Bibliography of The Golden Cockerel Press. January 1950–1961 December with a list of the prospectuses 1921–1962*. Compiled by Christopher Sandford and David Chambers. Middlesex: Golden Cockerel Press, 1963.

Cody, Morrill. 'Shakespeare and Company – Paris: Successfully Selling English Books on a French Side Street'. *Publishers' Weekly*, 12 (April 12, 1924). Appendix I. *The Letters of Sylvia Beach*. ed. Keri Walsh. New York: Columbia University Press, 2010.

Collier, Patrick. *Modernism on Fleet Street*. Aldershot: Ashgate, 2006.

Corbett, William. 'Cambridge'. *Harvard Review* 5 (Fall 1993), 104.

Cowley, Malcolm. *Exile's Return: A Literary Odyssey of the 1920s*. New York: Penguin Books, 1994.

Croft-Cooke, Rupert. *The Numbers Came*. London: Putnam, 1963.

Darnton, Robert. 'What is the History of Books?' *Daedalus* 111.3 (Fall 1982), 65–83.

———. *The Case for Books: Past, Present, and Future*. New York: Public Affairs, 2009.

———. *The Kiss of L'Amourette: Reflections in Cultural History*. New York: Norton, 1990.

Davies, Rhys. *Print of a Hare's Foot: An Autobiographical Beginning*. Bridgend: Seren, 1996.

Dell, Floyd. *Homecoming*. New York: Farrar, Rinehart, 1933.

Dettmar, Kevin J., and Stephen Watt. 'Introduction: Marketing Modernisms'. *Marketing Modernisms: Self-Promotion, Canonization, Rereading*. Ann Arbor: The University of Michigan Press, 1996.

Dodd, Marion 'The Long Way Around'. *Publishers Weekly*, 24 May 1919.
———. 'The Hampshire Bookshop'. *Publishers Weekly*, 16 March 1918.
———. 'What College Girls Read'. *Publishers Weekly*, 17 June 1922.
Abby Dune, 'Gotham's Quartier Latin'. *Los Angeles Times Illustrated Magazine*, 7 May 1922, VIII4.
'Editorial'. *Greenwich Village Quill*, October 1920, 5.
Emblidge, David, 'City Lights Bookstore: 'A Finger in the Dike'. *International Journal of the Book* 3.4 (2006), 27–34.
———. 'Isaiah Thomas Invents the Bookstore Chain'. *Publishing and Research Quarterly*, 28.1 (2012), 53–64.
———. 'The Gotham Book Mart: Location, Location, Location'. *International Journal of the Book* 9.4 (2013), 147–60.
———. 'The Old Corner Bookstore: "Rialto of Current Good Things, Hub of the Hub," *Concord Saunterer: A Journal of Thoreau Studies* 16 (2008), 103–18.
Ervine, St John. 'At the Play'. *The [London] Observer*, 28 October 1923, 11.
'Ex Cathedra'. *The London Aphrodite*, No. 2, October 1928, 160.
Eye Witness. 'Medillians Told Some Things on Book Reviewing'. *Chicago Tribune*, 17 March 1922,
Fabes, Gilbert H. *The Romance of a Bookshop:1904–1938*. Revised Edition. London: Privately Printed, 1938.
Felski, Rita, *The Gender of Modernity*. Cambridge, MA: Harvard University Press, 1995.
Fitch, Noel Riley. *Sylvia Beach and the Lost Generation: A History of Literary Paris in the Twenties and Thirties*. New York: Norton, 1985.
Fordham, John. *James Hanley: Modernism and the Working Class*. Cardiff: University of Wales Press, 2002.
Fox, R.M. *Smokey Crusade*. London: Hogarth Press, 1938.
'Frank Shay Dies: Wrote About Sea'. *New York Times*, 15 January 1954, 19.
'Frank Shay'. *Current Biography*. New York: H.W. Wilson, 1952.
Friedman, Susan Stanford. 'Definitional Excursions: The Meanings of Modern/ Modernity/Modernism'. *Modernism/Modernity* 8.3 (2001). 493–513.
Frost, Robert. *From Snow to Snow: The Hampshire Bookshop, 1916–1936, Twentieth Anniversary Week*. Northampton, MA: privately printed, 1936.
Frumpkin, Peter. *On Being Nonprofit: A Conceptual and Policy Primer*. Cambridge, MA: Harvard University Press, 2002.
Fryer, Judith. *Felicitous Space: the Imaginative Structures of Edith Wharton and Willa Cather*. Chapel Hill and London: University of North Carolina Press, 1986.
'Furnival Books'. *Times Literary Supplement*. 27 March 1930, 268.
Galow, Timothy W. 'Literary Modernism in the Age of Celebrity'. *Modernism/ Modernity* 17.2 (2010), 313–29.
Gardner, Jan. 'Grolier Poetry Book Shop Plans Fund-Raisers'. *The Boston Globe*, May 12, 2012. http://www.bostonglobe.com/2012/05/12/word/ WWCHuBIDa19ICWZz8QHSdM/story.html.

Gilbert, Julie Goldsmith. *Ferber: A Biography*. New York: Doubleday, 1978.

Glines, Steve. 'The Poetic Look'. *Boston Area Small Press and Poetic Scene*, 12 November 2005. http://dougholder.blogspot.com/2005_11_13_archive.html.

Goodway, David. 'Charles Lahr: Anarchist, Bookseller, Publisher'. *London Magazine*, June/July 1977. 46–55.

Gostick, Chris. *T.F. Powys's Favourite Bookseller, The Story of Charles Lahr*. London: Cecil Woolf Publishers, 2009.

Grant, Joy. *Harold Monro and the Poetry Bookshop*. Berkeley: University of California Press, 1967.

Gras, N.S.B. *Harvard Co-operative Society Past and Present, 1882–1942*. Cambridge, MA: Harvard University Press, 1942.

Guggenheim, Peggy. *Out of This Century: Confessions of an Art Addict*, foreword by Gore Vidal, introduction by Alfred H. Barr Jr. New York: Universe Books, 1979.

Hall, Donald. *Unpacking the Boxes*. Boston: Houghton Mifflin Harcourt, 2008.

Hamilton, Sion. 'Foyles Workshop'. *The Bookseller*, 22 February, 2013, http://www.thebookseller.com/feature/depth-foyles-workshop.html.

'Hampshire Bookshop Has Had Interesting History'. *Daily Hampshire Gazette*, 17 April 1936.

Hanley, James. *The German Prisoner*. London: 1930.

Hansen, Harry F. 'The Marshall Field Book Fair'. *The Publishers' Weekly*, 98, 17 (23 October 1920), 1251–52.

———. 'Ben Huebsch, Man of Causes'. *Chicago Tribune*, 23 August 1964, K8.

———. *Midwest Portraits*. New York: Harcourt Brace, 1923.

Harris, Luther. *Around Washington Square: An Illustrated History of Greenwich Village*. Baltimore: Johns Hopkins University Press, 2003.

Hemingway, Ernest. *A Moveable Feast*. London: Arrow Books, 2004.

Herbert, Rosemary. 'Books: A Haven for the Well-Versed'. *The Boston Herald*, 20 September 2002, 7.

Hibberd, Dominic. 'The New Poetry, Georgians and Others: The Open Window (1910–11), *The Poetry Review* (1912–15), *Poetry and Drama* (1913–14), and *New Numbers* (1914)'. *The Oxford Critical and Cultural History of Modernist Magazines*, Volume I, *Britain and Ireland, 1880–1955*, ed. Peter Brooker and Andrew Thacker. Oxford: Oxford University Press, 2009.

Hill, Murray. 'Murray Hill on Little Bookshops'. *The Bookman* 54.6 (February 1922), 528–33.

Hilliard, Christopher. 'The Literary Underground of 1920s London'. *Social History* 33.2 (May 2008), 154–82.

Holder, Doug. 'Interview with Louisa Solano'. *Wilderness House Events*, 24 July 2006. http://wildernesshouse.blogspot.ca/2006/07/interview-with-louisa-solano-guest-aug.html.

———. 'Louisa Solano Corner in Cambridge, Mass', *Boston Area and Small Press Scene*, 7 May 2008. http://dougholder.blogspot.ca/2008/05/louisa-solano-corner-in-cambridge-mass.html.

————, ed., *Louisa Solano: The Grolier Poetry Bookshop*, second edition. Somerville, MA: Ibbetson Street Press.

Holliday, Robert Cortes. *Men and Books and Cities*. New York: George H. Doran, 1920.

Hopkins, Kenneth. *The Corruption of a Poet*. London: James Barrie, 1954.

Hrushka, John. *How Books came to America: The Rise and Fall of the American Book Trade*. University Park: Penn State University Press, 2011.

Hudson, Holland. 'Progressive Bookselling: One Shop and its Methods'. *Publishers' Weekly*, February 12, 1921, 421–23.

Hutchison, Ruth B. *Women Building Chicago 1790–1990: A Biographical Dictionary*, ed. Rima Lunin Schultz and Adele Hast. Bloomington: Indiana University Press, 2001.

Israel, Betsy. *Bachelor Girl: The Secret History of Single Women in the Twentieth Century*. New York: William Morrow, 2002.

'Items of Interest'. *Bookseller, Newsdealer, and Stationer*, 1 July 1917, 31.

Jaffe, Aaron. *Modernism and the Culture of Celebrity*. Cambridge: Cambridge University Press, 2005.

James, C.L.R. 'Rogues, Scoundrels, and Liars'. Unpublished typescript written for David Goodway.

Jefferson, George. 'Charles Lahr, Publisher of D.H. Lawrence, Liam O'Flaherty, and H.E. Bates'. *The Book Collector* 113 (August 1993), 66–78.

Jenison, Madge. *Sunwise Turn, A Human Comedy of Bookselling*. New York: E.P. Dutton & Co., 1923.

Jewett, Eleanor. 'Art and Artists'. *Chicago Tribune*, 10 September 1922, E10.

Jury, Louise. 'Publish and Be Damned: A Defender of Free Speech – A Profile of John Calder'. *The Independent on Sunday*, 21 March 2007.

Kahane, Jack. *Memoirs of a Booklegger*. London: Michael Joseph Ltd., 1939.

Alissa G. Karl. *Modernism and the Marketplace: Literary Culture and Consumer Capitalism in Rhys, Woolf, Stein, and Nella Larsen*. New York: Routledge, 2009.

Kenney, Michael. 'Poetry Bash Makes a Splash'. *The Boston Globe*, 18 August 1997, C6.

Lahr, Sheila. *Yealm*, http://www.militantesthetix.co.uk/yealm/CONTENTS.htm.

Lang, Audrey, and Jo Royle. 'Bookselling Culture and Consumer Behaviour'. *The Future of the Book in the Digital Age*, ed. Bill Cope and Angus Phillips. Oxford: Chandos Publishing, 2006.

Laughlin, Clara E. *Traveling Through Life: Being the Autobiography of Clara E. Laughlin*. New York: Houghton Mifflin, 1934.

'Lectures at the Sunwise Turn'. *Publishers' Weekly*, 20 March 1920, 945.

Lefebvre, Henri. *The Production of Space*. Translated by Donald Nicholson-Smith. Malden, MA: Blackwell, 1991.

Leick, Karen. *Gertrude Stein and the Making of American Celebrity*. London: Routledge, 2009.

Lindsey, John. *Vicarage Party*. London: Chapman and Hall, 1933.

Hammel, Lisa. 'Boston Bookshop's Birthday'. *The New York Times*, 28 September 1983, C 13.

Loeb, Harold. *The Way It Was*. New York: Criterion Books, 1959.

Lowell, Amy. 'The Poetry Bookshop'. *Little Review* no. 2 (May 1915), 19.

MacDiarmid, Hugh. *Lucky Poet*, ed. Alan Riach. Manchester: Carcanet, 1994.

'Magazines are published by Greenwich Artists'. *The Oregonian*, 26 March 1922, 5.

Mandelbrote, Giles, ed. *Out of Profit and into Print: A History of the Rare and Secondhand Book Trade in Britain in the Twentieth Century*. London: British Library; New Castle: Oak Knoll Press, 2006.

Mangouri, Kaivan. 'Bookstores Forced to Turn a Page', *Boston.com*, 25 June 2011.

Marek, Jane E. *Women Editing Modernism: Little Magazines and Literary History*. Lexington: University of Kentucky Press, 1995.

Markham, Sheila. *A Book of Booksellers: Conversations with the Antiquarian Book Trade*. New Castle: Oak Knoll, 2007.

McCleery, Alistair, David Finkelstein, and Jennie Renton, eds. *An Honest Trade: Booksellers and Bookselling in Scotland*. Edinburgh: Birlinn, 2009.

McFarland, Gerald W. *Inside Greenwich Village: A New York City Neighborhood, 1898–1918*. Amherst: University of Massachusetts Press, 2001.

McFee, William. *An Engineer's Notebook*. New York: Frank Shay, 1921.

———. *Swallowing the Anchor*. Garden City: Doubleday, Page, 1925.

Mehegan, David. 'He Keeps a Haven of Poetry Alive'. *The Boston Globe*, 3 June 2006, D2.

Mencken, H.L. 'The Last of the Victorians', *Prejudices: First Series*. New York: Alfred A. Knopf, 1919.

Mercer, Jeremy. *Time Was Soft There: A Paris Sojourn at Shakespeare and Company*. New York City: St Martin's Press, 2005.

Miller, Laura, J. 'Shopping for Community: The Transformation of the Bookstore into a Vital Community Institution'. *Media, Culture & Society* 21.3 (May 1999), 385–407.

———. *Reluctant Capitalists: Bookselling and the Culture of Consumption*. Chicago and London: University of Chicago Press, 2006.

Mix, Deborah M. 'Gertrude Stein's Currency'. *Modernist Star Maps*, ed. Aaron Jaffe and Jonathon Goldman. Farnham, UK: Ashgate, 2010, 93–104.

Monnier, Adrienne. *Les Dernières Gazettes*. Paris: Mercure de France, 1961.

———. *Les Gazettes d'Adrienne Monnier: 1925–1945*. Paris: J. Julliard, 1953.

———. *The Very Rich Hours of Adrienne Monnier*. Translated by Richard McDougall. Lincoln, Nebraska: First Bison Books, 1996.

Monro, Craig. 'Lady Chatterley in London: The Secret Third Edition'. *D.H. Lawrence's "Lady": A New Look at Lady Chatterley's Lover*, ed. Michael Squires and Dennis Jackson, 222–35. Athens: University of Georgia Press, 1986.

Monro, Harold. 'The Bookshop', *Poetry Review*, 1 (November 1912), 498.

————. *Poetry and Drama*, 1.4 (December 1913), 387.

Monroe, Harriet. 'Comment: The Editor in England'. *Poetry: A Magazine of Verse* 23.1 (October 1923), 34.

Morley, Christopher. 'Wine That Was Spilt In Haste'. *Ex Libris Carissimis*. Philadelphia: University of Pennsylvania Press, 1932.

Morrisson, Mark S. *The Public Face of Modernism: Little Magazines, Audiences, and Reception, 1905–1920*. Madison: University of Wisconsin Press, 2001.

Mowbray-Clarke, Mary. 'The Sunwise Turn Bookshop – New York'. *Publishers' Weekly*, 26 May 1917, 1704–07.

Mumby, F.A., and Ian Norrie. *Publishing and Bookselling*. Revised Edition. London: Jonathan Cape, 1974.

Nancy, Jean-Luc. *On the Commerce of Thinking: Of Books and Bookstores*. Translated by David Wells. New York: Fordham University Press, 2009.

'New York Day by Day'. *The Miami Herald*, 23 November 1922, 8N1.

Nilsson, Rob. 'In Praise of Praise'. *cinesource*, 3 May 2012. http:// cinesourcemagazine. com/index.php?/site/comments/in_praise_of_praise.

Nin, Anaïs. *The Diary of Anaïs Nin: 1947–1955*. Volume 5. Ed. Gunther Stuhlmann. San Diego, New York, London: Swallow Press, Harcourt Brace Jovanovich, 1974.

O'Flaherty, Liam. 'Foreword'. *The Stars, The World, and The Women*. London: Jackson, 1930.

Ohmann, Richard Malin. *Selling Culture: Magazines, Markets, and Class at the Turn of the Century*. Hanover, NH: University Press of New England, 1996.

O'Leary, Janice, 'Poet Takes to Business with a Passion'. *The Boston Globe*, 30 April 2006, 11.

Oldenburg, Ray. *The Great Good Place*. New York: Paragon House: 1991.

Orwell, George. 'Bookshop Memories'. [1936] *Facing Unpleasant Facts*. Boston and New York: Mariner Books/Houghton Mifflin Harcourt, 2009, 38–43.

Palmer, Herbert E. *What The Public Wants*. London: E. Lahr, 1931.

'Pathology Des Dommagistes: Being Specimens for a projected Anthology to be issued in the U.S.A'. *The Monthly Chapbook (A Monthly Miscellany)*, no. 23, May 1921, 21–24.

Paulson, Amanda. '400 Square Feet of Poetic Punch'. *Christian Science Monitor*, 17 October 2002, 11.

Peiss, Kathy L. 'American Women and the Making of Modern Consumer Culture'. *Journal for Multimedia History* 1.1 (Fall 1998).

Pettigree, Andrew. *The Book in the Renaissance*. New Haven: Yale University Press, 2010.

Piper, Andrew. *Book Was There: Reading in Electronic Times*. Chicago: University of Chicago Press, 2012.

'Poetry Evenings at the Sunwise Turn'. *Publishers' Weekly*, 20 December 1919, 1620.

Pollnitz, Christopher. 'The Censorship and Transmission of D.H. Lawrence's Pansies: The Home Office and the 'Foul-Mouthed Fellow'. *Journal of Modern Literature* 28.3 (2005), 44–71.

Potter, Rachel. 'Obscene Modernism and the Sale in Salacious Books'. *Modernism/Modernity* 16.1 (2009), 87–104.

Pratt, Mary Louise. *Imperial Eyes: Travel Writing and Transculturation*. London: Routledge, 2007.

Provost, Claire, 'Grolier Book Shop to Close'. *The Harvard Crimson*, 18 March 2004. http://www.thecrimson.com/article/2004/3/16/grolier-book-shop-to-close-the/.

'*Publishers' Weekly* Thru 50 Years: Part III, 1872–1921'. *Publishers Weekly*, 15 January 1921, 108–09.

Putnam, Samuel. *Paris Was Our Mistress: Memoirs of a Lost and Found Generation*. London: Plantin Publishers, 1947.

Rainey, Lawrence. *Institutions of Modernism: Literary Elites and Public Culture*. New Haven: Yale University Press, 1998.

———. *Revisiting The Waste Land*. New Haven: Yale University Press, 2005.

Rak, Julie. 'Genre in the Marketplace: The Scene of Bookselling in Canada'. *From Codex to Hypertext: Reading at the Turn of the Twenty-First Century*, ed. Anouk Land, 159–74. Amherst: University of Massachusetts Press, 2012.

Rascoe, Burton. *Before I Forget*. New York: Literary Guild of America, 1937.

Raven, James. *The Business of Books: Booksellers and the English Book Trade*, New Haven and London: Yale University Press, 2007.

Rice, Anne. '"A Peculiar Power about Rottenness": Annihilating Desire in James Hanley's "The German Prisoner"' *Modernism/Modernity* 9.1 (2002), 75–89.

Roberts, Cecil. *The Bright Twenties*. London: Hodder and Stoughton, 1970.

Robinson, Frances Reed . 'The Hampshire Bookshop'. *Smith Alumnae Quarterly* (February 1976), 17.

Roger, W.G. *Wise Men Fish Here: The Story of Francis Steloff and the Gotham Book Mart*. New York: Harcourt Brace & World, 1965.

Rosen, Judith. 'Literary Thugs and Book Thieves'. *New York Times*, 17 May 2004, 19.

———. 'Grolier Poetry Bookshop Goes Nonprofit Route'. *Publishers' Weekly*, 22 June 2012, http://www.publishersweekly.com/pw/by-topic/industry-news/bookselling/article/52661-grolier-poetry-book-shop-goes-nonprofit-route.html.

Ross, Ishbel. *Ladies of the Press*. New York: Harper & Brothers, 1936.

Rota, Anthony. *Books in the Blood: Memoires of a Fourth Generation Bookseller*. Middlesex: Private Libraries Association; New Castle: Oak Knoll Press, 2002.

Ryan, Michael. 'Gordon Carnie–1895–1973'. *The Harvard Crimson*, 24 July 1973.

Sharkey, Alix. 'The Beats Go On'. *The Observer*, 3 March 2002, http:// www.theguardian.com/books/2002/mar/03/classics.features.

'Shay Defies the Draft'. *New York Times*, 23 September 1917, 21.

Shay, Frank. 'Bookselling on the Broad Highroad'. *New York Times Book Review*, 11 May 1924, 2.

———. *Drawn From the Wood*. New York: The Macauley Company, 1929.

Sims, George. 'Alida Monro and the Poetry Bookshop'. *ABMR: A Monthly Magazine of International Antiquarian Bookselling, Collecting and Bibliography* 9.7 (July 1982), 262–67.

'Six New Middle Western Bookshops: IV Fannie Butcher, Books – Chicago'. *The Publishers' Weekly*, 97, 14 (April 3, 1920), 1102.

'Smith College Book Store, Northampton, Mass., Incorporated'. (Business Notes), *Publishers' Weekly*, 6 May 1916, 1456; 27 May 1916, 1772.

Smith, Mary Byers. 'A Successful College Bookshop'. *Publishers Weekly*, 4 December 1920, 1753.

Snellings, O.F. *Rare Books and Rarer People: Some Personal Reminiscences of 'The Trade'.* London: Werner Shaw, 1982.

Snyder, Margery. 'Solano Bids Farewell to the Grolier Poetry Shop'. About.com, March 28, 2006. http://poetry.about.com/b/2006/03/28/louisa-solano-bids-farewell-to-the-grolier-poetry-book-shop/html.

Sproat, Elaine, ed. '"Woman and the Creative Will": A Lecture by Lola Ridge, 1919'. *Michigan Occasional Papers in Women's Studies* 18.18. http://hdl. handle. net/2027/spo.aaf0222.0018.001:02.

Sproehnle, Katherine. 'The Decay of the Customer'. *The Bookman* 56.5 (January 1923), 588–90.

Squires, Claire. *Marketing Literature: The Making of Contemporary Writing in Britain*. Basingstoke: Palgrave Macmillan, 2009.

Stallybrass, Peter and Allon White. *The Politics and Poetics of Transgression*. Ithaca, NY: Cornell University Press, 1986.

Stansell, Christine. *American Moderns: Bohemian New York and the Creation of a New Century*. New York: Metropolitan Books/Henry Holt, 2000.

Starrett, Vincent. 'A Gossip on Chicago Bookshops'. The *Publishers' Weekly*, 105.26 (June 28, 1924), 2007–11.

Stetz, Margaret. 'Sex, Lies, and Printed Cloth: Bookselling at the Bodley Head in the Eighteen-Nineties'. *Victorian Studies* 35.1 (1991), 71–86.

Stewart, Donald Ogden. *By a Stroke of Luck*. New York: Paddington Press, 1975.

Stirphas, Ted. *The Late Age of Print: Everyday Book Culture from Consumerism to Control*. New York: Columbia University Press, 2009.

Swan, David, and Terry Tatum, eds. *The Autobiography of Irving K. Pond*. Oak Park, IL: Hyoogen Press, 2009.

'Talks on Bookshops'. *Publishers' Weekly*, 28 January 1922, 212.

Tebbel, John. 'A Brief History of American Bookselling'. *Bookselling in America and the World: Some Observations and Recollections in Celebration of the 75th Anniversary of the American Booksellers Association*, ed. Charles B. Anderson. New York: Quadrangle, 1975.

———. *A History of Book Publishing in America*, 3 vols. New York: R.R. Bowker, 1972–1978.

'The Cytherea Prize Doll'. *Publishers' Weekly*, 1 April 1922, 973.

'The Gossip Shop'. *The Bookman* 14.1 (September 1921), 93.

'The Hampshire Bookshop'. *Smith Alumnae Quarterly* (February 1976), 14–17.

'The Hampshire Bookshop'. *Publishers' Weekly*, 3 May 1924, 1440.

'The Little Schoolmaster's Classroom'. *Printers' Ink*, 14 April 1921, 200.

'The Sunwise Turn: A Modern Bookshop'. *Publishers' Weekly*, 22 April 1916, 1361.

'Thirty-Six Birthday Poems for Gordon Carnie with Photographs of the Poets by Elsa Dorfman'. *Antioch Review* 30.3/4 (Autumn 1970–Winter 1971), 311.

Thomas, Jack. 'Closing Store has Them at a Loss for Words'. *The Boston Globe*, 1 December 2004. http://www.boston.com/ae/books/articles/2004/12/01/closing_store_has_them_at_loss_for_words/.

Thompson, John B. Mer*chants of Culture: The Publishing Business in the Twenty-First Century*. Cambridge, MA: Polity Press, 2010.

Tompson, Bonar. *Hyde Park Orator*. London: Jarrolds, 1936.

'Trade Winds'. *Saturday Review*, 43.1 (1960), 11.

Tranmer, Jeremy. 'Taking Books to the People: Radical Bookshops and the British Left'. *The Lives of the Book, Past, Present, and Future*, ed. Nathalie Collé-Bak, Monica Latham, and David Ten Eyck. Nancy: Presses Universitaires de Nancy, 2010.

'Transcript Writes of Hampshire Bookshop'. *Daily Hampshire Gazette*, 15 June 1922.

Turner, Catherine. *Marketing Modernism Between the Two Wars*. Amherst and Boston: University of Massachusetts Press, 2003.

Veblen, Thorstein. *The Theory of the Leisure Class: An Economic Study of Institutions*. New York: Macmillan, 1899; rpt. Dover Publications, 1994.

W.L.N. 'A Line O' Type or Two'. *Chicago Tribune*, 25 February 1920, 8.

Wagner, Erica 'Editorial'. *The Shakespeare and Company Literary Festival 2010: Storytelling and Politics*. http://www.festivalandco.com/index.php?page=517.

Walsh, Keri. *The Letters of Sylvia Beach*. New York: Columbia University Press, 2010.

Weld, Jacqueline Bograd. *The Wayward Guggenheim*. New York: E.P. Dutton, 1988.

Weller, Ken. *'Don't be a Soldier!' The Radical Anti-War Movement in North London 1914–1918*. London: Journeyman, 1985.

Wells, James M. *Portrait of an Era: Rue Winterbotham Carpenter and the Arts Club of Chicago 1916–1931*. Chicago: Arts Club of Chicago, 1986.

'What America Thinks, An interview with Mr St John Ervine'. *The [London] Observer*, 18 April18, 1920, 15.

Whitman, Sylvia. 'Shakespeare and Company and The Paris Magazine'. *The Paris Magazine*, ed. Fatema Ahmed. 4 (June 2010).

Who Was Who in America, 4 vols. (Providence, NJ: Marquis-Who's Who, 1951–1960), 3: 777.

Wicke, Jennifer. 'Coterie Consumption: Bloomsbury, Keynes, and Modernism as Marketing'. *Marketing Modernisms: Self-Promotion, Canonization, Rereading*, ed. Kevin J. Dettmar and Stephen Watt. 109–32. Ann Arbor: The University of Michigan Press, 1996.

Wickham, Anna. 'Meditation at Kew'. *Contemplative Quarry*. London: The Poetry Bookshop, 1915.

'Will Book Prices Have to be Increased?' *Publishers' Weekly*, 22 April 1916, 1362–63.

'Willa Cather Tells Purpose of New Novel'. *Chicago Tribune*, 12 September 1925, 9.

Wisker, Alistair. 'An Anarchist among the Floorwalkers: The Poetry of Lawrence Ferlinghetti'. *The Beat Generation Writers*, ed. A. Robert Lee. 74–94. London: Pluto Press, 1996.

Woodcock, George. *Letter to the Past*. London: Fitzhenry & Whiteside, 1982.

Woodress, James. *Willa Cather: A Literary Life*. Lincoln and London: University of Nebraska Press, 1987.

Worthen, John. *D.H. Lawrence: The Life of an Outsider*. London: Allen Lane, 2005.

Yost, Karl. *A Bibliography of the Works of Edna St Vincent Millay*. New York: Harper, 1937.

Index

Printed and bound by CPI Group (UK) Ltd, Croydon, CR0 4YY

01/05/2025

01858454-0002